Prescriptive Psychotherapy

PRESCRIPTIVE PSYCHOTHERAPY

A Practical Guide to Systematic Treatment Selection

Larry E. Beutler
T. Mark Harwood

WITHDRAWI

OXFORD
UNIVERSITY PRESS

2000

OXFORD
UNIVERSITY PRESS

Oxford   New York

Athens   Auckland   Bangkok   Bogotá   Buenos Aires   Calcutta
Cape Town   Chennai   Dar es Salaam   Delhi   Florence   Hong Kong   Istanbul
Karachi   Kuala Lumpur   Madrid   Melbourne   Mexico City   Mumbai
Nairobi   Paris   São Paulo   Singapore   Taipei   Tokyo   Toronto   Warsaw

and associated companies in
Berlin   Ibadan

Library of Congress Cataloging-in-Publication Data
Beutler, Larry E.
Prescriptive psychotherapy : a practical guide to systematic treatment selection /
Larry E. Beutler, T. Mark Harwood.
p.   cm.
Includes bibliographical references and index.
ISBN 0-19-513669-1
Psychotherapy. 2. Psychotherapy—Research.   I. Harwood, T. Mark. II. Title.
[DNLM: 1. Psychotherapy—methods. WM 420 B569p 2000]
RC480.5 .B475 2000
616.89'14—dc21   99-042912

1   2   3   4   5   6   7   8   9
Printed in the United States of America
on acid-free paper

Preface

Organization of This Volume

This book is designed to help experienced, practicing clinicians acquire and skillfully apply the knowledge and principles for selecting and fitting therapeutic procedures to various and particular patients. It is intended to serve as a detailed manual, supplementing the rationale and procedures described in *Systematic Treatment of the Depressed Patient* (Beutler, Clarkin, & Bongar, in press). This is not intended to be a manual like other treatment manuals, however. Most extant manuals require that the therapist who applies them comes to believe, or at least accept, the underlying model or theory of psychopathology and change on which the manual was built, and that they then learn a set of new techniques and procedures that are consistent with that theory.

We believe that this usual procedure fails to capitalize on the experience and skills that experienced therapists have developed and implicitly conveys a lack of regard for the importance of this experience. We also believe that these are among the reasons that research-developed manuals have not often been adopted in practice. Psychotherapists, especially if they are experienced, do not like the inflexibility that is required to learn and practice according to most manuals. The current manual, therefore, is unique in that it works from a set of general, empirically informed principles that can be transferred across different theories, rather than from one or another theoretical model or from a finite list of techniques. These principles inform therapists in the use of strategies and allow them to select techniques from their own particular experience and training. Thus, it is not a manual of cognitive therapy or psychodynamic therapy, or any other theory of psychotherapy. Nor is it a description of techniques that can be applied in treatment. Instead, it provides a set of principles that can be used from a variety of theoretical perspectives and that can be applied by means of a variety of different techniques.

The principles that underlie Prescriptive Psychotherapy, or prescriptive therapy (PT) for short, are intended to be broad ranging and to allow skilled therapists to draw from the techniques that work best for them and with which they are most familiar. Novice therapists and therapists-in-training, however, may benefit from learning theories and techniques. For these individuals, we illustrate how the principles might be applied within different theoretical systems. We also describe some exemplary techniques and illustrate how they and others might be used.

This book is organized around three tasks, the first two of which are the focus of the first section and the third of which organizes the second section of this book. The introductory section first provides a detailed description of the conceptual underpinnings of systematic treatment selection (STS; Beutler & Clarkin, 1990). As part of this description, we provide an overview of the principles and strategies that are critical to the understanding of Prescriptive Therapy, some of the techniques that might be used to work with these principles, and a discussion of the foundations for training in prescriptive treatments.

The second objective of this introductory section is to provide instruction to therapists in the acquisition of skill in the use of patient evaluation procedures that will allow effective and differential treatment planning and will describe the patient and treatment dimensions as well as illustrating the multiple theoretical frameworks from which these principles can be practiced. The evaluation procedures include an integration of patient and clinician perspectives and involve the application of conventional psychological tests, clinician observations, and less traditional, computer-interactive methods. Emphasis is placed on assessing both those transient states and durable traits that are directly relevant to planning treatment. Some of these methods are reiterated and extended in specific treatment chapters. These evaluations concentrate on identifying the processes and strategies of change that are likely to be the best fit for a given patient and problem.

The second section of this manual is organized around the third objective, that of providing to the practicing clinician a basic set of guiding principles and a corresponding set of differential treatment strategies for effecting change. It also identifies and familiarizes the therapist with the use of some specific but representative treatment methods that are sensitive to the important patient differences that can be detected through systematic evaluation. In this book, we organize the description of these methods around skills related to (1) establishing a therapeutic relationship, (2) adapting treatment to the patient's level of distress and impairment, (3) accommodating variations in patients' coping styles, and (4) responding to variations in patient resistance states and traits.

In identifying strategies that accommodate patient differences along these dimensions, we emphasize the interrelationship between the processes of assessment and intervention. We view the processes of clinical assessment and treatment as being both intertwined and ongoing. The informed clinician is one who can recognize and use clinically important and empirically derived patient qualities to initially plan a discriminating and differential treatment, with subsequent periodic reassessments and alterations of these plans to accommodate changes occurring in the patient's status.

Integration of Treatment Strategies and Procedures

The treatment-specific chapters of this manual follow a systematic order. Each chapter focuses on an aspect of therapy (e.g., preparing the patient for therapy) or a patient dimension (e.g., Patient Distress) that serves as an indicator for a differential treatment decision. These dimensions are identified by the chapter title. At the beginning of each chapter, we identify the principle or principles of change that will best guide the therapist's decision about working with patients who vary in the identified quality or characteristic. In addition, we identify the patient cues or the therapy situation that will illustrate, for the therapist, the presence and level of the particular treatment-relevant quality that will guide therapy. The exception to this organization is found in Chapters 5 and 6, wherein the material reflecting the differential treatment of patients varying in severity and coping style is divided in order to simplify the presentation.

We articulate the differential treatment strategies that are useful in applying the guiding principles to given patients. Examples of therapeutic processes and some representative techniques are described to illustrate these strategies. In the latter case, we describe specific treatment techniques and procedures that have been used successfully in outcome research to treat certain patient groups. These procedures should be seen as suggestive examples of how the principles have been applied. They are not mandatory procedures to learn. They are not described in great detail, therefore, but are presented only with enough detail as to illustrate how the techniques relate to the principles that guide their use. The therapist is encouraged to use his or her own initiative to develop and combine procedures that will be true to the principle and strategy of change being applied.

If a therapist does not possess the knowledge necessary to apply the principles and strategies, such as confronting a patient in a way that arouses and maintains motivation, then it is a signal that the therapist needs to seek out information about how to do so. We provide some support and direction in this quest by providing clinical examples of how treatment might be constructed. But, the therapist may need to expand his or her facility with specific techniques through additional training. Our illustrations do not encompass the array or diversity of techniques and strategies available. Therapists are encouraged to explore and creatively apply techniques that are consistent with their own evolving clinical style and expertise.

To further facilitate this process, this volume describes the procedures used to assess therapists' skills in the implementation of the needed strategies. These procedures reflect both the ability of the clinician and the response of the patient. In other words, the procedures reflect the degree to which the therapist is successful in accomplishing the aims that are intended by the relevant treatment principles. These procedures can be used both to ensure treatment integrity for clinical, research, and training purposes and to determine clinician readiness for applying the treatments in clinical practice.

We want to thank Drs. Lisa Firestone, Lynnette Glasman, Oscar Goncalves, and Robert Romanelli for their assistance in developing the concepts presented in this manual. We also want to thank all the students and staff who have worked with us on this project.

The term prescriptive "therapy" described herein should not be confused with similar-sounding interventions by other authors. In particular, we apologize to our good friend John Norcross for incorporating a term that he initially used to describe his own work. Simply, there are just too few words to serve the purposes of describing what therapists do. But we are reassured that John's approach and our own are very compatible and similar. Thus we take responsibility for this work, but we thank Dr. Norcross for his wisdom and for stimulating many of the thoughts expressed here.

In addition, we wish to thank Dr. Lisa Onken at the National Instute of Drug Abuse (NIDA) for her support and assistance. This work was supported, in part, from a grant from NIDA (DA09394) to develop this treatment and test its efficacy. It remains the focus of research efforts to further validate its use.

Finally, we dedicate this work to the therapists who have been so kind as to help us test these ideas: Deryl Goldenberg, Raissa Veronique, David Wasserman, Julie Bowden, Cassandra Delacoeur, Richard Kelliher, Jerome Yoman, Donna Genera, Linda Meehan, and Angie Maez.

LEB
TMH

Contents

Part I.

INTRODUCTION

Chapter 1
Introduction to Prescriptive Therapy

Background and Significance

Epidemiological surveys (Regier et al., 1988) indicate that approximately 30% of the U.S. population will qualify for one or more psychiatric diagnoses during their lifetimes. Recent estimates (Castro, 1993) indicate that only one in five individuals with a diagnosable mental disorder receives psychological treatment. Moreover, patients with psychiatric disorders as their primary diagnoses account for approximately one-quarter of all hospital days in America (Kiesler & Sibulkin, 1987). Giles (1993) maintains that, over the last decade, the cost of general health care has increased at approximately three times the national rate of inflation; however, mental health care expenditures, a major subset of general health care, have increased by more than 30% per year. The serious nature of mental health problems is highlighted by the high prevalence of psychiatric disorders, the undertreatment of these disorders, the reduction in productivity that results from impaired mental health, and the rising treatment costs that burden an already struggling health care system.

This text is intended to address the forgoing. Prescriptive therapy is specifically designed to provide targeted and highly effective treatment interventions that may be delivered in a treatment format that varies in length and intensity to fit a variety of problems, but for most applications it is a relatively brief (i.e., 20 or fewer sessions) intervention. Increasing the efficacy and effectiveness of therapy in an efficient, systematic fashion will improve treatment outcome and patient productivity while reducing the time in, and subsequently the costs of, treatment for both the patient and the health care system. The guidelines and strategies presented in the following chapters were developed from an understanding of depressive spectrum disorders but have

3

been found to have application to a wide variety of problems in which dysphoria and anxiety are present, including chemical abuse and anxiety based disorders (Beutler, Clarkin, & Bongar, in press).

Prescriptive therapy is specifically designed for application to complex (unipolar) depressive spectrum disorders. In view of the fact that depression is the most widely occurring comorbid condition, we believe that it is unfortunate that most guidebooks treat depression as if it were an independent mental health condition. In most instances, depression is complicated by many other factors, problems, and diagnoses. Among these, drug abuse and personality disorders are the most difficult comorbid conditions. This book is designed to address these kinds of complexities.

Because drug abuse is one disorder that represents a major social and behavioral health problem and because it is a frequent complicating factor in depression, it receives special emphasis in this volume. NIDA statistics suggest that 37% of the U.S. population have used illicit drugs (Smith, 1992) and as many as 23% of the work force regularly use illicit drugs in the work place (Barabander, 1993). Some statistics indicate that 3% of employees abuse heroin (Browne, 1986) and more than twice that figure may abuse cocaine (Abelson & Miller, 1985). Abuse, and the depression that underlies or is reflected in this abuse, or that is the consequences of it, affects family, work performance, and the survival of newborn children (Levy & Rutter, 1992).

Of contemporary concern, cocaine and methamphetamine abuse appear to represent major problems in the United States. This is due in large part to the severe addictive properties of this class of drug coupled with the high likelihood of polydrug abuse among its users. Moreover, the social and economic loss to society that accompanies use among employed middle-class groups, the population in which these are the drugs of choice, is a serious problem (Almog, Anglin, & Fisher, 1993).

Anecdotal evidence, both locally and nationally, indicates that methamphetamines are rapidly replacing cocaine as the street drug of choice among abusers. This appears to be both because it is cheaper and because it is easier to manufacture and make available. Researchers in the field of drug addiction and treatment have observed that depressive symptoms frequently occur among cocaine abusers and follow methamphetamine abuse (Weiss, Griffin, & Mirrin, 1992). Some retrospective, empirical evidence suggests that many substance abusers use cocaine and methamphetamine, as well as many other street drugs, to self-medicate an underlying depressive condition (Weiss et al., 1992).

The coexistence of cocaine/stimulant abuse and depressive symptoms suggests that psychobehavioral interventions that are effective in treating depression may be adapted usefully to the treatment of drug abuse. Our own research on which this manual is based (e.g., Beutler, Clarkin, & Bongar, in press) supports this conclusion. Thus, it is no surprise that cognitive therapy, though initially formulated for the treatment of depression, has been translated to a treatment for drug abuse (Wright, Beck, Newman, & Liese, 1993) and alcoholism (Wakefield, Williams, Yost, & Patterson, 1996). Likewise, psychodynamic (McLellan, Luborsky, Woody, O'Brien, & Druley, 1983) and interpersonal therapies (Rounsaville, Dolinsky, Babor, & Meyer, 1987) have been successfully extrapolated from the treatment of depression and anxiety disorders to the treatment of a variety of substance abuse disorders. Interestingly, in making the translation, none of these treatments, which were initially defined for work with depressed patients, identifies depression as a concomitant focus of these treatments when adapted to work with chemical abuse.

Except, perhaps, for some promising new developments, chemical treatments for cocaine and amphetamines have largely been ineffective and when tried are generally contraindicated because of the danger of compounding the problems of illicit drug use with the use of a prescribed medication. Psychological and behavioral approaches to the treatment of substance abuse have yielded some good initial effects on patterns of use and abuse; however, long-term effects are virtually nonexistent and both dropout and relapse rates are very high, particularly among cocaine abusers (e.g., Carroll, Rounsaville, & Gavin, 1991; Kang et al., 1991). Thus, new psychobehavioral treatments are needed to pursue the promising initial effects obtained, and extrapolating from those that have been helpful in other problem areas is a reasonable place to begin this process.

Among therapies for substance abuse and cocaine abuse in particular, it is especially important that the treatment be flexible and multifaceted in order to both address the high rates of noncompliance and dropout and the high level of complexity and comorbidity that typically characterizes these problems. For example, a broad-band treatment that is flexible enough to address both depressive spectrum symptomology and habit problems is critical. Although there is debate as to whether depression is a precursor to drug abuse, a direct (i.e., biological) consequence of withdrawal, a transitory condition of distress that dissipates upon entering treatment, or an indirect correlate of rehabilitation, there is general agreement (Hoffman, DiRito, & McGill, 1993; McLellan et al., 1983; Rounsaville, Weissman, Kleber, & Wilber, 1982; Rounsaville et al., 1991; Weiss et al., 1992) that the successful treatment of drug abuse hinges on the alleviation of coexisting depressive symptoms.

Using Treatment Manuals to Enhance Training and Practice

The application of psychotherapy to the many problems that affect people's lives is largely a post–World War II (WWII) phenomenon. The late 1940s and 1950s saw an expansion of the role of psychotherapy and a climate that fostered an increase in the number of psychotherapists in North America, as the federal government attempted to address the vocational and mental health needs of returning veterans. Psychologists and social workers, and eventually marital, behavioral, alcohol, and family counselors came to be recognized, along with psychiatrists, as experts in the treatment of various mental and emotional problems. An expanded list of diagnoses, often drawing their symptoms from experiences that were common to normal people, broadened the range of problems that mental health professionals were called on to address.

Over the period of three decades, the number of recognized and diagnosed problems expanded from approximately two dozen to more than 400. War neuroses, depression, chemical dependency, and finally the full array of diagnostic conditions came under the purview of the new army of mental health practitioners and psychotherapists.

Prior to the post-WWII expansion in the variety of training backgrounds considered to be appropriate for the training of psychotherapists, psychoanalytic thought dominated the mental health field. Indeed, Freud's psychosexual view dominated American psychotherapy and was even accepted as embodying fundamental "truths" about human development by the public. Themes based on this viewpoint were incorporated as standard fare in the plots of theater and cinematic productions during the 1950s and continued well into the 1970s. The cadre of psychotherapists expanded after WWII along with the number and variety of perspectives through which mental health problems were conceptualized. In the postwar years, and at the same time they were becoming accepted in the public media, psychoanalytic theories began to lose favor among segments and subgroups of professional psychotherapists. Concomitantly, new theories arose and developed in an effort to address various weaknesses with the prevailing psychoanalytic model. The 1960s saw the introduction of various models of behavior therapy; the 1970s saw the widespread acceptance of experiential, existential, and systemic therapies; the 1980s saw the introduction of a plethora of cognitive change and interpersonal therapies. Well over 400 different theories were available to the practitioner by the mid-1980s (Beutler, 1991; Herink, 1980).

As the number of available and practiced theories grew, so did disillusionment with the original hope that one of them might hold the truth about how problems occurred and could be changed. By the late 1970s, 50% of practicing psychologists identified themselves as eclectic (Garfield & Kurtz, 1977), indicating by this choice that they had given up the effort to find a single-theory viewpoint that was consistently valid as a way of viewing or treating psychological problems. In subsequent years, more and more professionals came to forsake single-theory frameworks and adopted a poorly defined eclecticism as their preferred model of practice (e.g., Norcross & Prochaska, 1988). As many as 70% of members of some professional groups now identify themselves as eclectic in orientation and practice (Jensen, Bergin, & Greaves, 1990). These psychotherapists have sought to add interventions drawn from several different treatment models to their array of available procedures in order to increase their ability to address the widely different needs of those who seek their services. This movement probably reached its peak during the human potential movement of the 1970s and 1980s when great emphasis was placed on freedom and flexibility.

The inevitable results of introducing so many new theories included a decline in the consistency of how treatment was conducted and an increase in the variety of techniques and procedures used. Theories and methods came to be applied to vague groups of patients and problems according to varying standards. While psychotherapists began to acknowledge the importance of integrating interventions across theoretical lines, this was usually accomplished in the absence of an organizing, integrative theory. Each therapist was left to his or her own devices to implement treatment, without guidance about how to select the specific procedures that would be especially effective for a given patient or condition.

By the mid-1970s it became apparent that the diversity of psychotherapy practices, even within a given theoretical model, was too great to disentangle the effects of the different interventions used. Psychotherapy research of the late 1970s and 1980s emphasized the need to reliably identify the components of psychotherapeutic treatments, to homogenize patient groups to which treatments were applied, and to compare models that were founded on different theoretical premises. Accordingly, the Treatment of Depression Collaborative Research Project (TDCRP; Elkin, 1994; Elkin et al., 1989) introduced the use and comparison of treatments that were conducted via standardized manuals, each reflecting a different theoretical conceptualization and a different array of interventions. These manuals were applied to diagnostically homogeneous samples of patients, establishing diagnosis as the basis for grouping and identifying patients.

The introduction of manuals has been heralded as a "minor revolution" (Luborsky & DeRubeis, 1984, 5) in psychotherapy research and has been seen as a promising means of increasing the reliability and effectiveness of training and practice. The use of manuals in supportive research has even been accepted as a major criteria for determining a proposal's acceptance for federal funding, for identifying those treatments that have received sufficient empirical support to warrant transfer to practice (Chambless et al., 1996), and for determining what treatments should be included in the curriculum of major graduate training programs (Maki & Syman, 1997). Indeed, research has demonstrated that using manuals improves the reliability and coherence of applying therapeutic interventions and suggests that technical compliance increases treatment efficacy (Beutler, Machado, & Neufeldt, 1994; Dobson & Shaw, 1988).

In spite of their several advantages, three problems with extant manuals have not been resolved. First, manuals remain inordinately rigid and inflexible. Even when patients are diagnostically homogeneous, the variation among them requires a higher degree of flexibility than permitted by most contemporary, single-theory manuals. This point was emphasized by Anderson and Strupp (1996), who interviewed 59 highly selected and diagnostically similar patients who were treated either before or after their therapists received training in a short-term dynamic psychotherapy. They found that the most effective therapists departed from the manualized rules when particular situations arose and concluded that then existent manuals did not allow sufficiently for the therapist to adapt treatments to the multitude of important nondiagnostic states and needs of particular patients. From such findings, it is clear that structured treatment manuals allow a needed degree of technical consistency, but they do so by sacrificing therapist flexibility.

Second, there is some indication that manual-based training actually increases the presence of countertherapeutic attitudes on the part of therapists. Henry, Strupp, Butler, Schacht, and Birder (1993) found that the therapists who were most compliant with manualized demands, were more rigid, angry, insensitive, and rejecting than those who were less compliant. This pattern of results arose both from a tendency for those therapists who were initially rejecting and angry to get more out of the training than less angry ones and a tendency for training itself to reduce one's empathic sensitivity. Thus, while increasing technical proficiency, manual-based training also reduces empathic attunement and attitudinal readiness.

Finally, and perhaps because of these counteractive factors, systematic, research comparisons of psychotherapies that are conducted according to different manuals have failed to demonstrate that their distinguishing methods and theories translate to differences in outcomes among any of a wide variety of patient problems. Indeed, most empirical comparisons have indicated that different treatments exert essentially equivalent effects—the so-called Dodo Bird Verdict (Luborsky, Singer, & Luborsky, 1975). The selection of diagnosis as the criteria on which to group patients has clearly lacked sensitivity to the specific and selective demand characteristics that distinguish different psychotherapies and to the different patients for whom they may be best suited. Indeed, the relatively weak evidence that either experience, training, theoretical model, or type of intervention makes a substantial difference in outcomes among patients has led some to suggest that we abandon, altogether, advanced psychotherapy training in techniques, procedures, and theories (e.g., Christensen, & Jacobson, 1994).

To overcome these various shortcomings, an effective treatment manual must encourage the use of a structured treatment but also must foster the development of intuitive judgment. In addition, manuals must maintain ecological validity by drawing from a multitheoretical base and by incorporating an emphasis on the many ways that patients differ. Finally, effective manuals must also take into account the nonspecific qualities that account for so much of the benefits of treatment.

Prescriptive Therapy

The concepts of PT have been developed as a general approach to psychosocial treatment. They have been developed and tested in samples of those with depressive spectrum disorders, reactive anxiety, alcoholics, and in general out-patient populations. The finalization of these principles were developed under the auspices of a research grant from NIDA. In this latter project, PT was designed as a psychobehavioral intervention for patients with comorbid substance abuse (cocaine and/or methamphetamine) and mild to moderate depression. In its current form, the text has been expanded to accommodate its original purpose, to provide a set of guidelines for psychotherapy that can be applied to a wide range of conditions and problems. It is our experience, formulated in practice and validated in our research, that patients who have mood, anxiety, and/or substance abuse disorders have symptoms of depression and disturbed relationships that are somewhat similar. Although different diagnostic groups also have distinctive symptoms, dysphoria is nearly universal and heralds the presence of conflict and problems. It signals a need to make adjustments and change. The symptoms that constitute distinctive diagnoses represent targets of change, but the procedures and mechanisms of change to which people with these diagnoses respond depend on qualities and characteristics that cut across diagnostic groups. Variations in these nondiagnostic qualities, including both enduring traits and transitory, symptom-related states, allow us to develop indicators for response to different classes of intervention that can be applied in a similar way to people with different specific problems and diagnoses.

Said another way, there is no universal personality type, living environment, or lifestyle that characterizes all people who present for treatment, and, accordingly, research literature strongly suggests that no particular treatment works for everyone. However, research also suggests that some of the variations that exist among people predispose them to be receptive to different treatments, and that this pattern of reaction is similar across a wide variety of problems.

Most of the psychosocial treatments that have been researched to date ignore both: (1) the complications presented by the common occurrence of psychiatric comorbidity (e.g., depressive symptomology and substance abuse are among the most common comorbid conditions), and (2) the wide variability of receptivity to treatment among patients who present with complex (recurrent) and chronic problems. Prescriptive therapy is intended to address the differences that exist among patients more effectively than the currently available treatments. Current treatments draw from theoretical models that are not compatible with all patients; however, PT extracts strategies and techniques from several different theoretical models to provide the best fit for individual patients.

The companion volume to this manual (Beutler, Clarkin, & Bongar, in press) undertook an intensive review of literature on both the nature of depression and its treatment. From the combination of this literature review and cross-validational studies, the authors extracted a set of hypothetical guidelines or principles that could be used to guide treatment selection for specific patients. These guidelines were then cross-validated on a multisite sample of 289 patients representing depression, chemical abuse, and their combinations. The authors concluded that, among other things: (1) depression/dysphoria, more than being a disorder in its own right, is a signal of stress in the system and this is why it is the most frequently observed co-existing condition with both medical and psychiatric disorders; and (2) effective treatment of both depression and chemical abuse are predicted by similar parameters and patterns of patient-therapy, and patient-treatment matching variables.

From these premises, Beutler, Clarkin, and Bongar modified and refined the original hypothetical principles to coincide with the findings from their cross-validation study. The result was a set of 18 general principles that could be used as guidelines for selecting and matching treatments to patients across a variety of conditions in which depression and dysphoria was present as a marker of distress and difficulty. These principles allowed one to determine and select short-versus long-term treatments, psychological versus pharmacological treatments, and multiperson versus individual treatments and to select among a variety of psychotherapeutic strategies.

In the current manual, we have focused on the 10 principles (of those that were defined in the companion volume) that apply to the specific case of individual psychotherapy. We have selected this focus because it is the central and most frequently recommended mode of treatment and (arguably) the most complicated of the treatment procedures and formats.

Drawing from the 10 principles for guiding the application of individual psychotherapy, PT focuses on four patient characteristics that can be identified at the initiation of treatment and across a variety of problems. These four patient characteristics have been identified in previous research and cross-validated in our own research programs as ones that correlate with a distinguishable response to different families of interventions. These patient characteristics, which we describe in greater detail later, are (1) level of functional impairment, (2) characteristic ways of coping with stress, (3) level of current, experienced distress, and (4) trait-like levels of interpersonal resistance to external influence.

The rationale for defining the qualities of treatment that constitute a "fit" with these patient dimensions is derived from research on differential treatments and the demonstration that patient qualities can serve as indicators and contraindicators for employing different strategies, in the form of classes of intervention. The framework for these decisions derives from STS (Beutler & Clarkin, 1990; Beutler & Consoli, 1992; Gaw & Beutler, 1995), an empirically grounded structure that uses extant research evidence to define state and trait-like patient indicators and contraindicators for the use of various strategies and techniques of mental health interventions. This PT manual is a refined and up-to-date reflection of the STS model, it incorporates the latest research, and is presented here as a guide in broad clinical use.

The Underpinnings of Systematic Treatment Selection

Noting the general failure for the effects and effectiveness of various treatments to be distinguished, Beutler and Clarkin (1990) suggested that research and practice shift focus from efforts to find a singularly effective treatment for a singular condition to a focus that inspects the problem of treatment planning in a more complex manner. They suggested that patient diagnosis had largely failed as a basis for selecting among treatments but offered empirical evidence that dimensions of patient response and adaptation may moderate treatment effects. They proposed a decisional model for selecting among treatments, based on families of interventions rather than broad theories of psychopathology, and guided by empirical distinctions among patients rather than diagnostic symptoms. This is the model that initially guided the efforts of Beutler, Clarkin, and Bongar (in press) and that subsequently was modified as a result of their multisite study of treatment.

This latter research confirmed the original view that treatment could be usefully framed within a perspective of levels. Four levels or decision points were identified, each of which is interactive and sequential. Thus, decisions must be understood as having accumulating influence. In this framework, single decisions about treatment are considered to be high risk. The validity of decisions is best thought to reflect the cascading influence of each decision on the other.

The first level of decision making involves a determination of the *patient predisposing qualities* that are predictive of varying prognoses and that serve to mediate the effects of different treatments. The extant literature of the time suggested that at a minimum, these qualities should include aspects of normal adjustment (coping style, interpersonal attitudes, etc.), attention to the patient's environment (social support, role demands, expectations, etc.), and aspects of the problem presented (symptoms, severity, impairment, distress, chronicity, etc.). As Beutler and Clarkin (1990) initially proposed, and as our research has subsequently confirmed, patient predisposing variables are implicated in treatment planning at two subsequent levels, one that relates directly to prognosis (e.g., social support and subjective distress) and the one that determines the correct or best fit of a treatment to a patient's needs (e.g., coping style, functional impairment, and expectations).

In the organizational framework, the second level of decision making involves selection of the *context* of treatment. Context decisions include those related to the intensity of treatment required (beginning with the decision of whether to treat at all), the setting in which treatment would be offered (e.g., inpatient or outpatient), the modality (medical vs. nonmedical), and the format (individual vs. multiperson treatment). Available literature suggested that while patient diagnosis was often attributed as a factor in these decisions, more often clinicians looked to patient functioning, previous episodes, chronicity, flexibility, cooperation, and other indicators of severity as determiners of treatment context. Indeed, empirical evidence has generally supported these contentions and indicated that prior history of similar problems along with levels of impairment may be particularly important in deciding issues of context.

As the research of Beutler, Clarkin, and Bongar (in press) confirms, only after decisions about the context of treatment had been resolved can one usefully employ patient predisposing qualities to guide treatment selection at the third level: *relationship and therapeutic procedures.* This research found that the nature of a treatment relationship varied by the setting in which it occurred and could best be adapted within a known treatment context. Thus, effective treatment planning is a reflection of how well the assigned therapist or clinician adapts both to the patient and to the context in which treatment is offered and, at the same time, provides procedures that are effective and useful within that environment.

Relationship and procedural decisions are proposed to take place at several different levels. These decisions include the selection of therapists whose views and expectations are compatible with those of the patient, the use of procedures that enhance these expectations and facilitate the treatment alliance, and the availability of skills and professional experiences that are fitted to the level of patient need. The particular therapist, skills, experience, procedures, and techniques all function as predisposing patient qualities. Empirical evidence supports the contention that some procedures are relatively effective across patients but arise from different levels of training, skill, perspectives, and knowledge.

The fourth level in the STS model provides the most refined level of treatment planning. At this level, the evidence suggests that a clinician can fit particular interventions to the changing needs of each patient. Only after taking into account the therapeutic process and the therapeutic relationship can one usefully and differentially select certain treatment techniques and strategies to fit the particular and specific needs of each patient. For example, effective treatment is most likely if the therapist adjusts the level of directiveness and guidance to the patient's ability to tolerate external control (resistance level), if the use of symptom-removal and/or insight interventions are applied based on an assessment of how patient's acquire and adapt to new information (coping style), and if the use of abreactive and affect reduction procedures are consistent with the patient's level of motivation and distress (level of emotional arousal and subjective distress). The focus on adapting and changing the nature of the intervention to fit patient qualities was at contrast with the still prevalent effort to find a single type of intervention that surpasses all others in effects and value. Instead, PT is intended to fit the setting as well as the patient and to match the dispositions of the clinician to the predilections of the patient.

Guiding Objectives of Prescriptive Therapy

Several important contradictions are infused into the practice of mental health treatment. These contradictions reveal the presence of contrasting and opposing value systems. For example, the field is characterized by the contrast between (1) reliance on structured, single-theory manuals that have guided research versus the multitheory perspectives that characterize most practitioners, (2) the practical necessity of relying on empirically validated treatments versus the clinician's faith in personal experience and clinical judgment, and (3) the conclusion of many academic scientists that all treatments are essentially equivalent versus the clinical belief that all interventions are accompanied by indicating and contraindicating conditions.

These contrasting views of clinical treatment have contributed to mutual distrust between practitioners of psychotherapy and clinical scientists (Beutler, Williams, & Wakefield, 1993; Beutler, Williams, Wakefield, & Entwistle, 1995). The history of treatment development, and especially the development of psychotherapy, is characterized by a failure to develop a reciprocal appreciation among scientists and practitioners. Any hope of bridging this chasm relies on the ability of treatment models to stimulate two-way communication between clinicians and academic investigators.

Systematic treatment selection attempts to establish the scientific bases of the assumptions that are inherent in psychotherapeutic practice. It provides a model for selecting interventions differentially to accommodate a variety of patient qualities and characteristics. In this process, STS advocates using multicomponent methods of intervention derived from a variety of systematic approaches to psychotherapy. Like all available prescriptive treatment models, the STS model eschews comprehensive clinical theories of either psychopathology or of psychotherapy as guides to intervention. Instead, it focuses on identifying specific and individual patient characteristics that dispose the use of equally specific treatment strategies. The application of a truly prescriptive and differential psychotherapy requires that the clinician learn to identify the patient cues that reliably indicate the presence of treatment-relevant traits and states, assess the levels at which these qualities occur, and then select appropriate therapeutic interventions to fit these qualities and levels.

For example, 1 of the 10 guiding principles to be discussed in this volume asserts that *"therapeutic change is greatest when a patient is stimulated to emotional arousal in a safe environment until problematic responses diminish or extinguish."* This is a principle of exposure and extinction. Rather than mandating the use of specific procedures such as response prevention, however, as means of implementing this principle, prescriptive therapists are asked to identify the procedures within their own range of skills that may be employed to confront, raise, and extinguish the avoidant response. Thus, one therapist may use the technique of *in vivo* exposure, another may use imaginal desensitization, and still another may use role-playing exercises. In the case of clear, single-symptom conditions, the procedures derived may be very similar, but when complex and comorbid problems are present, a system based on the identification of techniques becomes cumbersome and unwieldy. The therapist who applies it is a technician rather than a behavior change expert. Guidelines that emphasize principles of practice over techniques are likely to be more flexible and adaptable, by comparison.

Concomitantly, the strategic focus of PT is not compatible with the conventional practice of rating and judging therapists on their level of compliance and skill in applying a set of technical procedures, independent of the impact of these procedures on the patient. Instead, for example, this model assesses therapist skill in terms of the degree to which he or she has been successful at increasing the patient's fear response, holding it at escalated levels in the presence of the feared object until diminishment of response occurs. Thus, the focus becomes the success of the therapist in accomplishing a particular change in the patient's response rather than simply the compliance of the therapist with some standard of technical fidelity. Moreover, a principle of change does not simply define how to treat a particular condition such as a phobia; change principles address a host of behaviors that arise from emotional avoidance. This shift in perspective ensures the exercise of maximal flexibility and creativity on the part of the therapist.

Dimensions of Patient and Treatment Matching

Cross-Theoretical Applications

As we have noted, one disadvantage of conventional manualized therapies as used in contemporary clinical trial studies is that they often are insufficiently flexible to address a given patient's needs (Anderson & Strupp, 1996; Henry, Schacht, Strupp, Butler, & Binder, 1993). Single-theory formulations prescribe against (proscribe) the use of interventions that are inconsistent with their theory, even if those interventions have been observed to be effective in independent research studies. The limited range of these interventions, however, do not accurately reflect the pragmatic, cross-theory "eclecticism" that characterizes most psychotherapists (Norcross & Prochaska, 1988; Garfield & Kurtz, 1977). Nor do these manuals adequately allow for combining treatment methods from multiple conceptual models in order to tailor them to comorbid conditions, as is typically done in practice. A combined intervention, or PT, promises a wider range of applications than single-theory models. An effective test of such interventions requires a defining set of markers that would allow interventions from different theories to be applied in a systematic way to fit the particular patient without losing the assurance of consistency and integrity.

The patient dimensions that focus the remainder of this manual are (1) level of functional impairment; (2) patient coping style, particularly level of externalization and impulsivity; (3) level of patient resistance; and (4) level of patient distress. These qualities represent continuous dimensions of patient functioning and, collectively, include both state and trait qualities.

The corresponding dimensions along which PT will be designed to vary include (1) high versus low treatment intensity, (2) skill building and symptom focus versus insight and awareness focus, (3) high versus low therapist directiveness, and (4) emotional confrontation versus support. The bidirectional quality of these latter dimensions correspond with the mediating role played by patient dimensions and identify the range of strategies that the therapist must have at her disposal in order to work with patients who vary in the identified quality.

As reviewed by Beutler, Clarkin, and Bongar (in press), these matching dimensions have been tested, both prospectively and retrospectively, in several studies. However, except for the archival and retrospective results reported by these latter authors, these dimensions have only been tested separately, as embedded constructs within different single-theory manuals (i.e., cognitive therapy [CT]; Yost, Beutler, Corbishley, & Allender, 1986; Wakefield et al., 1996; focused expressive psychotherapy [FE]; Daldrup, Beutler, Engle, & Greenberg, 1988; supportive-self-directed therapy [S/SD]; Scogin, Hamblin, & Beutler, 1987), for depression, alcoholism, and chronic pain.

The systematic linkage of several of these patient and treatment dimensions at once, within a single treatment (Beutler, Clarkin, & Bongar, in press; Gaw & Beutler, 1995; Beutler, Consoli, & Williams, 1995), has never been tested in a prospective, controlled study. The cross-validation study by Beutler, Clarkin, and Bongar (in press) was an archival or retrospective study rather than a prospective one. Readers who are interested in a more in-depth treatment of these issues are referred to Beutler, Clarkin, and Bongar (in press).

Specific Patient Characteristics

Main effect differences between pure types of psychotherapy account for approximately 10% of the variation in outcomes among mixed-patient groups (e.g., Lambert, 1989; Lambert & DeJulio, 1978; Smith, Glass, & Miller, 1980). The preponderance of the effects of psychotherapy can be attributed to general procedures that are employed to enhance and support the development of a trusting and empathic working relationship between patient and therapist. These qualities are not differential; they seem to work in a similar way across most models and types of psychotherapy, leading some to even suggest that they are the bases of change in all therapies (Frank & Frank, 1991; Garfield, 1980, 1994). However, even after extracting the proportion of outcome attributable to such general or common qualities, wide variations of unaccounted for outcomes remain within any treatment comparison. The use of manualized therapies and diagnostically pure subject groups does not eliminate this within treatment variance (Howard, 1989). Howard observes that in virtually all scientific comparisons, regardless of the diagnostic group on which it is conducted, each psychotherapy is effective for some patients and is ineffective for others. These findings indicate the need to more specifically identify both the characteristics of patients and the nature of treatments that account for this level of differential effectiveness.

Empirically, across diverse patient groups, including samples of substance abusers, the patient variables that have been found to interact most successfully with treatment procedures are coping styles (Beutler, 1979; Beutler & Mitchell, 1981; Sloane, Staples, Cristol, Yorkston, & Whipple, 1975), level of resistance (Beutler, Engle et al., 1991; Beutler, Mohr, Grave, Engle, & MacDonald, 1991; Shoham-Salomon & Hannah, 1991), and aspects of problem severity and distress (Imber et al., 1990; Luborsky, McLellan, Woody, O'Brien & Auerbach, 1985). Although these dimensions appear to be relatively independent of one another, patients may vary on several of these treatment indicators/contraindicators at once. The typical manualized treatment is applied relatively independently of patient variability, and may unintentionally include treatment components with offsetting effects (e.g., the power of CT for externalizing patients may be offset by its poor effects among poorly motivated patients).

Within these constraints, evidence indicates that among patients with symptoms of depression and anxiety (1) therapies that target symptom removal or the acquisition of behavioral skills through contingency management (e.g., Higgins, Budney, & Bickel, 1994) and cognitive change methods are more effective among impulsive or externalizing patients than are those that attempt to facilitate insight, an effect that appears to be reversed among patients with less externalizing coping styles (Beutler, Mohr et. al., 1991; Beutler, Engle et. al., 1991; Calvert, Beutler, & Crago, 1988; Sloane et al., 1975); (2) nondirective and paradoxical interventions are more effective than directive ones among patients with high levels of pretherapy resistance (i.e., "resistance potential"), and this effect is reversed among those with low resistance (Beutler, Mohr et al., 1991; Beutler, Engle et al., 1991; Shoham-Salomon & Hannah, 1991; Forsyth & Forsyth, 1982); and (3) therapies that raise emotional tone and intensity are more effective than those that do not raise the level of emotional arousal (Beutler & Mitchell, 1981; Greenberg & Safran, 1987; Mohr et al., 1990; Orlinsky & Howard, 1986).

Accordingly, effective prescriptive treatment strategies coordinate and balance the focus of treatment along dimensions of symptomatic, insight, and thematic change; altering level of therapist confrontation and direction; and raising or lowering emotional tone and intensity. It will also include varying the level or intensity of care, emphasizing or deemphasizing personal and background differences between the patient and therapist, and deciding how medical treatments should be incorporated into treatment.

Introduction to the Therapeutic Principles, Strategies, and Techniques of Training in Prescriptive Therapy

We believe that the selection of strategies and techniques of effective treatment is best derived from an understanding of basic principles of therapeutic change. The guidelines presented in the STS model of treatment selection by Beutler, Clarkin, and Bongar (in press) are based on a three-tier program in which clinicians are taught sound principles of behavior change; these principles are designed to lead the clinician to construct strategies for implementing change; strategies are transmitted through the use of procedures and techniques. Each level of implementation provides more opportunity for flexibility and creativity but does so in the context of remaining faithful to the nature of guiding relationships among patients, treatments, and outcomes. This progression from firm principle to creative application of technique stands in contrast to the usual method of constructing treatment guidelines that increasingly restrict treatment options in the application of technical procedures.

Here we present the basic principles that are used in individual therapy to promote change and to induce differential rates of response. Subsequent sections expand on these principles and on the associated implications for procedures and strategies. The principles of therapeutic change represent the broadest conceptualization of treatment. Attention to these principles via the selection of appropriate strategies and techniques will increase the likelihood or magnitude of change. These principles are:

1. Therapeutic change is greatest when the therapist is skillful and provides trust, acceptance, acknowledgment, collaboration, and respect for the patient and does so in an environment that both supports risk and provides maximal safety.
2. Risk and retention are optimized if the patient is realistically informed about the probable length and effectiveness of the treatment is, provided with support and comfort, and is provided with a clear understanding of the roles and activities that are expected of him or her during the course of treatment.
3. Benefit corresponds with treatment intensity among functionally impaired patients.
4. Therapeutic change is most likely when the patient is exposed to objects or targets of behavioral and emotional avoidance.
5. Therapeutic change is greatest when the relative balance of interventions either favors the use of skill building and symptom removal procedures among externalizing patients or favors the use of insight and relationship-focused procedures among internalizing patients.
6. Therapeutic change is most likely if the initial focus of change efforts is to build new skills and alter disruptive symptoms.
7. Therapeutic change is most likely when the therapeutic procedures do not evoke patient resistance.
8. Therapeutic change is greatest when the directiveness of the intervention is either inversely correspondent with the patient's current level of resistance or authoritatively prescribes a continuation of the symptomatic behavior.
9. The likelihood of therapeutic change is greatest when the patient's level of emotional stress is moderate, neither being excessively high nor excessively low.
10. Therapeutic change is greatest when a patient is stimulated to emotional arousal in a safe environment until problematic responses diminish or extinguish.

The second and third principles are what Beutler, Clarkin, and Bongar (in press) have called basic guidelines because they are general and can be implemented without direct observational feedback from observing the psychotherapy sessions. The remaining eight principles are what these authors have identified as "optimal guidelines" because they are designed to be selective and differentially applied and require direct feedback through observations of the treatment relationship.

The principles, when restated to identify the nature of treatment for a specific patient, constitute treatment strategies. Strategies represent families of interventions or techniques that share a common objective. They operate within and originate from the principles of therapeutic change, but do so in a manner specific to a given patient. For example, principle 9 emphasizes that patient stress should be moderate. Translated to a particular patient, however, this principle may mean that the patient's level of distress should be lowered and that procedures should be employed to reduce it from high to moderate levels. The reduction of affective arousal may be an indicated strategy and reflections, closed-ended questions, stress-management procedures, and the provision of structure are techniques that may be implemented by different therapists to comply with this objective strategy.

In a similar manner, at a minimal level, effective strategies for implementing the other principles will:

- Provide a safe and respectful environment.
- Expose the patient either to the external precipitators of the symptom or to the internal experiences that are avoided (e.g., via *in vivo* exposure, repeated interpretation of a consistent dynamic theme, adopting a here-and-now focus on daily problems and relationship change).
- Adapt level of treatment to the level of patient impairment (e.g., adjusting frequency and length of sessions, assigning group and/or individual treatment).
- Select interventions that either build skills and alter symptoms or that evoke insight and awareness, applying them differentially to reflect differences in patient coping styles.
- Adopt either a directive or nondirective role with the patient to lead him/her toward action and change (e.g., alter level of directiveness, utilize paradoxical interventions, behavioral contracts, and/or evocative support).
- Provide either support or confrontation and exposure to fit the patient's level of emotional distress (e.g., structure and support if emotional arousal is high and confrontation, experiential and open-ended/unstructured procedures if arousal is low).

The remainder of this book describes how these strategies may be developed for individual patients and how they may be used to guide treatment selection.

Conclusions

The belief that all treatments are equal flies in the face of the experience and beliefs of most clinicians. The perpetuation of the statistically correct, but factually suspect conclusion that experience and training are irrelevant may well rest in the failure of research to disaggregate patients in logical ways to reveal their distinguishing responses to the things that a therapist might do (Howard, Krause, & Lyons, 1993). In contrast to the broad diagnostic symptoms and criteria to which research looks for differential response indicators, clinicians tend to look to patterns of interpersonal styles and emotional response states as guides to make treatment decisions. These patient qualities, most of which are not captured in the diagnostic nomenclature, are used by clinicians to avoid using some strategies and intervention styles and to selectively use others. Taken together, an effective manual would guide the therapist to adapt to patient differences and would demonstrate that doing so would improve the level of treatment effects beyond that of single-theory models and associated manuals. Prescriptive therapy is an effort to provide such a manual and structure for treatment.

Research on PT has provided support for the conclusion that patient distress and impairment, coping style, and resistance behaviors are implicated in predictable ways in the selection of psychotherapeutic strategies for treating depression, substance abuse, or both (Beutler, Clarkin, & Bongar, in press; Beutler, Goodrich, Fisher, & Williams, in press). These findings suggest that some aspects of treatment planning can be based on an understanding of qualities that patients bring with them to treatment and that invoke certain kinds of responses regardless of other patient factors. Such considerations can be expressed as basic treatment guidelines. In the list of 10 guidelines that we have offered, we have included two basic guidelines (numbers 2 and 3) relating to the importance of addressing the patient's need to be informed of the nature and objectives of treatment and the need to intensify treatment in accordance with the patient's level of impairment.

One other principle (number 1) is also general in that it applies to all individual treatment, but we have identified it as "optimal" rather than as a basic guideline because its verification requires a time-intensive observation by an external observer, a procedure that cannot always be routinely implemented. Specifically, this principle emphasizes that treatment be based on a caring relationship enacted in a safe environment, but therapists are frequently not good observers of the presence of such a relationship. Feedback from the patient and from external observers are usually required.

The remaining seven principles also constitute "optimal guidelines" and address the problem of altering procedures to fit patients of different types. They address the need to adjust the intensity of treatment, the symptomatic versus thematic levels of change, the need to adapt to the patient's level of resistance, and the desirability of maintaining a motivational level of arousal and distress. Validation of these principles requires observation of the internal workings of the psychotherapy.

Within these principles, our research suggests that the clinician can be guided to make several decisions, the net result of which is to develop a comprehensive strategy of treatment that is compatible with the particular needs and attributes of the patient and that is distinguished from patient to patient. For example, a differential treatment:

- Confronts the patient with the objects or targets of behavioral and emotional avoidance.
- Implements direct efforts to change focused symptoms related to such symptoms as substance abuse and risk.
- Avoids evoking therapeutic resistance, and adapts the level of directive guidance to the patient's current level of resistance.
- Maintains the patient at a level of arousal that motivates change.
- Confronts the patient with avoided behaviors and experiences until they diminish or extinguish.

In later chapters, we expand on these principles and translate them into working diagrams of treatment. We begin with a further description of the procedures and rationale for training therapists in the use of PT and follow with a description of how patients may be evaluated to help the clinician identify their standing on those variables that are used in the construction of treatment. We then describe methods of responding to the basic guiding principles that direct the initial development of a working relationship. Finally, we proceed to a discussion of each patient dimension, in turn, with a focus on its implications for adapting therapeutic interventions.

Chapter 2
Training Objectives and Rationale

As we pointed out in chapter 1, the theory-specific and diagnostic concepts that drive and direct the use of most psychosocial training manuals do not allow adaptation of the treatment to the unique characteristics of different patients. Together, the focus of these treatment manuals is on diagnostic groups and theoretical perspectives (psychoanalytic, behavioral, cognitive, etc.). This narrow focus results in both a sterile profile of the patient and an inflexible therapy. All patients of a given diagnostic class (e.g., those with depression, eating disorders, or anxiety disorders) are treated similarly within the scope of a particular manual, with minor modifications to account for different symptom patterns. The research purposes for which these manuals were originally developed implicitly assume that diagnostic homogeneity translates to patient homogeneity and explicitly assumes that it is desirable to treat all patients within a defined diagnostic class in a virtually identical way to eliminate factors that obscure the effects of treatment in statistical analysis.

In attempting to maintain a consistent approach for all patients of a diagnostic class, these treatment manuals embody a significant degree of external overinclusiveness. That is, researchers who employ manualized therapies in controlled studies assume a higher degree of similarity among patients within a defined diagnostic class than is warranted. In point of fact, clinicians have always been impressed with how much variability there is within any given diagnostic group. Accepting the assumption that patients within a diagnosis are homogeneous has led to manualized treatments for depression, anxiety disorders, personality disorders, eating disorders, and so forth. These are treatments for *disorders*, not people, and there are many similarities in treatment procedures across these disorders as a function of the theoretical model used. Thus, by their descriptions, cognitive therapies for depression are more similar to cognitive therapies for eating disorders than they are to interpersonal psychotherapy for either of these conditions. The therapist, in turn, is constrained to adopt the interventions that are prescribed for application by the theoretical model to the major presenting symptoms and their variations. Missing are treatments that are designed to fit the unique aspects of how people adapt and adjust to life circumstances. Such inflexibility is all the more important because diagnostic dimensions are largely irrelevant to most differential treatment decisions (Beutler, 1989, 1991).

Because they are insensitive to patient variability and because they proscribe interventions that are incompatible with the theory that drives it, each manual underrepresents the number and types of potentially effective therapeutic interventions. That is, the reliance on a single and particular theory of symptom development or psychopathology binds them to a restricted range of interventions. These interventions are taught and assessed as techniques that are wedded to the spawning theory. Any particular theory, whether cognitive, interpersonal, psychodynamic, or other, embodies a limited view of psychopathology and of the interventions that are consistent with the theory. This proscription of treatments occurs even when the excluded interventions are demonstrably effective. As a general rule, a therapist who is "approved" to use a given approach must not only accept the importance of using these techniques but must accept the validity of the theory from which they derive as well.

Contemporary research literature on treatment indicators, contraindicators, and correlates provides little support either for the relative weight given to diagnostic symptoms over normal variations in interpersonal response or for the allegiance that is prescribed for adhering to a single model of treatment. While diagnostic variables are certainly important as criteria by which to assess change and improvement, there is virtually no evidence that any treatment has effects that are restricted to particular diagnostic symptom classes or to one or another model of symptom development. Indeed, we even are unable to find evidence that the validity or veracity of a theory is related to the effectiveness of the treatment based on it. In fact, there is more than a little evidence that good practices can arise from bad theory and, conversely, that ineffective and even dangerous practices can arise from sound theory (e.g., Beutler, Bongar, & Shurkin, 1998; Beutler, & Guest, 1989).

In contrast to the usual single-theory formulations of psychotherapy, prescriptive psychotherapy models assume that the effectiveness of each treatment is a function of the degree to which it is able to accommodate the treatment plan to the unique needs and responses of a given patient. The most highly visible models of prescriptive psychotherapies (e.g., multimodal psychotherapy, transtheoretical psychotherapy, and STS) hold in common the attempt to address the need for flexibility without sacrificing the empirical need for reliability and structure. Systematic Treatment Selection (STS) is a treatment planning model originally developed by Beutler and Clarkin (1990) and subsequently translated to identify the strategies that appear to underlie the effective use of specific operations and procedures, independent of their spawning theories (Gaw & Beutler, 1995; Beutler, Consoli, & Williams, 1995). We provide some examples of specific procedures and techniques that illustrate ways to employ the principles of STS and may provide a guide for clinicians to planfully and reliably alter the interventions they use in order to accommodate the nuances of particular patients within and across diagnostic groupings.

A software package using STS logic has been added to the use of standardized psychological tests to assist in the assessment process. This program includes an interactive data base and descriptions of more than 40 treatment manuals, helping therapists select among the most promising treatment options for a variety of particular patients (Beutler & Williams, 1995).

Prescriptive therapy is designed to resolve the paradoxical needs for flexibility, on the one hand, and structure, on the other. It accomplishes this by specifying guiding principles, identifying a limited number of patient variables that have been empirically demonstrated to be predictive of a differential response among varieties of psychotherapy, and operationalizing choice points that index the activation of differential strategies and that can be applied to distinctively different patients. Thus, instruction in PT will present (1) methods of measuring treatment-relevant characteristics of patients, (2) a description of principles and differential strategies that fit these characteristics, (3) examples of procedures that will help operationalize these strategies, and (4) methods for assessing compliance with the application of these strategies.

Because PT may be taught and employed in graduate training programs (similar to our training program at the University of California—Santa Barbara [UCSB]), we provide guidelines for training both advanced practitioners as well as graduate student trainees.

Foundations of Training in PT

The techniques and procedures we have chosen are largely drawn from cognitive therapy, relationship-oriented therapy, experiential therapy, and self-help manuals. Purposely, in PT, we plan, integrate, and institute treatment at the levels of principles and differential strategies rather than at either the level of theory or technique in order to ensure greater therapist flexibility and to foster therapist creativity. Specific techniques and applications are selected by therapists to be consistent with guiding principles and are responsive to differential treatment plans that are predicted to be most effective with given patients. Therapists, thus, are encouraged to develop, select, and use techniques in creative and new ways (i.e., tailored to each patient's needs and remaining consistent with the strategies selected) within the context of the guiding principles. Concomitantly, concerns with reliability and stability of interventions are addressed at the level of strategy rather than at the level of technique, to ensure and encourage therapist flexibility. By evaluating and giving feedback to therapists about how well their strategies fit patient qualities, the therapist can also learn to be self-observing and self-correcting, increasingly honing therapeutic and decisional skills for tailoring treatment.

Therapist Skill Development

Becoming an effective clinician-psychotherapist begins in one's infancy with a process of becoming socialized, learning to accept and tolerate intense emotions, and being presented with models of emotional sensitivity and acceptance that are provided by the fortune of inheriting a congenial family. Therapeutic development is continued in adolescence and high school as one develops an intrinsic sense of values, along with the capacity for self-reflection and critical observation. The process of developing attitudes conducive to being an effective psychotherapist is well entrenched by the time the individual enters college, and even more so as he or she enters graduate education and professional specialization. At these latter levels, such attitudes can only be reinforced and supported; if an individual has failed to develop them, it is unlikely that undergraduate, graduate, or postdoctoral training will help him or her do so.

The process of training in PT has been developed, in our program, to include the preparation of students who plan to enter professional training at some later point in their careers. At this level, usually in the undergraduate years, we endeavor to facilitate the development of the knowledge needed to integrate research and practice, including an understanding of the relationship between patient assessment and psychotherapy.

In contrast, at the level of doctoral training, we employ the STS model of treatment planning to prepare professional psychologists to assume roles as researchers and practitioners. At this level, training in techniques occupies a large portion of the student's activities. While the major objectives of training are related to teaching students the guiding principles and differential strategies that guide treatment selection, these students must also have a foundation of techniques and procedures available to them. Thus, training is aimed at providing scientific knowledge that forms the basis of skill development and teaching the techniques that are espoused by a variety of theoretical models. Following the goals of systematic treatment selection, we teach graduate students to (1) use methods of measuring treatment-relevant characteristics of patients, (2) become aware of optimal strategies and associated interventions that can be used with patients whose identified characteristics vary, and (3) employ methods for assessing their compliance with the application of effective psychotherapeutic procedures.

However, it is not enough to train a professional to competence at one point in his or her career. Doing so lacks an understanding that continuing training and monitoring is necessary to ensure that knowledge is current and levels of effectiveness are maintained. The effective use of PT, for example, requires a modification of principles with the accumulation of new research knowledge. Training in PT can be more limited and condensed, less focused on technique development, than is true of training at the undergraduate and graduate levels. Fundamental skills are achieved and honed through original practice and continued experience. Advanced clinicians have acquired those skills that are routinely employed in their practices. Thus, the focus of continuing training is on the new principles and knowledge that support the refinement of treatment. This level of training places much more emphasis on acquiring a working knowledge of the principles and differential strategies that guide technique selection than on the techniques or theory.

In our program at UCSB, training focuses on a relatively small number of patient variables and matching treatment dimensions that will be most useful for the advanced education of experienced clinicians and those newly entering the helping professions. The procedures taught represent a beginning and a movement toward addressing the complexity of patients and treatments that we believe have been ignored in prior training.

Consistent with the STS model, the treatment procedures that form the basis of training in PT are drawn from a wide array of models and strategies, without regard to the truth of the spawning theories. Suggested strategies are derived from a wide variety of theoretical models, each selected on the basis of demonstrated effects and each unhampered by the proscriptive rules of a particular theory of symptom development. Instead, the application of procedures and strategies is guided by empirical evidence of the efficacy and effectiveness of the strategies and techniques themselves. The methods of self-evaluation, moreover, embody empirically based and verifiable guidelines for the selection of these strategies and interventions.

In the following pages, we describe the basic structure of psychotherapy training and illustrate the application of these principles in regard to graduate (doctoral) and advanced (professional, postdoctoral) training in psychotherapy. Contrasting the training of graduate and postgraduate professionals illustrates the perspective that we hold on the relative value of principles of change, differential strategies, and specific techniques. It also illustrates, what we hope, advanced practitioners entering the PT training program have acquired through their prior training and experience.

Applications to Training in Psychotherapy

There are six keys[1] to being an effective psychotherapist: attitudes, knowledge, tools, techniques, time, and creative imagination. Effective therapy begins with *attitudes* of respect, optimism about the patient's potential for growth and change, empathic sensitivity, curiosity, and self-awareness. These attitudes are the foundation for the interpersonal and listening skills that are the nucleus of the powerful healing forces that contribute to the benefits of all forms of effective psychotherapy. Some experts think these attitudes are the basis for all psychotherapeutic change—the common factors model of psychotherapy. They are also thought by some to be placebos. In contrast, we believe that these attitudes are far from being placebos in the traditional medical sense. That is, placebos are, by nature, inert (from a purely biological perspective); however, therapeutic attitudes have powerful psychological effects. Therapeutic attitudes are active and necessary to the change process, though not always sufficient to ensure that such changes occur. But, they are also largely independent of formal academic training. Indeed, if contemporary educational programs affect these attitudes, it is as likely to be in a negative as in a positive direction.

As we have noted, therapeutic attitudes are probably developed in the process of one's very early social development, within the experiences offered to them by a supportive and caring family or alternative support system. The absence of caring role models in childhood and adolescence may even constitute a negative indicator for the ability to develop therapeutic attitudes, though there is no research on this topic to our knowledge. Creating therapeutic attitudes, in fact, may be out of the reach of postsecondary formal education. Yet they are essential and a therapist must never lose sight of their importance and never cease trying to develop them further. With these attitudes alone, one can be an effective clinician and therapist for most people who seek their services.

Knowledge of the principles that guide clinical change is important but never subsumes or replaces, in importance, therapeutic attitudes such as respect and caring. However, knowing the principles that tell us how changes occur in the feelings, struggles, and behavior of people adds to the power of therapists' humane and helpful attitudes. To maximize the power of psychotherapy, one must have a sound understanding of fundamental principles of change in addition to appropriate therapeutic attitudes. Knowledge of principles derives from studying the empirical basis of clinical work and knowing the patient qualities that temper or mediate the effects of various interventions. That is, the therapist must know how to identify relevant patient characteristics and how to select and use compatible interventions. Unlike the pessimism with which we approach the likelihood of being able to teach adults a therapeutic attitude, we are optimistic that graduate and advanced training in psychotherapy can produce a sound basis of knowledge. Thus, we will be emphasizing the principles of change that derive from sound clinical experience and clinically relevant research.

Together, the knowledgeable application of *tools* and *techniques* of psychotherapy comprise the therapist's level of *skill*. The tools include the psychological assessment procedures, materials, office arrangements, and equipment necessary for a patient to establish a sense of safety and predictability in the treatment environment. Tools include the procedures for physiological monitoring and computer hardware and software that are often needed for interpreting, applying, or integrating psychological observations and interventions. The tools must be applied through a medium of well-developed and empirically valid techniques and they only achieve maximal power when applied in a skillful way. Thus, we view tools and techniques to be the basis of skill; however, skill also includes the therapist's willingness to modify and alter the interventions applied in a flexible fashion. We prefer to emphasize the inseparability of tools and techniques by invoking the more general term, therapeutic "skill." Throughout this volume, we refer to therapist skill as the integrative and flexible combination of attitude, knowledge, tools and techniques. A skillful therapist can shift among a variety of therapeutic procedures in a seamless fashion, knowing when to persist and when to alter directions and focus. Most of this manual is devoted to training these skills.

Time is the fifth key to success and also is inherently related to therapist skill. The skillful therapist is able to time interventions and permits the patient the time necessary to change. Rushing to effect change is a sure recipe for failure, but so is overreluctance to enter the fray. In the service of helping therapists manage time, we focus in this manual on identifying the indicators that suggest when to intervene, not just on identifying what they might do. The indicators for treatment are time sensitive and the therapist who is aware of state-like changes, as well as trait-like qualities, is prepared to intervene in a timely fashion.

The therapist's attitudes, knowledge, skills, and timing come together through the use of creative *imagination*. Imagination is the creative foundation of flexibility. Like any art, the art of psychotherapy does not and cannot discard the importance of physical laws. However, one can learn to apply these physical principles in new and creative ways. The application of old principles to new and novel environments is the epitome of therapeutic art and flexibility, as it is with any art. For example, the creative painter knows that the principles of color mixture cannot be discarded but is able to apply these principles in new and interesting ways. The musician does not discard the principle of chords or knowledge of melodies but uses this knowledge to create new patterns and to evoke new responses in an audience. Others may copy the work of the painter or musician, using the same combinations of color and sound; however, these people are technicians, not artists. The artist is the individual who initially sees how to adapt and use principles of color and sound in new and effective ways. The artist has the idea; the technician copies it.

The artistic psychotherapist does not—indeed, cannot—work outside valid principles of change and relationship, any more than the painter or musician can work outside the physical laws that govern sound and color. But, like other artists, the artistic therapist is able to work within the principles that guide relationship and change to adapt to the ever-changing and ever-different qualities and characteristics that each patient presents. This is the basis of effective, prescriptive psychotherapy. It is our goal to help therapists learn the principles and use creative imagination to employ them in novel and productive ways to adapt to new situations and the endless variety of behavior that characterizes people.

Training at the Graduate Level

In identifying and applying prescriptive interventions to graduate training, one of two different models are in conventional use by various training centers: (1) therapists are trained in two or more particular (often, manualized) therapies and are taught to select one of the available models to fit each patient, or (2) therapists are trained in a variety of specific procedures and models and apply treatments to particular patients by constructing a new intervention package that includes procedures from several different models. The advantage of the first training model is that it applies a preexisting package of treatments that are integrated in a systematic and tested way. As we have already noted, its disadvantage is that it underemphasizes the similarity of problems and treatments that work among diagnostically similar patients, and it is too rigid for the tastes of most clinicians. The second approach is designed to overcome these weaknesses but does so by bringing procedures together in a way that is not always systematic or theoretically logical. While the relative value of these two approaches is yet to be determined, STS emphasizes the latter model, with the addition of defining crosscutting principles and differential strategies.

Training in systematic eclectic and prescriptive psychotherapy, based on the STS model of treatment selection, is similar in some ways to that developed and espoused by Arnold Lazarus (1981) for training in multimodal therapy (MMT). Specifically, it emphasizes the acquisition of technical skills for identifying patient qualities, learning how to apply interventions, and then systematically assessing one's own competence. Compared to MMT, PT training places relatively less emphasis on techniques and relatively more on learning to use guiding principles and differential strategies. The goal of training is to achieve a point at which principles and technical skills are so well learned that one applies them automatically and seamlessly, with endless permutations of adaptation to each patient's uniqueness.

The identification of patient qualities requires the availability of sound methods of assessment as well as training in their reliable use. In the graduate training program at UCSB, we emphasize instruction on the selection and use of psychological tests to measure relevant treatment planning dimensions. An *advanced clinical appraisal* course is organized around the STS model, using graduate-level textbooks (Beutler & Berren, 1995; Groth-Marnat, 1997) that relate various instruments to dimensions of importance to treatment decision making within the STS framework.

The STS model emphasizes the importance of learning to identify demographic qualities of the patient and four additional patient qualities that are useful for tailoring treatments to individuals. These qualities are levels of *problem complexity, functional impairment, social support, subjective distress, coping style*, and *resistance*. These patient qualities, representing both state and trait-like dimensions, have been identified by systematic research as being predictive of both good and poor treatment results. That is, they can serve both as indicators and contraindicators for the application of different families of intervention. Thus, at the level of graduate school instruction, the concentration is on identifying and developing skill in using traditional assessment procedures to identify these dimensions. The dimensions are then used to formulate treatment recommendations and responding to referral questions about prognosis, treatment, and level of impairment.

Advanced Postgraduate, Professional Training

There are four major differences between the procedures used with advanced practitioners and those used for graduate students. First, in training experienced practitioners, we recommend placing relatively less emphasis on learning a battery of psychological tests. Second, we feel it is redundant to provide advanced practitioners and clinicians with a grounding in the diversity of theories that guide psychotherapists. Third, we do not attempt to teach basic concepts of psychopathology and diagnosis to experienced practitioners. Fourth, we do not introduce experienced practitioners to as many patient and therapy matching dimensions as we teach our full-time graduate students. Instead, the focus of training at the advanced practitioner level emphasizes the principles of *cue recognition* and the understanding of *differential strategies* that allow practitioners to select and adapt good treatment elements to the needs of patients who vary along four dimensions: *level of functional impairment, level of subjective distress, coping style*, and *level of resistance*. These are the dimensions that most directly relate to psychotherapy, as opposed to broader treatment decisions that include the context of treatment, the use of medication, the selection of group and multiperson interventions, and the like.

In the postgraduate training on prescriptive treatment planning, advanced clinicians are trained to use computer-assisted evaluation procedures (Beutler & Williams, 1995) to identify treatment directions, rather than relying on the use of specific psychological tests. This computer interactive assessment procedure is a time-efficient method of coaching the experienced clinician through a series of questions designed to assess the same treatment-related dimensions identified for graduate students in the advanced clinical appraisal course. It helps the clinician acquire skills in identifying patient status on relevant dimensions and planning treatment in a consistent, patient-specific, and empirically validated way. The interrogatory software is used to translate clinician-obtained information into scores and narrative descriptions of compatible treatment plans. It is applied after the clinician has used his or her preferred clinical methods to obtain and gather information about the problem and its history.

Prior to the application of the STS computer software, the clinician typically conducts a clinical interview, administers a number of self-report measures, completes objective and/or projective personality tests, and obtains historical and medical records. In applying the STS computerized assessment system, the computer iterates a series of summarizing questions, to which the clinician responds. The computer algorithms then summarize the clinician's responses to derive information about the seven general areas used in general treatment planning:

1. Patient demographics
2. Functional impairment
3. Subjective distress
4. Coping style
5. Resistance
6. Problem complexity
7. Social support

The process of completing the STS software procedure takes from 20 to 40 minutes, the length and depth of the prompted interview varying as a function of the amount of treatment-relevant information that has been obtained by the clinician through the use of appropriate and reliable, objective test scores. The computer is able to ingest a variety of scores from formal psychological tests, shortening the length of the clinician's involvement with the computer. Once the computer has incorporated the information, it constructs summary scores based on patient demographic background, personality traits, emotional states, problem characteristics, and environmental supports and generates several charts and summaries. Computer-generated reports include the following:

1. Narrative reports in which empirically derived treatment strategies are suggested
2. Projection of treatment course based on all similar patients in the usable data base
3. Graphs of the patient's relative standing on each of the assessed variables
4. Assessment of probable risk level and concomitant prevention strategies
5. List of the most pressing problem
6. Series of brief minimanuals for each problem area, along with references to research and descriptions of research that supports their use

If there are a number of different therapists at the particular clinic in which the patient is being assessed, the computer also profiles the clinicians and identifies (by code number) those who have been particularly successful with patients who present with similar profiles. A method for tracking patients is also included. Patient weekly progress is compared to the projected course of change based on groups of similar patients in order to identify when an individual is changing at either a particularly rapid or slow rate.

As with graduate training, it is important that the experienced clinician learn to identify the dimensions that define the degree of match between patient qualities and various therapy procedures, independently of the computer program. With a little assistance from the computer-based assessment and from decision forms, clinicians can learn to recognize and distinguish among interventions in their own repertoires that are, for example, *skill or symptom focused versus conflict focused, emotion arousing versus emotion reducing, confrontive versus supportive*, and so forth. It is a simple step from there to teach advanced clinicians to compare each patient characteristic with a corresponding aspect of the therapy process, to obtain an index of the degree of match and mismatch between the patient and the treatment offered. The creative integration of procedures from one's own armamentarium is then adjusted and integrated to maximize the fit between procedure and patient.

The use of computer technology for the application of treatment planning has certain advantages over efforts to teach experienced clinicians to use a variety of specific psychological tests, as is done in graduate training. Learning such procedures is a time-consuming task and is not well suited to the continuing education format that forms the basis of most postprofessional training. Moreover, because the matching algorithms used in the computer-assisted procedures are empirically derived, it is also easier to allow the computer to integrate and interpret the meaning of patient-treatment match scores that vary in level and magnitude. Whereas clinicians can easily learn to evaluate the general degree to which their own treatment efforts are consistent with the application of a well-tailored and effective treatment for a patient with a given background, set of environmental supports, pattern of emotional states, and particular personality traits, the computer helps them do this in a reliable and consistent way.

Moreover, because the data base on which computer-generated patient variables are assessed and treatment qualities are tracked is continually expanding, it is also possible to build into the process of computer-assisted evaluation, research that seeks to improve and identify the indicators for the use of specific formats and environments, group or family-based interventions, intervention in environmental systems, use of psychoactive medication, and unique implementations of a variety of specific techniques (e.g., response prevention, two-chair work, active listening, and communication skills).

As applied to training in the employment of psychotherapy procedures, it should be understood that by necessity, the training period for established practitioners in STS methods is shorter and more limited than that used for full-time graduate students. This is possible if we assume that experienced practitioners have a more solid grounding in theory and practice than do graduate students. Indeed, our PT training program for professionals assumes that established practitioners are familiar with a wide array of techniques, whether or not they use them regularly, and have acquired a heightened level of clinical sensitivity to patient problems and to indicators of patient distress and resentments.

To expand the experienced practitioners' exposure to treatment procedures, we introduce them to examples and training materials that can be used to update their technical proficiency. We assume that experienced practitioners have a body of skills and procedures that can serve them well. We seek to help them to expand on their technical repertoire and to use at least a few of these techniques in a selective and effective method in order to apply them to corresponding patient dimensions.

In this manual, we identify the patient dimensions that guide treatment selection. Then we review the formal test measures and the computer-assisted methods of evaluating them. In addition, we introduce the various principles of change that govern the selection of interventions for patients who vary on a given dimension, outline the strategies that logically arise from applying these principles to that patient dimension, and then present examples of representative procedures and techniques that can be used to implement the resulting treatment plan. The final step in discussing each patient dimension is to present information that will assist the experienced clinician in evaluating his or her skill in adhering to the treatment principles. This evaluation will entail both a self-assessment of the degree to which the clinician's methods fit with patient dimensions and will include an estimate of the overall skill and flexibility with which the clinician uses the indicated strategies of psychotherapy.

Principles, Strategies, and Techniques

Principles, strategies, and techniques differ along a dimension of specificity. As indicated earlier in Chapter 1, principles are general guiding rules, strategies specify a differential application of these principles, and techniques are specific procedures. Although techniques are specific, their application is not necessarily so. A given technique can be applied in a variety of ways and to various strategic objectives, depending on the therapist's skill and flexibility. For example, interpretation of transference may be offered softly as a way of facilitating awareness and insight or it may be offered more stridently as a way of confrontation that induces arousal. Similarly, questions can be used both to provide support and to promote self-exploration. Even active strategies such as directed imagery may be used on one occasion or by one therapist to provide a sense of comfort and safety and on another occasion or by another therapist to evoke feeling awareness. Thus, the effective therapist must not become bound by a finite list of techniques and should remain mindful of the objectives or strategies and the guiding principles that direct treatment, as he or she applies technical interventions.

Clinicians are and should be taught a large variety of techniques; however, in the PT training program, they learn to place greater emphasis on understanding the principles of extinction, exposure, and paradoxical intervention as mediators and differential contributors to change. They must also come to recognize the indicating patient qualities that invoke the use of each principle. Effective training will challenge therapists to find and develop new techniques based on sound guiding principles rather than binding them to carry out the specifics of desensitization, *in vivo* exposure, reframing, paradoxical injunctions, and other specific techniques. We recommend that coursework and individual supervision both encourage therapists to find new ways of employing or activating the principles of change to fit the circumstances that characterize each new patient.

Summary

PT training assumes that no two patients and problems are alike. The central challenge for practicing psychotherapists is to be able to adapt the nature of treatment to each new patient and problem. Each patient represents a particular challenge in how to adapt the principles that will effect change. We believe that the effective therapist is one who can apply the principles of change within the context presented by a particular patient and can do so in a creative and flexible manner.

The therapist must know the principles of behavior that describe how confidence and hope are affected in relationships and must possess the skills to apply these principles in ways that fit a particular patient's fear, sense of defeat, and life circumstances. Thus, in contrast to programs that simply teach that patient confidence and hope are important correlates of change, we endeavor to provide an understanding of the principles that will allow a clinician to develop creative plans for infusing patients who are rebellious and uncooperative with this hope and support. Likewise, instead of teaching students that the therapeutic relationship is important, we aim to teach clinicians the principles of relationship that will allow them to create an interpersonal climate that encourages change. Because of their importance, we emphasize the following (summarized here and presented in greater detail previously in this chapter) in pursuit of translating a growth-enhancing attitude, knowledge, skill, time, and creative imagination into a form that will facilitate the development and maintenance of a sound therapeutic relationship:

1. A therapeutic *attitude* is one characterized by being warm, optimistic, interested, and accepting.
2. Therapeutic *knowledge* is used to define the course, length, and process of therapy, including the therapeutic roles that the participants will adopt.
3. Therapeutic *skill* includes the use of tools and techniques to reflect patient feelings and acknowledge patient anger and fear without becoming defensive.
4. *Timing* includes the ability to apply interpersonal pressure to facilitate self-exploration and to withdraw pressure when the patient makes therapeutic movement.
5. *Creative imagination* is the enactment of the therapist's curiosity and excitement with the process of discovery.

To expand their effectiveness, clinicians must be challenged to discover and practice techniques that enhance the power of the relationship and support the processes of change. For example, we know that patient hope and trust are important. But, we also know that few patients have these qualities at the time they seek help. We also know that these qualities tend to increase if the therapist applies a therapeutic attitude of trust and respect, if the nature and goals of treatment are structured, if the patient's feelings are acknowledged and reflected, if the therapist's interventions are offered at moments of conducive emotional arousal, and if therapists provide a model of interested excitement in the process of discovery. The challenge to the clinician, then, is to instigate a treatment that provides these attitudes, this knowledge, the skill, the timing, and the imagination that will allow the patient to have a successful experience.

Central to these efforts, students must be taught to be self-observing and to evaluate the degree to which the procedures employed accomplish their intended purposes. This requires that the objectives of intervention be clearly specified. In turn, it requires that treatment decisions are closely linked to relevant patient dimension and that these interventions are reliably assessed for their intended impact. The results of this assessment should be available as feedback to the clinician and can be used to help guide the process of refining treatment.

Learning to apply selected interventions is intimately related to the self-assessment and correction of deficits by therapists. Hence, these two objectives of training are inseparable. Training in prescriptive therapies focuses on the acquisition of sound principles of change and the construction of creative ways of applying these principles to the peculiarities of different patients. Feedback from an assessment of patient change and of personal skill and compliance with change principles are necessary aspects for correcting and changing the interventions applied.

In subsequent chapters, we describe the principles, strategies, and methods of assessment that may be developed for patients representing different combinations and patterns of indicating characteristics. We also provide examples of ways to translate strategies into the specific level of techniques. However, as we have said many times, the level of principle and strategy will serve as our primary focus, not that of techniques. We assume that you, as an experienced practitioner, already have an understanding of many different types of procedures and can call them into play as the situation warrants.

Note

1. These keys to success were borrowed from an unlikely source. They were extrapolated, with thanks, from P. Parellis's description of the successful natural horseman (Parelli, 1993). The first author has found many parallels between the nonpunitive, relationship-oriented methods that have become central to modern methods of "natural" animal training and the desirable attributes of a skilled psychotherapist. Parelli's keys to success are among these parallels.

Chapter 3
Patient Evaluation

Objectives of Assessment

Unlike conventional diagnostic evaluation, the assessment of patients who seek treatment for complex disorders that include affective disruption, chemical abuse, and behavioral problems includes attention both to general symptomatology and specific problems, symptoms, and maintaining behaviors. We provide here a general description of the principles and practices that have application to a wide variety of problems.

Each dimension that is assessed plays a particular role in deciding the nature of the treatment program or assessing its effects. The evaluation of patients is guided by eight objectives that are roughly arranged in the order of their occurrence. Although all eight objectives are a part of each phase of the study, different ones are more or less important during different phases. The eight objectives of assessment are:

1. Establish the diagnostic and medical eligibility of potential participants for this model of prescriptive therapy.
2. Identify skill deficits, assets, symptoms, and levels of risk, including risk of drug use and self-destructive acts.
3. Establish baseline levels of problematic symptoms (e.g., substance abuse) and mood disturbance against which to later assess treatment effects.
4. Establish the patient's level of functional impairment.
5. Establish the patient's level of impulsivity and external coping.
6. Establish level of interpersonal resistance.
7. Identify patient level of subjective distress and problem severity.
8. Evaluate the quality of the working relationship and the outcomes of treatment.

In the following section of this manual, we describe how information will be gathered to achieve each of these eight objectives.

Measurement Procedures

In the following paragraphs, we have identified examples of the types of instruments we find useful in the assessment of individuals to ensure a broad perspective of the patient's problems. Some of these instruments are self-administered; others are administered by the therapist or by an independent clinician (psychologist or psychiatrist). This list is not exhaustive, nor is it exclusive. It should provide both for evaluation of general characteristics and qualities that cut across diagnostic groups or problems and also of specific problems related to particular conditions. The latter represent symptoms and patterns that can be used to assess how effective treatment is; the former are more usefully used to plan strategies for effective treatment. Of course, we cannot here report and describe ways of evaluating all of the specific problems and symptoms that may be useful from time to time to evaluate change; thus we have selected two for illustrative purposes. Depressive symptoms are presented as one outcome measure that is useful across conditions and diagnoses as a general expression of patient sense of well-being. In contrast, the assessment of chemical abuse patterns is presented here to illustrate how diagnostically specific symptoms might be assessed and used in evaluating treatment effectiveness.

The instruments we describe are examples. They are not the only ones available for measuring the identified dimensions. They are a representative sampling of the type of instruments that may be useful in treatment planning. Their use is drawn from our own research and experience. When specific tests are described, we provide, in later chapters, more specific information on what scales and formulas are used to help identify important patient qualities that relate to the guiding principles of PT.

Objectives 1–3: Diagnosis and Medical Eligibility, Risk Behaviors, and Baseline Levels of Symptoms and Deficits

While we do not consider a diagnostic label to provide sufficient information on which to base a distinguishing and helpful treatment, it is valuable for both record keeping and to assist a comparison of treatment effects to established research literature. Frequently, a setting proscribes treatment if a prospective patient does not qualify for a formal diagnosis. However, diagnostic decisions are quite unreliable, even in this day of the DSM-IV. The maximal reliability and information will be forthcoming if the diagnosis is based on a careful, standardized assessment. This type of assessment also provides information on the level of patient impairment. The *Structured Clinical Interview of DSM-IV* (SCID; Spitzer, Williams, & Gibbons, 1986) is the current standard in the field, and is used for both assigning diagnosis and for assessing level of impairment or severity. We will discuss its use further in the next section.

It is imperative that a diagnostic designation be supplemented by an additional information in order to enhance its usefulness. Assessments of symptoms, resources, assets, and risk-related behaviors help fill out of the picture. Specific symptom and functioning measures will be covered in the following sections. It is important to observe here, however, that one must ensure that the setting is endowed with the expertise and resources that will allow them to adequately address the patient's problems.

The nature of any clinical setting limits the types of patients for whom maximal protection and care can be provided. It is important to determine the nature of these limitations and to consider the patient within these parameters.

For example, the treatment of children, the physically challenged, older adults, and those with serious medical problems usually require specialized services and facilities. Such populations also require access to professionals who have special knowledge about the types of problems and circumstances that characterize the lives of these individuals. Though it seems self-evident, it should not be taken for granted that a treatment facility has addressed each of the following issues:

1. Availability of facilities to accommodate patients whose medical conditions and special needs are consistent with those to be treated.
2. Clinicians who are familiar with the cultures and fluent in the languages spoken by patients who are being identified for service.
3. Materials that are consistent with the levels of education presented by the identified patients.
4. Clinicians who are trained to obtain the information needed to determine the history of patient problems and to assess patient background and symptoms.
5. Clinicians who are familiar with the symptoms and risks associated with both acute and chronic substance abuse, and who know the procedures for detoxification, medication management, and risk management.
6. Formal and valid methods of assessing levels as well as symptoms of dysphoria and depression.
7. Procedures for ensuring that patients understand the nature of treatment demands, are offered viable alternatives, and assured that their rights to privacy are respected.

Only when one is assured that a clinical setting offers the foregoing resources, can we have some reassurance that the environment will afford an opportunity for the patient to experience maximal benefit. Having thus obtained this reassurance, then the process of evaluating the baseline symptoms and level of risk posed, can proceed. The instruments described in the following paragraphs exemplify the types of assessment used at this stage.

The Beck Depression Inventory (BDI-II; Beck, Steer, & Brown, 1996) is an easily administered self-report device for assessing changes in depressive symptoms. It is readily applied in a repeated-measures design and reliably assesses depression level (Beutler & Crago, 1983). This instrument is usually used for two related purposes: (1) to assess patient status with respect to depression and (2) to establish a baseline by which to evaluate subsequent change in patient dysphoria. Generally, mild to moderate depressive symptoms are characteristic of those who seek assistance for chemical abuse disorders; however, it is not uncommon to identify severe depression among those presenting with substance abuse problems.

The *Hamilton Rating Scale for Depression* (HRSD; Hamilton, 1967) is a clinician-based measure of depressive symptoms and patterns that often provides a second view of patient depression. The scale taps such areas as sleep disturbances, libido and sexual functioning, somatic complaints associated with depression, suicidal ideation, guilt, and anergia. The HRSD is a standard measure in treatment research and consists of a series of symptom ratings that are made both after the initial assessment and at the end of treatment. We recommend that the rating be made by an individual (advanced graduate student, psychologist, or psychiatrist) who has received specialized training in HRSD administration.

The *SCL-90R* (Derogatis, 1977) is a 90 item, self-report instrument that yields nine symptom scores and three global summary scores. The primary summary score, GSI, reflects overall subjective symptom severity. The brevity of the SCL-90R is especially useful in situations requiring rapid assessment. It may be used to assess both initial levels of psychological disturbance and change over time.

Firestone Assessment of Self-Destructive Thoughts (FAST; Firestone, 1988) is a self-report inventory that is used both to establish suicide risk and to evaluate the significance of destructive cognitive patterns over time. A revised version of the FAST, designed to help discriminate between trait and state characteristics of the client, is particularly useful. This instrument assesses the presence and intensity and destructiveness of internal injunctions, asking clients to endorse which of a series of representative self-destructive thoughts are present. Three responses are sought from the respondent on each item: (1) Have you ever experienced this thought during your life? (2) How frequently have you experienced this thought at the time you were the most depressed? (3) Have you experienced this thought during the last 2 weeks and how frequently?

An *AIDS Risk Evaluation* is particularly necessary in the treatment of substance-abusing patients in order to identify high-risk behaviors for AIDS/ HIV. The assessment of such risk behaviors is especially important in the treatment of chemical abuse disorders. The items on the scale we developed solicit information on the method of drug use (needle, free base, crack, etc.), HIV status, and current sexual practices. Thus, it provides information on AIDS risk and is a method of tracking the mode of use as a function of the effectiveness of treatment.

Medical Review/Evaluation is conducted to rule out physical problems that may be associated with chronic drug use. It is helpful to review each patient's medical history in conjunction with the history of drug use, depression, family background, past and current medication use, and medical/psychiatric symptoms. A formal reference to a checklist of physical symptoms allows on going monitoring of changes.

Objective 4: Establish the Patient's Level of Functional Impairment

Once availability of the requisite facilities and materials is assured, the clinician can begin the process of employing these materials in assessment of patient predisposing qualities. These are the characteristics of patients that determine their functioning and response to treatment. The following procedures are examples of those that may be used to assess aspects of psychiatric and social functioning. They are not exhaustive but should be taken as representative and as well enough established to resolve most questions of instrument validity.

The Addiction Severity Index (ASI; McLellan, Luborsky, Woody, & O'Brien, 1980) is a standard, structured interview that derives information on drug usage as well as psychosocial functioning, and psychiatric symptomatology. Scores on the ASI both establish the diagnosis of substance abuse and assess baseline levels of psychological disturbance.

Seven subscale scores are derived indicating severity of the following problem areas: (1) Medical; (2) Employment, (3) Alcohol, (4) Drug, (5) Legal, (6) Family/Social, and (7) Psychiatric severity. Those who administer this interview must recieve special training in order to ensure that they obtain reliable ratings. Even with such training, however, the possibility of patient distortion and misinterpretation around issues of substance abuse is very high, especially when issues of legal allegations are in question. To help overcome this problem, drug use reports are typically cross-checked with urine or blood tests to increase the level of reliance warranted by patient reports.

The ASI is frequently used to help assess the effects of treatment (i.e., amount of change achieved). In addition, therapists can use feedback from periodic follow-up evaluations to adapt their therapeutic work accordingly. For estimates of benefit, indices of initial drug use may be compared to later administrations of this instrument.

The Structured Clinical Interview for DSM-IV (SCID; Spitzer, Williams, & Gibbon, 1986) is used to determine the degree to which patients meet diagnostic criteria. While decisions of treatment are largely independent of diagnostic criteria, such criteria are important as an assessment of treatment effectiveness and they also offer a confirmatory check on the use of illicit drugs and provide a cross-check with the information obtained on the ASI Drug Abuse indices. The SCID has modules for assessing both Axis I and Axis II disorders and may be used to identify the presence of personality disorders and situational disturbances. The interview format is determined strictly by the DSM-IV criteria. This SCID procedure may be cross-checked by follow-up in the form of a clinical interview. The decision tree format allows reliable evaluation of substance abuse disorders, psychotic disorders, suicidal behavior, and the presence of organic symptoms.

Objective 5: Patient's Level of Impulsivity and External Coping

Externalizing coping style is an enduring trait and, in prior research, has been most widely measured by various combinations of scales from the *Minnesota Multiphasic Personality Inventory* (MMPI; Dahlstrom, Welsh, & Dahlstrom, 1972). We find that this measure is helpful in providing a reliable, self-report estimate of relevant personality patterns. The results can help the therapist plan the nature of treatment offered to the patient.

The *Minnesota Multiphasic Personality Inventory-2* (MMPI-2; Butcher, 1990) is a well-established, 567-item true–false scale designed to assess personality traits and response dispositions. It is a self-report measure and combinations of various subscales derived from it have been found to be stable predictors of treatment differential response in numerous studies.

STS Clinician Form—Computer Version (STS; Beutler & Williams, 1995) is a computer-interactive clinician assessment procedure that is specifically designed to assess the dimensions of importance to PT treatment, from the clinician/therapist's perspective. Ordinarily, the evaluating therapist or clinician completes the STS evaluation, both after the first therapy session and again after each session in order to track change and affirm progress.

Objective 6: Level of Interpersonal Resistance

A patient's level of resistance potential must also reflect both aspects of in-dwelling behavior (trait-like patterns) and responses induced by a demanding situation (state-like patterns). Three measures are used to assess various aspects of resistance in the current study. The most used scales for this purpose are drawn from the MMPI-2 and the *Therapeutic Reactance Scale* (TRS; Dowd, Milne & Wise, 1991).

The MMPI-2 has been widely used for developing a composite measure of patient trait-like resistance to treatment. Several subscales reflecting dominance, resistance to control, and problems with authority are used as a composite measure of trait resistance potential.

The TRS (Dowd et al., 1991) is a self-report measure that was developed specifically for predicting resistance to therapist directives in clinical populations. Dowd and his colleagues have provided both normative, reliability, and initial predictive validity data on this instrument among mixed clinical samples.

The STS (Beutler & Williams, 1995) also contains a measure of a form of resistance that is more situation specific than the MMPI measure but not as specific to psychotherapy as the TRS. This subscale is completed by therapists after the first treatment session and is employed as an additional measure of resistance patterns. It is often helpful to reassess the level of resistance periodically to make alterations in the nature of the treatment strategies used.

Objective 7: Patient Level of Subjective Distress and Problem Severity

Subjective distress is both a trait-like and a state-like quality, both of which change with treatment. The SCL-90R (previously described) is valuable for assessing aspects of distress and problem severity that are relatively stable across time. In addition, it is helpful if each patient completes a measure of state-like or situational distress before each session. A measure like the STAI-State, administered prior to each PT session, complements the use of measures of functional impairment and distress.

The *State Trait Anxiety Inventory-State* (STAI; Spielberger, Gorsuch, Lushene, Vagg, & Jacobs, 1983) is a 40-item, multiple-choice, self-report inventory. This is a revision of the Spielberger, Gorsuch, and Lushene (1970) scale and is a quickly administered method of assessing anxiety states. This instrument may be used to help therapists select and tailor strategies and procedures that are designed either to increase or decrease patient arousal.

The STS (Beutler & Williams, 1995) allows clinician-referenced cross-validation of patient distress, level of impairment, and problem severity. These three subscales are separately extracted. The subjective distress evaluation consists of three subscales. These subscales include therapist ratings of patient distress, clinical indicators of distress, and ratings of self-esteem. These three subscales are combined into a single measure of subjective distress that is used to evaluate changes over time and is helpful as a cross-check on the SCL-90-R measure of distress (i.e., the GSI subscale).

Objective 8: Quality of the Working Relationship and Outcome

To evaluate the comparability of treatments, it is also advantageous to maintain an ongoing evaluation of the nature and quality of the working relationship in psychotherapy. Self-report and clinician-rated measures of the therapeutic relationship typically are obtained at the end of treatment as indicators of the general quality of the relationship throughout the treatment program. These measures are used to evaluate the role of nonspecific relationship factors in effecting changes.

Barrett–Lennard Relationship Inventory (BLRI; Barrett-Lennard, 1972) is a self-report measure of four therapist qualities that relate to therapist facilitative skill. The BLRI has been found reliably to reflect both the facilitative skills of the therapist as perceived by the patient and the probability of positive treatment effects (Gurman, 1977). This test is administered at the end of treatment only and captures a stable aspect of the therapeutic alliance related to patient perceptions of therapists.

California Psychotherapy Alliance Scales (CALPAS; Gaston, 1991) is a shorter alternative to the BLRI, though it views the relationship from a somewhat different theoretical perspective. The CALPAS has been successful in discriminating the processes of cognitive and dynamic therapies (Gaston, Marmar, Thompson, & Gallagher, 1988). The CALPAS is a revision of an earlier version and is completed both by the therapist and the patient. It consists of a series of 7-point ratings on the nature of the treatment relationship and yields the following five subscales: patient working capacity, patient commitment, goal consensus, working strategy consensus, and therapist understanding and involvement. The CALPAS is administered to therapists and patients after every five sessions. Because of its brevity, this instrument can be administered more frequently than the BLRI and can be used to identify ruptures or changes in the therapeutic process that may subsequently be disruptive to treatment outcomes.

The Helping Alliance Questionnaire (HAq-II; Luborsky, Diguer, Schweizer, & Johnson, 1996) is an easily administered 19-item self-report inventory that is useful for describing and measuring the therapeutic alliance. The Haq-II comes in both a patient and therapist version that allows a measurement and description of the alliance from both perspectives. The Haq-II is reported to have excellent internal consistency and test–retest reliability and it has also demonstrated good convergent validity with the CALPAS (Luborsky et al., 1996).

STS Therapy Rating Scale (appendix A) provides an assessment of still an additional aspect of treatment. This measure is designed to ensure that the treatment procedures used are in compliance with the intended methods of PT. This measure is completed by supervisors and consultants to provide feedback to the therapist, but the therapist can also complete the ratings as a self-evaluation. The measure includes the following subscales: (1) Induced Patient Emotional Arousal, (2) Therapist Use of Behavioral versus Insight Procedures, and (3) Therapist Directiveness. These subscales will be used to construct measures of treatment "fit" by comparing them to corresponding measures of patient (1) subjective distress, (2) externalized coping style, and (3) patient interpersonal resistance. In addition, the measure includes some additional subscales that provide a cross-check on the quality of the therapy processes: (1) therapist skill, (2) therapist verbal activity, (3) degree of physical movement of therapist (4) patient verbal activity, (5) patient physical movement, and (6) therapeutic alliance.

Treatment Decision Points

Relationship Between Emotional States and Enduring Traits

Prescriptive Therapy is developed and adjusted in response both to what is presented by the patient and the way it is manifest. Some of the patterns of behavior and manifestations of symptoms on which treatment decisions are made are enduring or "trait-like" qualities and others are temporary or "state-like" affects and moods. However, the demarcation between state-and trait-like qualities is not clear and unvarying. There is a continuum of situational changeability, along which is distributed all human attributes. At one extreme are reactive moods and thoughts that are situationally dependent. These situationally determined subjective states are very changeable. At the other extreme are long-standing, well-learned, and biologically determined demographics that undergo little change after one enters adulthood. It might be expected, for example, that interpersonal needs, patterned methods of coping with stress, and temperaments, will be enduring and stable because they are not strongly dependent on momentary situational conditions. These are trait-like characteristics.

Between these extremes are qualities that respond to the environment but do so somewhat slowly. These are usually qualities that are reflected in recurrent patterns of behavior or life themes. They are well learned and historically developed patterns that are activated by particular situations but are governed more by their symbolized significance than by the situation itself. They transcend any one situation. One's resistance against external pressure, for example, may arise quickly to threat, but it may also build up and dissipate over the course of days and weeks in a recurrent and predictable way to usual life events. Likewise, although most moods and emotions are very situationally dependent, when there is a long history of learning patterns, some moods may take weeks to dissipate. Even further, depressive dispositions and emotional thresholds of sensitivity may systematically differ from one person to another and be manifest as depressive or excitable temperaments. These qualities may be stable enough that we think of people as having depressive or cyclothymic personality types.

The speed with which one's behaviors and responses change is usually a function of the nature of the environment to which one is exposed at any given moment, the genetic loading of that characteristic, and the consistency of past learning that formed the response tendency. Accurate measurement of rapidly changing subjective states requires an ongoing process, whereas measurement of slowly changing dispositions and trait-like habits and enduring qualities are less time-consuming. In the case of true traits, a single measurement in time is often sufficient.

For the purposes of prescribing and reliably implementing PT, the criteria and decisions that are dependent on the assessment process can be reduced to three major questions. The answers to the questions themselves are dependent on the status of four patient qualities. For simplicity of illustrating the application of PT, we have ordered the relevant patient dimensions along a continuum from most to least trait-like. That is, the range from the least situationally determined to the most responsive to situational change. Approaching the task of identifying patient qualities and linking each of these to a treatment decision in this way improves our ability to organize what is otherwise a rather complex process. This ordering of the variables of focus, moreover, allows us to order the decisions from the most general to the most specific interventions. That is, the sequential decision will make treatment increasingly refined and time efficient.

The patient-based cues that we use to assign corresponding treatment strategies in PT will be reiterated at the beginning of each of the subsequent chapters of this manual in order to reinforce the connection between patient variables and treatment decisions. In this preliminary review, the patient dimensions of interest are described in general terms only.

1. How impaired is the patient in daily functioning and how in need is the patient of obtaining new sources of social support? The first treatment decision is related to the intensity of treatment to be offered. This decision hinges on the level of social impairment and the access of the patient to sources of social support and assistance. This ordinarily is a decision that is made at the beginning of treatment and changes in functioning may be incorporated into estimates of improvement over time. However, the initial decision to implement a treatment at a given level of intensity rests with the level of initial impairment noted.

2. How does the patient typically interact with others and cope with stressful events? Whereas the first treatment decision hinges on the ability to identify the patient's level of impairment, the second decision relates to identifying the enduring pattern of coping used by the patient when adapting to stress and change. This decision need only be made at the beginning of treatment. For all intents and purposes, coping styles remain stable during the adult life of a person. But the way of cataloguing coping styles varies from theory to theory. There are passive and active styles, emotional and behavioral styles, styles linked to diagnostic categories, and styles that reflect one or more of the five personality factors that are thought to be the building blocks of personality (Costa & Widiger, 1994). For simplicity in the application of PT, we work with only a single dimension that reflects how one generally interacts with the interpersonal world, especially when attempting to cope with change and distress.

We use a descriptive quality to identify this pattern that is both most easily observed and most consistently accepted across theories, albeit by a number of different terms. Virtually all personality taxonomies identify an enduring disposition to act out, to be impulsive, to be socially active, and to be aggressive as a central quality. We use the term "Externalizer," to identify those who have this trait-like quality. These individuals are those who tend to be undercontrolled, move against people rather than with them, and usually have interpersonal difficulties that reflect the presence of excessive rather than insufficient behaviors. Thus, externalizing patients tend to act out, overeat, overdrink, overdiet, overreact, actively avoid confronting problems, and overdramatize their emotions and physical complaints.

The end-point objectives of these behaviors are generally accepted as being to increase stimulation, to ensure or maintain personal autonomy, or to control and manipulate other people's responses. The components of this dimension are seen in the various terms by which it is defined by different theorists—externalization, stimulation seeking, extroversion, sociopathy, and so on. By whatever terms, externalizing behaviors help one avoid certain internal or external experiences, and reinforce the boundaries between self and others. Boundaries and emotional distance are maintained either by diverting focus away from one's self or by placing the blame for one's behavior elsewhere.

External coping styles are relatively easy to observe, but that is not true of behaviors at the other end of this continuum. By definition, internalizing behaviors are more difficult to identify than externalizing ones. Internalization includes such behaviors as compartmentalization, self-criticism, overcontrol, and a variety of other internal processes. Because the behaviors are difficult to observe, "internalization" is a concept that is much more theory dependent than is "externalization." However, internalization can be identified by a variety of personality measures and by the relative absence of externalizing behaviors. Empirical research suggests that adequate treatment differentiation can be accomplished by defining externalization and internalization as a single dimension. Thus, we base differential treatment decisions on a ratio of indicators of externalization and internalization behaviors. This means that decisions are made simply by differentiating patients who, on a relative basis, are either exhibiting or lacking impulsive, aggressive, directly avoidant, and socially gregarious behaviors.

In PT, a patient's dominant coping style is defined as a ratio between measures of extroverted, impulsive, and externalized behaviors to self-reflective, self-critical, and ruminative tendencies. Ratios favoring externalization and internalization are used to select treatments that are either symptom focused (externalizers) or theme/conflict focused (internalizers).

The measures of externalzing and internalizing patterns include subscales from standard personality tests (MMPI-2, CPI Socialization subscale) and from therapist ratings on the STS Coping Style subscale. The patient's relative standing on the externalization ratio is provided to each PT therapist and supervisor in advance of the initiation of treatment so that a distinguishing treatment can be planned. This score is used to direct the focus of the treatment plan, either to begin and maintain directed efforts to change symptoms and problematic behaviors or to gradually shift from a symptomatic to a thematic focus, emphasizing insight and emotional awareness objectives. These interventions comprise procedures that expose the patient to either internal experience or external events that are feared and avoided by patients and to help them develop more adaptive skills. The principles, procedures, and strategies that are implied in this decision are discussed in chapter 5, along with illustrations of some specific techniques that seem to be consistent with these differential objectives.

3. Is this patient likely to resist therapeutic influence and interventions? Obtaining an answer to this question is a little more complex than the answer to the first two questions. This is because resistance is both a situational (state-like) and an enduring (trait-like) aspect of patient behavioral propensities. Thus, the PT therapist evaluates both the trait-like tendencies of a patient to resist the influence of authorities and variations in their moment-to-moment receptivity to therapist-initiated interventions.

The trait-like aspect of resistance, "*resistance potential*, is defined by a collection of personality scores derived from the MMPI-2, the TRS, and the STS–Reactance subscale. Variations in resistance potential will be used to decide whether and what kind (highly specific or self-directed) of homework will be assigned to patients. Chapter 6 outlines the nature of these decisions.

Compared to the identification of an enduring disposition to resist external influence, it is much more difficult to identify the resistance behaviors of patients that are situationally determined by the changing demand characteristics of a particular treatment session. To accurately determine when these rapidly changing levels of receptivity dictate a shift of therapeutic procedure within a treatment session, a therapist must learn to accurately read the verbal and postural patterns of patients from moment to moment. Research has established that the patient's voice level (soft or loud), expressive intensity, facial expression, and posture provide a reliable basis for identifying a patient's level of receptivity to therapeutic influence.

Even more important, research has demonstrated that therapists have considerable difficulty in dealing with patients who express high levels of situationally induced resistance. Thus, while PT identifies ways that a therapist can identify in-dwelling defensive patterns, it is even more important to learn ways of coping with resistance when it arises within therapy sessions. Thus, in chapter 6, we outline a procedure for selecting among nondirective and paradoxical strategies and techniques. It is important to integrate these decisions with the process of supervision, however, to provide greater support and assistance in overcoming the therapist tendency to respond defensively to patient resistance. Supervision can help the therapist guard against the tendency to become angry and defensive, and can support the resolve to remain reflective, open, and focused on the patient–therapist relationship.

4. *Are the patient's emotions sufficiently aroused to motivate changes?* The fourth question reflects our concern with the role of patient subjective distress and discomfort in sustaining motivation for change. This is the most difficult of all dimensions to assess both because it changes quickly, requiring an assessment of state-like behaviors within sessions, and because its relationship to discrete psychotherapy strategies is probably curvilinear. That is, the therapist must try to maintain a level of moderately high distress and discomfort rather than very low distress. Low distress is accompanied by poor motivation for change. On the other hand, high distress is associated with inadequate ability to remain focused on problem resolution. If distress is too high, therefore, it may interfere with life functioning, and direct efforts are indicated to reduce this stress. If it is too low, the patient is unmotivated and efforts are required to induce arousal. That means that the therapist must not only assess the level of distress that is usually present and the level that is present in a particular moment in time but also the impeding effects of both of these types of distress.

Because it is changeable, formal measures of subjective distress are obtained immediately before each treatment session. In PT, this information is provided to therapists as the session begins in order to assist in the selection of treatment strategies. Periodically (about every fifth session), this score is checked against measures of distress that are less state-like, in order to confirm the stability of distress levels over time. These latter, stable measures are the SCL-90R (GSI subscale) and the STS–Subjective Distress subscale. We also obtain an estimate of the degree to which the patient's level of subjective distress impairs flexibility and adaptation to external demands. This determination is made by estimating the patient's level of functional impairment as assessed by a modified version of the Global Assessment of Functioning (GAF) included in the STS Clinician Rating Form. The rating is made by external clinicians and cross-validated by the therapist.

PT therapists are taught to develop their perceptive skills and abilities for identifying moment-to-moment changes in distress. These judgments are used to make adjustments in the interventions applied. Identification of changing, moment-to-moment states is facilitated by assessment of nonverbal behavior. The therapists learn methods of identifying behaviors that have been found to be related to subjective distress and are trained to rate them reliably. The noncontent aspects of patient presentations that most closely relate to level of distress include speed of speech (number of words per minute) and frequency of physical movement. At the same time, verbal dysfluency, circumstantial associations, and frequent change of topic serve as the basis for making formal ratings of moment-to-moment changes in functioning. These clinical, nonverbal indicators serve to guide the therapist to alter the treatment by introducing supportive or confrontational procedures.

Initially, levels of subjective distress that are higher than the 75th percentile (outpatient norms for the SCL-90-R GSI subscale) indicate the advisability of employing treatments that are designed to provide direct support and anxiety reduction. Scores below the 25th percentile, in contrast, are taken as indicators for employing confrontational and abreactive procedures that tend to increase patient arousal and distress.

Concluding Comments

This chapter has suggested and described procedures that are used to evaluate patients in selecting treatment procedures. There are at least three reasons for this evaluation. Some procedures are used for screening patients for treatment eligibility. Other procedures are used to evaluate treatment progress and change. Still other procedures are used to select among differential treatment strategies. These three objectives of assessment should be kept distinct.

Although therapists should be aware of the methods for selecting and screening potential patients, they do not need to know either how to administer most of these assessment procedures or the details of their use. The particulars of assessing outcome are also of limited use to therapists, but they should know the nature and content of the assessment procedures. This knowledge ensures that therapists are able to assess their own progress and success in meaningful ways. The specific measures used help make these determinations more reliable and meaningful.

Prescriptive therapists must be quite familiar with the strengths and limitations of the methods that are used to identify the decision points that inform and guide the application of different treatment strategies. Specifically, the therapist should know the difference between state and trait measurement and the associated decisions. This knowledge helps the therapist identify and recognize which aspects of patient functioning are likely to change rapidly and which are likely to change slowly.

For example, coping styles and resistance potential are enduring qualities that set the threshold and changeability of patients, but all patients may become resistant under certain circumstances and all vary in their emotional tone and response to confrontive interventions. To effectively plan and implement treatment, therapists must learn to recognize when a reaction is situational and to differentiate this reaction from those conditions when it is characterological. Accordingly, this knowledge allows therapists to know when to apply a set of focused procedures and when to allow the patient to move through the normal processes of adjustment and change.

Clinicians conventionally rely on subjective judgment and personal observation to measure many of the patient qualities that change quickly over time. Research assures us that this is a hazardous procedure in spite of the great faith that clinicians have in their own judgments. Thus, reliance on formal measures must be developed, much like the airplane pilot who must learn to trust and give credence to the instruments on his panel more than on his physical sensations. This is a hard skill to acquire but one that is likely to be especially rewarding in helping the clinician accurately assess patients' needs for confrontation or for support, among other decisions.

In the chapters that follow, we outline the principles and strategies that govern the specific application of this version of PT. We emphasize the importance of therapist self-reliance and creativity, but we also must emphasize that the assessment process is designed to be of service to clinicians and to help make their decisions more replicable and informed. Learning to balance self-trust with the informed use of instruments of measurement is an important task for increasing the effectiveness of the prescriptive therapist.

Part II.

TREATMENT PRINCIPLES AND STRATEGIES

Chapter 4
Establishing a Therapeutic Relationship

Two fundamental tasks guide the therapist's activities in the early stages of virtually any effective psychotherapy. These tasks are important to the goal of establishing and then maintaining the patient's collaboration and motivation during treatment. They are mediating in that their successful completion significantly improves the likelihood and magnitude of therapeutic changes. The tasks are (1), to establish a sound working relationship and (2), to develop a guiding set of objectives and expectations that will both serve as a contract and provide a focus for therapeutic work. The nature of objectives and focus of treatment will be partially determined by the nature of the patient's coping style (chapter 5), but the development of a relationship that supports and encourages the patient to take risks is a general consideration and must be addressed early and then readdressed whenever a therapeutic tear occurs in the relationship.

The therapist's success in accomplishing the tasks of early treatment reflects the degree to which he or she is able to apply the six keys to success we introduced and described in chapter 2 and to apply them to a process that enhances the therapeutic relationship.

1. A therapeutic *attitude*, as applied to relationship building, is one of respect, kindness, and caring. A therapist who typifies this set of attitudes is optimistic and tuned to the patient's achievements and strengths, not just to problems and weaknesses.
2. Therapeutic *knowledge*, that enances relationship power, includes an understanding of how people form impressions, respond to structure, and become motivated to initiate and maintain change.
3. Therapeutic relationship *tools* are those vehicles used to translate the therapist's knowledge into a structure that enhances the patient's view

of the relationship. Tools include an office structure and a receptive environment that conveys the therapist's attitudes and knowledge.

4. Relationship *techniques* include a variety of verbal and nonverbal procedures that are designed to reduce symptoms or relationship problems. Together, the attitude, knowledge, tools, and techniques of therapy constitute therapeutic skill in establishing a process of open negotiation. The skillful application of techniques to establishing the relationship is a demonstration that the process of treatment is flexible and responsive to the patient.

5. Therapeutic *timing* is seen in relationship development by a correspondence between patient readiness and treatment intervention. Timing is critical to maintaining a treatment alliance when the therapist initiates direct action, recommends treatment, removes structure, and alters course.

6. *Creative imagination* is reflected at all stages of therapy by how the therapist patterns and organizes various interventions to adapt them to the unique and specific qualities of the patient. As applied to the development of the relationship, imagination contributes to understanding and sensing what is possible between two people and being able to place one's self in the role of the other.

This chapter is devoted to describing the process of establishing the initial relationship and maintaining this relationship as threats are posed by the struggles of therapeutic work. Necessarily, our focus is on the attitude, knowledge, tools, and techniques of treatment, though this should not be taken as a diminution of the other keys to therapeutic success. These former keys are emphasized here simply because we know more about them and their function.

Guiding Principles

Two principles guide the therapist during the early stages of treatment. The first of these principles addresses the means to enhance the likelihood of change, and the second principle addresses the task of increasing the magnitude of change.

1. Therapeutic change is greatest when the therapist is skillful and provides trust, acceptance, acknowledgment, collaboration, and respect for the patient and does so in an environment that both supports risk and provides maximal safety.

2. Risk and retention are optimized if the patient is realistically informed about the probable length and effectiveness of the treatment, provided

support and comfort, and given a clear understanding of the roles and activities expected of him or her during the course of treatment.

Indexing Cues

The principles of developing the relationship are quite universal and are relatively independent of patient trait-like characteristics. They are indirectly related to a variety of patient variables as we will see over the next chapters. The first of the cues that one must recognize in order to activate the principles of relationship development is temporal. The other cues occur when certain state-like reactions emerge.

1. *At the beginning of therapy.* Early in the treatment the therapist should be focused on the development of a warm, accepting, and safe relationship. As a rule of thumb, at least half of the therapeutic time in early sessions should be devoted to conveying the therapeutic attitudes, knowledge, and skills that increase patient attachment and productivity.

2. *Following therapeutic tears in the relationship.* Psychotherapy proceeds by a process of tearing and repairing the relationship. That is, progress is a process of rupture and healing. Whenever the therapist intervenes, he or she creates the potential for a tear to occur in the treatment relationship. Tears occur when the therapist confronts, responds in a nontherapeutic way, suggests an action, or provides an interpretation of the patient's behavior. In other words, it most likely occurs when the therapist acts as an expert. A sudden change in patient mood or attitude or a relatively sudden decline in patient energy and investment may index the presence of a tear and can be taken as a cue for the therapist to institute processes that are aimed at repairing this tear. Following a tear, a therapist may helpfully increase the effort and time devoted to following these principles, relative to those to be described in later chapters. Returning to a focus on the principles of relationship development and enhancement are the avenues to producing reparative healing.

3. *Patient expresses anger at the therapist.* Anger at the therapist is expressed in either passive or active forms, and in either direct or indirect ways. Some anger is overt—directly expressed. It is directed either at the lack of progress, at some characteristic of the therapist, or at something the therapist has done. This is the most difficult anger to which the therapist must respond because he or she must not respond in kind (except in unusual circumstances), choosing instead to accept, acknowledge, and support the patient's expressions of rage. More obscure expressions of anger are conveyed through less obvious cues: facial expressions, sudden loss of energy, and expressions of disagreement or requests for changes in the treatment. All these behaviors should

serve as cues that the patient may be dissatisfied with the therapist, with the speed of progress, or with the nature of treatment. Such behaviors should evoke an effort on the part of the therapist to initiate a reparative response.

As in cases of directly expressed anger, the therapist is called on to respond with acknowledgment, acceptance, understanding, and attention, avoiding the urge to become defensive. Therapeutic attitudes include an acknowledgment of the patient's feelings, an acceptance of their expression, and a willingness to consider the possibility that patients may be justified or even right in their perceptions.

Fostering Collaborative Objectives and Expectations

Generally, the strategies for developing and enhancing the treatment relationship is to gain the patient's collaboration, provide evidence of caring and support, and to assure the patient of the safety of the environment. The most accepted strategies provide structure, reinforce the joint nature of the therapeutic effort, and ensure that the therapist behaves in a consistent and nonjudgmental way.

The first major task of the therapist is developing a sense of collaboration and establishing realistic expectations. The collaborative task of relationship building requires that the therapist comes to see and then to convey the processes and goals of treatment as shared responsibilities. This basic strategy is generally associated with the use of three more specific procedures and techniques: (1) by formally preparing the patient for therapy, (2) by using language that fosters a perception of therapy as a mutual process, and (3) by securing the patient's expressed permission for implementing directed change activities.

Techniques in Pretherapy Preparation

Preparation of the patient begins before the first treatment session. The techniques that one may use to prepare patients may vary widely. Written materials that describe the clinic, treatment facilities and options, parking arrangements, and special facilities for the physically challenged and that outline the billing procedures is one method for preparing a patient for the process of psychotherapy. These materials, if not provided in excess, can reduce a patient's uncertainty and overcome some of the fears that might keep the patient from coming to the first therapy session. For patients who are new to treatment or those who have special needs that are accommodated by the treatment setting, this material may be especially useful and should describe the purposes of therapy, the processes to be followed in interviewing, and the amount of time required to complete these phases of the assessment and treatment processes. Audiotapes, video presentations, and computerized instruction may be alternatives to a great deal of written material and may be especially helpful for those whose have some deficit reading skills (Beutler & Clarkin, 1990; Beutler, Machado, & Neufeldt, 1994). Because they require some special equipment, visual presentations may be made available to the patient to use in the waiting room prior to the appointment.

By whatever means presented, the preappointment material should be complemented by the procedures for introducing the patient to treatment at the time of their first visit. The reception room staff should be friendly. Staff members can receive and check the completeness of the materials previously sent to the patient's home. They should invite the patient to sit, ensure their comfort, and then introduce whatever intake forms and introductory materials are to be used for speed entry and preparation. Staff should be especially careful to avoid the appearance of criticism or negativity if patients have failed to complete their forms or have completed them incorrectly. Many patients do not complete the forms and expect to be criticized for this failure. A danger of sending materials to the patient's home, in fact, is that the patient may find it difficult to attend a scheduled session if, for some reason, he or she has not completed the forms in advance. The staff, to counteract this tendency, should take special care to invite the patient to ask questions and then offer to help the patient complete the necessary forms.

The therapist also should be prepared at the time of the patient's appointment. He or she should know what information was given to the telephone interviewer or receptionist, should be familiar with whatever materials were sent in advance of the patient's arrival, and should carefully review these materials immediately before the patient's appointment time. The therapist should also be familiar with the clinic's procedures and with the purposes for which information is gathered.

The therapist should meet the patient in the waiting room, introduce him or herself in a formal manner and indicate how he or she would like to be addressed (e.g., "I'm Doctor Johnson—you may call me Carl. I'll be meeting with you today"), and then invite the patient into the office. Seating should be comfortable but without physical obstruction between the patient and therapist. The patient should be invited to sit, queried about how he or she would like to be addressed ("What name would you like to have me use when we talk, Mr. Dollard?" or, "How would you like me to address you?"), and invited to provide feedback about the initial scheduling procedures (e.g., "Were you able to get all the information and answers you needed through the material that we sent?"). Then, assuming even a more open questioning style, the therapist invites the patient to reveal the story of his or her problem (e.g., "Now, please tell me about what brought you here?").

In this first interview, the therapist seeks to obtain answers to three basic questions and then to give information to the patient about future treatment. The three questions that guide the interview are: (1) *Why* are you here? (2) Why are you *here*? (3) Why are you here, *at this time*? (Beutler, & Berren, 1995). The first question seeks to know the nature of the problem; its history, patient background, and family; and the history of prior treatment. The second question seeks to know the nature of the referral, the process of selecting among options, and the patient's expectations about what treatment will be like. The third question draws attention to whether the problem is acute or chronic, whether it is pressing, and whether the events that evoked a search for help were internal to the patient's distress or the result of external demands and threats.

At the conclusion of the first interview—only rarely does this need to be delayed until a second interview, the therapist provides feedback and recommendations to the patient about the nature of treatment. This formulation and plan should not use technical terms or labels, though sometimes a descriptive diagnosis is permissible. Neither is it necessary or even helpful to describe the details of the anticipated treatment. What benefits the patient is to know what the therapist believes to be the goal or goals of treatment, what form the treatment is expected to take (group or individual or family), how long treatment is likely to take, and the results that might be expected within that length of time. Whereas most research programs offer somewhat limiting choices at this point, it is important to communicate that the patient can choose to opt out of the research and that there may be options for other facilities or other therapists within the current facility. The patient should be questioned about his or her response to the therapist (e.g., "Do you think that we can work together?"), with special encouragement to describe any reservations that the patient has about the therapist, in particular. The possibility of changing therapists should be raised at this time (e.g., "If, for some reason, you find something about me that you think might make it difficult to work with me, we can probably make arrangements at this point to change therapists"). This is an especially important insertion for the resistant patient and introduces an important choice while fostering the sense of control.

As a final preparatory procedure, the therapist suggests both a length of treatment and a meeting schedule. The therapist then, again, asks for suggestions about specific times and dates, modifying the schedule within the limits that are tolerable to the setting and objectives. The discussion about treatment format and demands should be open-ended, with the therapist both seeking and providing feedback from the patient, using the input to guide decisions about the type of therapy that might be helpful to the patient's needs and problems. This procedure ensures that the patient will be an active consumer of therapeutic processes and sets an important precedent for the therapist to seek and use feedback from the patient in the course of psychotherapy.

Techniques for Developing Collaborative Language

Collaborative language is another method for conveying and reinforcing the mutuality of the psychotherapeutic process. It is a useful procedure both in the initial phase of treatment and in the later stages of repairing tears in the relationship. Luborsky and colleagues (1985) have demonstrated that words such as "we" and "our" are more frequent in the language of therapists and patients during successful therapy than are personal, singular references such as "mine" and "I". By emphasizing these words when talking about the psychotherapy experience, goals, and processes, the therapist cements the perspective that the venture is one that is jointly created.

There is frequently a delicate balance between what should be included under language that uses first person plural pronouns such as "us," "we" and "our." Personal responsibility for the development of problems must be balanced with joint responsibility for finding solutions. Simply, the patient's problems and the consequences of his or her associated behavior should not be subsumed by the therapist. They are identified as belonging to the patient. By identifying choices, consequences, precipitators, and correlates of problems as having personal rather than joint ownership, the patient's responsibility and control are reinforced. However, the responsibilities for finding solutions, through psychotherapy, are the domain of both therapist and patient. Thus, these things are identified by the use of collaborative language.

Techniques of Securing Patient Permission

Securing permission is a useful procedure in all therapeutic sessions. It is not restricted to the early phases of treatment, when expectations are being established and treatment contracts are being negotiated. It is a strategy that is especially important if and when a patient is showing some resistance to the directed procedures of the treatment. In sum, the therapist asks and obtains permission before implementing any active treatment strategy or technique (e.g., "Would you be willing to try something with me?" Or, "Would it be all right if we focused a little more closely on that issue?"). Whenever the therapist introduces new material, changes directions, seeks to confront, or introduces a directive, such permission should precede the introduction of this material.

Frequently, it helps if active procedures that are introduced and to be directed by the therapist are described as "experiments." Indeed, they are experiments in that neither the therapist nor the patient knows where they will ultimately lead. This framework may also foster a questioning attitude on the part of the patient and presents the therapy process as a collaborative venture in which both seek to discover new experiences and new meanings. Thus, the therapist might ask, "Would you be willing to undertake an experiment to see where it takes us?" Active procedures, except in the most extreme of circumstances, should not be initiated unless the patient is willing to give the permission requested. This is intended to ensure that if the patient is highly resistant, he or she is not threatened by either loss of personal control over circumstances or by the therapist's perceived knowledge or power.

Relationship Facilitation

The second major task of the therapist, once initial collaboration has been established, is to solidify a relationship that is congenial to beginning a process of working toward the collaborative goals. The strategy is to facilitate a perception that the relationship is supportive and that the therapist is caring and nonjudging. The task of developing these perceptions is one to which the therapist will return throughout the treatment relationship, especially as tears and disruptions occur. It is especially important when therapy is active and therapist directed.

Developing and maintaining the "working" or "therapeutic" relationship is the fundamental strategy for change in PT and is central to any model or type of therapy. It is a foundation for all other work that is done. Developing or redeveloping a working relationship occupies a good portion of the first few sessions. It is an aspect to which the therapist must return at the beginning of every session as well as whenever the relationship is declining or shows evidence of being torn.

Much has been written about the therapeutic relationship and a great deal of research has testified to its centrality in producing beneficial outcomes. A positive therapeutic relationship accounts for most of the therapist-initiated changes that occur in almost any mental health condition. By whatever name applies, therapeutic alliance, facilitative relationship, working alliance, and so on, an effective relationship is one in which the patient feels acknowledged, understood, and accepted. It is also one in which the patient views the therapist as credible, knowledgeable, accepting, caring, respectful, and empathic. Both therapist and patient contribute to the processes of establishing this relationship, but the patient's positive perception of the therapist is the defining characteristic of what makes a relationship important (Strupp & Binder, 1984).

Techniques of Relationship Enhancement

Beginning with Carl Rogers (1957), empathy and acceptance have been considered the foundation stones of a persuasive and helpful relationship. Rogers's "necessary and sufficient" conditions represented an articulation of strategies for achieving therapeutic change. His reliance on reflection of feelings is an example of a specific technique that was designed to be consistent with the strategy.

Rogers's work emphasized the importance of maintaining a safe therapeutic environment, at least insofar as the therapist's warmth, nonjudgmental attitude, empathy, and consistency can establish it as such. It also hinges on the changing and growing ability of the patient to hear the level of understanding and empathy being conveyed. These general qualities have now been incorporated into the foundation work of most of psychotherapy and work on the therapeutic alliance or working relationship has turned more to defining what the therapist can do to facilitate the patient's recognition. In this process, the concepts of empathy, warmth, acceptance, congruence, and understanding have taken on broader and more varied roles in psychotherapy than Rogers may have originally supposed. Research has turned more and more to studying interactive qualities that foster patient motivation and focus. This has been done under the general scope of studying the therapeutic alliance, but these newer concepts have almost always been found to be highly correlated with the qualities originally proposed by Rogers (e.g., Beutler, Machado, & Neufeldt, 1994).

Several authors besides Rogers (e.g., Orlinsky & Howard, 1987) have suggested that it is advantageous to distinguish among several different therapist qualities. However, to keep the process as simple as possible, in the current context, we discuss the various relationship qualities that are designed to convey a sense of safety, support, caring, and understanding under a single term, "empathic support." Empathic support implies not only that the therapist experiences these characteristics but that they are conveyed to and perceived by patients themselves (Beutler, Machado, & Neufeldt, 1994; Orlinsky, Grawe, & Parks, 1994). Empathic support, in this broad definition, includes patient perceptions that the therapist is credible, has persuasive potency, is understanding, possesses warmth, is caring, is capable of emotional understanding, and provides supportive encouragement. To convey these impressions, the therapist must be judged to be sensitive or attuned to the meanings and feelings that lie beneath the overt communication and words used by the patient. Only when one can convey that he or she has been attentive to these hidden feelings and meanings, as much as to the obvious ones, is the patient likely to feel truly understood and valued. A central aspect of therapeutic work, particularly early in the treatment relationship, is creating and strengthening these perceptions (Beitman, 1987).

General Techniques

Empathic support is fostered both by what the therapist does and what the therapist does not do. That is, there are both *prescribed* and *proscribed* strategies and techniques that, together, enhance the development of a set of positive patient perceptions. Prescriptive strategies are ones that, by their presence, are used to induce positive perceptions, whereas proscribed strategies are ones that foster the relationship by their absence. On the positive side, prescribed strategies include the following:

1. Acknowledge the presence of patient's feelings.
2. Achieve and express authentic understanding of these feelings.
3. Achieve a phenomenological understanding of the patient's meanings and perceptions.
4. Be a nonauthoritarian, knowledgeable expert.
5. Achieve and communicate genuine caring about the patient's suffering.
6. Achieve and express acceptance for characteristics of the patient that are unusual, frightening, or unacceptable to the patient.
7. Ensure that the environment, records, and processes are safe and secure.
8. Be trustworthy—keep commitments to the patient.

These are illusive concepts both because they require the development of an internal state of understanding, acceptance, and trustworthiness and also because they require the ability to communicate these attributes. The specific ways and techniques that communicate these attributes are not completely known, but research has discovered a number of procedures and techniques that are clearly related to the process.

Interestingly, the nature of proscribed strategies can be more easily specified than the prescribed ones; however, they are much more difficult to maintain than to identify. Proscribed strategies foster a positive alliance by avoiding certain behaviors. For example, an effective therapist *does not*:

1. Criticize or correct the patient.
2. Place a moral (right versus wrong) judgment on, or evaluate the worth of what the patient describes.
3. Assume that he or she knows what the patient thinks or believes.
4. Attempt to persuade the patient to have a change of mind.
5. Discount or minimize the patient's view of what is either real or valuable.
6. Interrupt the patient's flow of thoughts and feelings.
7. Violate the patient's trust expectations.

8. Become defensive, angry, or distressed by the patient's expression of strong thoughts and feelings.

The last of these proscriptions is particularly important. Strupp and Binder (1997) point out that even among a sample of experienced and successful therapists in the Vanderbilt projects, none were able to deal effectively and nondefensively with patient anger. Indeed, each of these proscriptions will, occasionally, be breached, with a concomitant decline in the patient's sense of receiving empathic support. Indeed, most therapeutic procedures and therapeutic models specifically call for the therapist to violate one or more of the proscriptions in the course of implementing procedures and techniques that are designed to induce change. Doing so indicates the need to spend some time reconnecting and reinforcing the therapeutic relationship.

For example, the therapist may tear the relationship whenever he or she identifies certain thoughts as "illogical" or "invalid" and suggests a correction, becomes angry at something the patient has said, infers the presence of certain thoughts and feelings, or labels certain behaviors as inappropriate, illogical, or unproductive. The therapist must strike a balance between doing things that enhance the sense of empathic support and guiding the patient to change or confronting the obstacles to treatment, recognizing that engaging in these latter procedures is accompanied by a weakening of the therapeutic relationship. Violating the proscriptions produces a tear in the relationship while adhering to the prescribed relationship behaviors repair the tears in the fabric of the relationship. Therapy proceeds in this tear-and-repair fashion, but one must maintain a balance that favors the presence of prescribed behaviors most of the time.

Although a positive balance between prescribed and proscribed strategies must be maintained for progress to occur, the particular nature of the balance varies from patient to patient and from moment to moment. Maintaining a positive balance requires clear and careful judgment and measurement on the part of the therapist to know when the critical balance is tipping toward a negative value. In virtually all cases, however, the beginning phases of therapy must be heavily balanced toward raising the patient's perceptions of the therapist's empathic support—the patient should come to feel understood and valued. Thereafter, a balance is sought that never allows the perceived positive nature of the relationship to drop below a point at which it is recognized as being more dominant in the interaction than the perception of receiving support and empathy. Maintaining a balance that favors the salience of empathy thus fosters the patient's optimism, faith, and motivation and ultimately allows the tears in the relationship to heal. If the relative balance between tears and repairs does dip in favor of the former, at least more than momentarily, one can see it in the patient's loss of motivation and increased anger and by other disruptive reactions. The maintenance of a negative balance is likely to eventually result in the patient abandoning therapy altogether. Thus, the balance between providing a prescription for developing a positive relationship and introducing the proscriptions noted previously requires that the therapist be constantly attuned to indicators of patient resistance and rejection.

Angry or resentful feelings expressed directly to the therapist are clear signals that the balance has swung toward proscribed behaviors, but these clear signs may not occur until the relationship has been irreparably damaged. Earlier signs that the prescribed behaviors may be inadequately represented in the balance of these interventions include irritability in the patient's voice, withdrawn posture, a declining mood, looks of irritability and boredom, and sundry passive and noncooperative behaviors (nonattendance or lateness, homework noncompliance, rejection of suggestions, etc.). As noted earlier, the therapist must learn to recognize these communications and use them as signals to alter the balance between proscribed and prescribed behaviors.

Specific Verbal Techniques and Procedures

A variety of largely evocative and verbal behaviors have been identified for enhancing the quality of the therapeutic relationship and conveying the prescribed attitudes. Briefly, and in abbreviated form, we identify these positive interventions as consisting mainly of reflections, restatements, acknowledgements, and reassurance.

Reflection is a therapeutic procedure initially proposed by Rogers both to induce awareness of one's feeling states and to convey empathy. It requires that the therapist be attuned to the patient's emotional reactions and consists of identifying and labeling, in a nonjudgmental fashion, the feelings that underlie a patient's comments. A good and productive reflection is one that identifies a feeling state of which the patient is either barely aware or reluctant to express aloud. Thus, most feelings that are the objects of reflection are negative in tone, because these are the ones that are most likely to be suppressed.

Identifying feelings is different than identifying hidden thoughts. In efforts to catalogue the primary (fundamental, irreversible) emotions, those with negative connotations include sadness, anger, fear, and disgust. Variations and mixtures of these primary emotions may include hurt (anger), jealousy (fear and anger), rage (anger), depression (anger), revulsion (disgust), apprehension (fear), and the like. However, the act of labeling feelings is complicated because people often identify their thoughts as well as their affective and mood states as "feelings." Reflections are aimed at feelings, not at thoughts. If a therapist labels a thought, it becomes an interpretation—a tearing procedure. The distinction is more than semantic. Reflections are aimed at raising consciousness; interpretations are aimed to foster insight. Thoughts are interpretations made by the patient *about* events, including feelings. They may serve as cues that give rise to feelings but are not the feelings themselves. Accurate reflection requires the therapist to be empathetically attuned (similar to Kohut's concept of "empathic attunement").

To help make the distinction between reflection and interpretation, it may be helpful to think about the construction of the sentences that are used in communication, both by the patient and by the therapist. When a person says, "I feel depressed," he or she is expressing a feeling. When he or she says, "I feel that I am depressed," that person is interpreting the meaning of his or her experience. Even though patients like the one in this example may use the word, "feeling" to describe the experience, the statement identifies a thought, not a feeling.

A reflection by the therapist, in the first instance, might be, "You feel hopeless." This response takes the patient's expression of feeling and adds a dimension of severity, focusing on the accompanying feelings of hopelessness and helplessness.

In the second example, the reflection might take a different tact such as, "You seem to be really confused and maybe a little frightened because you don't know what the meaning of all your symptoms are." Here the therapist focuses on the fear that can be assumed to be present when one is uncertain about how she is feeling. To do this well, the therapist must be highly tuned to the emotional tone and signs that the patient presents in voice, language, and body. In both this and the previous example, the empathic therapist attempts to identify the feeling behind the statement and to allow it to be expressed, increasing the patient's awareness and cementing the sense of being understood on an emotional plane.

Both in the language of the patient and in the response of the therapist, it is important to differentiate between thoughts and feelings. A thought or interpretation can be distinguished from a feeling by two tests: (1) one can logically insert the word "that" prior to the feeling word, and (2) one can substitute the word "think," or one of its derivatives, for the use of the word "feeling" without changing the meaning. Thus, in the foregoing example, the interpretative/cognitive nature of the patient's comment is unmasked by the fact that the sentence loses no meaning when it is changed to, "I *think* that I am depressed". Likewise, a therapist who responds "you *feel* abused" is reflecting. One who says "you have been abused," or you feel [believe] you've been abused," is providing an interpretation.

A productive reflection is usually indexed by the patient's response. This takes the form of an acknowledgement of the correctness of the reflection and often is accompanied by the expression of some surprise or delight in recognizing a new element in the subjective feeling state (e.g., "Wow! Yes, I guess I really was angry and it didn't even dawn on me"). Thus, the patient is able to acknowledge a somewhat different or even new feeling state. Such an awareness not only fosters emotional awareness but leaves the patient with the sense of being understood by the therapist at a fundamental, emotional level.

Restatement is a less powerful therapist response than reflection. It does not capture the emotional meaning but simply clarifies and summarizes the patient's preceding verbal response(s). Restatement provides nothing new to the patient's remarks and is specifically designed to foster the feeling of being understood at an intellectual level. It conveys an attitude of attentiveness and confirms that the therapist is listening.

In its simplest form, a restatement uses many of the same words as those used by the patient but adds the therapist's emphasis (e.g., "You really *did* feel rejected"). Thus, although not changing the meaning, the therapist may change the value reflected in certain elements. In complicated forms, restatement uses different words to add or emphasize the elements of significance (e.g., "It seems that things were getting out of your control"). The distinction between such a restatement and an interpretation is that the restatement follows immediately upon a similar statement by the patient (e.g., "I wasn't able to cope anymore"). Without this degree of correspondence between the patient and the therapist's overt and expressed meaning, the therapist's response becomes an interpretation, rather than a restatement.

Acknowledgment is a statement that is specifically designed to affirm either the correctness or the value of the patient him-or herself or what the patient has described. Thus, it more directly conveys the beliefs and values of the therapist than either reflection or restatement. Such an acknowledgement may be aimed at the content of the patient's communication ("Yes, you are right about things being a little unclear in what your mother meant"), or it may be more personal. A personal acknowledgement confirms the worth or value of individuals rather than the truth of their proclamations (e.g., "You really are worthwhile, you know") and is usually offered when the patient seems to be in doubt about such matters or is struggling to gain self-esteem. Individuals who have suffered from feeling unacknowledged may be particularly needy of such affirmation by the therapist, particularly in the beginning stages of therapy.

The immediate impact of acknowledgement is probably proportional to the degree of its personal focus. A personal acknowledgement is likely to have a significant impact, but it is also likely to have short-lived benefits. While a short-term boost to one's emotions is often helpful in bringing an individual through a transition, reflections and responses that evoke thought are likely to have longer-lasting effects. Thus, mixing provocative comments and reflections with personal acknowledgements may gain more ground than acknowledgement alone in the long run.

Reassurance is a class of comments designed to provide immediate comfort and to reduce anticipatory anxiety. It offers structure, predicts positive consequences, and inserts reminders of past accomplishments. Reassurance also expresses the therapist's desire and optimism—a desire to help the patient achieve treatment goals and the optimism that the patient will be able to do so. In this process, reassurance reduces the anxiety associated with uncertainty and cements the perception that the therapist is confident, assured, and available.

Most reassuring comments are aimed at either supporting past behaviors of the patients, about which the patients is uncertain, or predicting positive consequences for current and anticipated acts. Like acknowledgement, reassurance reveals the therapist's beliefs and values quite directly. And, also like acknowledgement, reassurance is more useful for facilitating a therapeutic bond than for making substantial changes.

The therapist may comfort the patient by such comments as, "I'm sure that everything will turn out all right," or in less direct ways by general comments such as, "Remember that most of the time, your decisions have been good ones." Such comments and statements are useful for helping a person through a crisis but need to be coupled with more provocative interventions to sustain long-term change. They are helpful for reminding patients of their strengths and enhancing self-esteem when patients have been damaged, but their primary role is to imbue the therapist with a persona of being constant, knowledgeable, and available. Therapists should use such comments sparingly when patients are acutely distressed and uncertain, resorting to more enduring and evocative strategies (e.g., accurate reflection through empathic attunement) to build the relationship when acute stress has passed.

Assessing the Quality of the Therapeutic Relationship

The Pennsylvania Therapeutic Alliance scale is one of several conceptually related measures of the quality of the working or therapeutic relationship. It is reprinted in Table 4.1 for use by external raters to judge and evaluate the degree to which the therapist's attitudes, knowledge, skill, and creative imagination are being expressed during the therapy session. These aspects of the relationship are tapped by two separate subscales, one reflecting assessments of general relationship skill and the other aspects of a collaborative relationship.

Such external assessments of therapeutic quality can be supplemented by directly questioning the patient. The therapist is well advised to seek feedback about how the patient perceives the relationship, including the technique of asking about the patient's dissatisfaction with the direction the treatment is taking or the way topics are resolved. This is especially critical when there are hints that the patient is dissatisfied or angry. The therapist who directly

TABLE 4.1. Pennsylvania Helping Alliance Scale

Type I Alliance

Type I therapeutic alliance emphasizes the therapist's ability to establish a warm, supportive relationship.

1. The therapist is warm and supportive.

1	2	3	4	5	6	7	8	9	10
Very little or none		Some			Moderate amount		Much		Very much

2. The therapist conveys a sense of wanting the patient to achieve treatment goals.

1	2	3	4	5	6	7	8	9	10
Very little or none		Some			Moderate amount		Much		Very much

3. The therapist conveys a sense of hopefulness that treatment goals can be achieved.

1	2	3	4	5	6	7	8	9	10
Very little or none		Some			Moderate amount		Much		Very much

4. The therapist conveys a sense that he or she feels a rapport with the patient, that he or she understands the patient.

1	2	3	4	5	6	7	8	9	10
Very little or none		Some			Moderate amount		Much		Very much

5. The therapist conveys feelings of acceptance and respect for the patient as opposed to behavior in which the patient is put down (e.g., by jokes at the patient's expense).

1	2	3	4	5	6	7	8	9	10
Very little or none		Some			Moderate amount		Much		Very much

Type II Alliance

Type II is working alliance based on the sense of working together in a joint struggle against what is impeding the patient. The emphasis is on shared responsibility for working out the treatment goals and on the patient's ability to do what the therapist does.

6. The therapist says things that show that he or she feels a "we" bond with the patient, that he or she feels a sense of alliance with the patient in the joint struggle against what is impeding the patient.

1	2	3	4	5	6	7	8	9	10
Very little or none		Some			Moderate amount		Much		Very much

7. The therapist conveys recognition of the patient's growing sense of being able to do what the therapist does (indicates needs to be done) in terms of the basic tools of the treatment (e.g., ability to introspect and analyze his or her own behavior).

(continued)

TABLE 4.1. (continued)

1	2	3	4	5	6	7	8	9	10
Very little or none		Some			Moderate amount		Much		Very much

8. The therapist shows acceptance of the patient's increased ability to understand his or her own (the patient's) experiences.

1	2	3	4	5	6	7	8	9	10
Very little or none		Some			Moderate amount		Much		Very much

9. The therapist acknowledges and confirms the patient's accurate perceptions of him or her (the therapist).

1	2	3	4	5	6	7	8	9	10
Very little or none		Some			Moderate amount		Much		Very much

10. The therapist can accept the fact that the patient also can reflect on what the patient and he or she have been through together, building up, as it were, a joint backlog of common experiences. (References by the therapist to past patient-therapist exchanges sometimes may fit here).

1	2	3	4	5	6	7	8	9	10
Very little or none		Some			Moderate amount		Much		Very much

and nondefensively queries about the presence of negative feelings is likely to improve the therapeutic bond.

In addition, the therapist is advised to work to create a perception that the responsibilities of treatment are shared, including the failures and setbacks. The intentional use of first-person-plural pronouns (we and us) may advance these perceptions. Language structure alone will not turn the trick, and it is necessary that the patient see the tasks and goals of treatment as being shared and mutually accepted. Complementing language structure with a formal definition of how the roles are shared, through the use of preparatory role induction interviews, may further foster a positive bond.

Concluding Comments

The use of efforts to instill the perception of collaboration must be supported by true collaborative efforts on the part of the therapist. The therapist's task is to remain flexible and responsive to variations among patients. The strategies of instilling collaboration extend to the techniques that can be applied even within the time-limited framework of PT. This adaptation and flexibility is best represented in the process of proposing a plan and contract for treatment. Proposing a course of treatment and then modifying the length of treatment, appointment times, treatment processes, and treatment goals or objectives in response to patient input and preferences provide confirmation of collaboration. Thus, the treatment contract, in the best of all worlds, is a mutually accepted and agreed upon plan. Although there are some limitations that both good therapy and research impose on this process, the therapist can always find some ways to accommodate the patient. These accommodations should be made explicit, both in the initial contract and periodically throughout the treatment, to reinforce the patient's perception of being a partner in the process. The contract is and should be a true compromise between the recommendations of the therapist and the wants of the patient.

Although neither good clinical judgment nor the research protocol allows unlimited modification of the therapeutic processes and goals, some modifications can be made. For example, the initial contract can vary in the following ways:

1. The number of contracted sessions can vary. The most usual form of time-limited PT calls for an initial contract of from from 15 to 20 sessions, but contracts may be renegotiated or extended several times.
2. The nature of homework assignments can be modified to address problems that are of direct concern to the patient.
3. The time of appointment can be of any mutually acceptable time.
4. The therapist can be reassigned to address preferences for one of a different sex.
5. Alternatives to PT (general psychotherapy, 12-Step programs, family or couple therapy, etc.) should be available for the patient to receive treatment.

Thus, as the foregoing decisions and plans are discussed, the therapist might advance a suggestion or proposal and then seek feedback. Disagreements or differences of viewpoint are opened to negotiation. Especially as the therapist presents the treatment plan and the available choices, he or she should use collaborative words. Thus, "our" goals, treatment methods, and expected outcomes should be preferred and used, rather than "my" or "your" goals, and so on, whenever it is possible to do so. When compromises are achieved, a summary statement that emphasizes the final agreement is helpful. For example, the therapist might summarize a disagreement by pointing to the initial differences in objectives and then to the accepted common agreement:

"As I see it, *we* each initially pointed to a somewhat different set of priorities for treatment, but *we* both agree now that *we* should start with getting your drug use under control, see how that affects your depression, and then *we* can proceed to work on understanding how your marriage and family relationships might be involved in all of these things. Do *we* agree now about that?"

Note, in this example, the therapist does not attempt to subsume the patient's problem but only to identify the mutuality of the goals and treatment directions. Thus, the patient's responsibilities are still identified and ownership is identified with the patient; it is the solutions that are indexed as a joint responsibility. If the insertion of plural inclusive language is truly more than a linguistic exercise, it will support and reflect the other efforts to ensure that collaboration is a reality of the experience.

Chapter 5
Adapting Treatment to Patient Level of Impairment and Coping Style: Part I

This chapter is the first of two that addresses the two decisions made at the point that one begins to focus on the coping and functioning of the patient: (1) assigning a level of care for the patient and (2) determining the patient's coping style so that an appropriate family of interventions can be assigned.

Patient level of impairment is determined by the level of support available to the patient and the areas of functioning that are impaired. The determination of impairment will in turn determine the frequency and intensity of treatment provided.

Patient coping style is a personal quality that is defined as the typical and usual way an individual interacts with others and responds to a threatened loss of safety and well-being. Because of their stability across situations and time, the nature of the interventions that are differentially compatible with patient coping styles can be identified early in the treatment process and applied throughout the course of treatment. Prescriptive therapists will initially select one of two general treatment strategies, each defined by a different point of focus, the selection of which will depend on the patient's coping style. One strategy is to employ interventions, throughout treatment, that are focused on either building behavioral skills or reducing symptoms. The second strategy begins similarly to the first but rapidly replaces the symptomatic and skill-building focus with one that is designed to facilitate insight and self-awareness.

The Nature of Coping Styles

It is useful to define patient coping styles descriptively and atheoretically. This allows us to avoid becoming embroiled in arguments about the etiology of various response dispositions, whether they are unconscious or conscious, and the nature of the motives that drive and activate them. That is not to say that PT does not make assumptions about the nature of coping styles. Indeed it does, but these assumptions involve only minimal extrapolation, interpretation, and inference. They stay as close to observable and empirical data as we can make them without losing their clinical utility.

We make two basic assumptions about coping styles: (1) they are predictable and recurrent behaviors that are observed in interpersonal relationships, and (2) they are most obvious when a person's sense of stability and safety is threatened. Coping styles are characteristic ways of either achieving wanted goals or avoiding unwanted experience. However, as they apply to clinical problems and treatment, it is reasonable to assume that coping styles are ritualistic ways of coping with unwanted experience—they are styles of avoidance.

A coping style is conceptually distinct from a defensive style or ego defense. The latter concepts are closely defined by a particular theoretical framework and, accordingly, are assumed to be unconscious and are usually considered to be motivated by invisible, internal conflicts. Coping styles define efforts both to acquire positive goals and to avoid negative experience. They may be either conscious or unconscious; however, neither these attributes nor the presence of unconscious motives needs to be inferred for the construct to be useful. In contrast to ego defenses, one can identify one's coping style without reference to nonobvious events. It is identifiable by reports of others or by self-descriptions of interpersonal behavior. Thus, coping styles are broader and more general qualities than either ego defenses or defensive styles are assumed to be, although one who is so disposed can probably identify certain characteristic ego defenses that correspond with one's coping style.

Systematic Treatment Selection, and hence PT, views one's coping style as an enduring propensity or disposition that characterizes interpersonal interactions. Thus, a coping style is an inextricable aspect of a person's personality. But, to say it is a part of personality does not imply that a coping style is invariable. People's characteristic behaviors vary, depending on whether they are occurring in response to desired or unwanted experience. Because most of the behaviors and symptoms that cause one to have difficulties arise from efforts to avoid unwanted experience, the aspects of coping style that direct clinical treatment are patterns of behavior that exist around factors and events: (1) that have resulted in the patient initiating treatment and (2) that tend to evoke socially inappropriate or personally distressing reactions. We can refer to these evoking conditions as stressors.

Stressors are events that evoke experiences that the patient seeks to avoid. Thus, they initiate disruptions to one's behavior. "Treatment-relevant stress" consists of the events that initially moved the patient to seek treatment and those conditions that evoke socially or personally unacceptable behaviors.

People can be roughly categorized into one of two groups depending on whether their characteristic response to stress is to focus on personal responsibility and internal experience (internalizers) or other's responsibility and external experience (externalizers) (Beutler & Clarkin, 1990). People within each of these two groups, of course, vary widely in how consistently they behave; however, it is possible to identify them with the dominance of one of these general patterns. Those people who focus internally may feel overwhelmed by distress, they may blame themselves or their own feelings for problems, they may be self-depreciating, they seek solace in avoiding other people, or they develop stress-related physical symptoms such as headaches or stomach aches. These symptoms reflect a general investment in the effort to control and manage stress by constricting and minimizing the intensity of emotions.

In contrast, those who focus on external events may blame other people or outside circumstances for their problems; they may make active efforts to remove themselves from external stressors, they seek comfort and solace in the company of others, and they may become aggressive and angry at the events and people whom they believe are obstacles to their comfort or happiness. Thus, they control their subjective distress by exaggerated emotional expression, by increased social involvement, or by exaggerated behaviors that can become offensive and disruptive to others. In research literature, externalizers have been observed to be gregarious while internalizers are generally more socially avoidant (Millon & Davis, 1995).

As a general rule, internalizers have more tolerance of emotional distress than do externalizers. Externalizers find negative emotions (anxiety, sadness) to be intolerable, though they do tend to seek external stimulation and heightened excitement. To compensate for this intolerance, they develop a nearly ritualistic drive for direct avoidance. In some individuals, these avoidance patterns are observed in the form of compulsive rituals, bingeing and purging, phobias, and restrictive eating. In others, they are observed in superficial attachments, aggressive behaviors, and interpersonal distrust.

The link between coping style and treatment assignment is seen in the fact that one of the cross-cutting objectives of PT is to expose an individual to avoided experience. Thus, psychotherapy poses an intentional threat and induces stress with which individuals must cope, not unlike other events in their lives. Psychotherapy introduces a change in one's usual and expected environment, and it does so intentionally. The demand characteristics of PT are designed to draw forth usual but ineffective coping strategies and to link them with a consequence that is different than usual—it allows the ineffective coping styles to cease paying off in stress reduction, and so on. Psychotherapy does this by introducing information that is often unacceptable or incompatible with the patient's usual beliefs—it induces cognitive dissonance and associated anxiety. It does this within a safe environment that encourages the exploration of behaviors that are new and unpracticed, and by exposing the patient repeatedly to feelings and sensations that are novel and uncomfortable. By so doing, psychotherapy interventions are expected to evoke, and then undermine, behaviors that are typically employed to restore safety and comfort. These behaviors must prove to be ineffective in the avoidance of distress if psychotherapy is to be effective.

To activate healing experiences, effective psychotherapy must use procedures that are compatible with the patient's dominant ways of coping. External coping styles are addressed by externally focused interventions; internalizing coping styles are addressed by internally focused interventions. Thus, externally focused interventions aim to disarm the patient's efforts to avoid external events; internally focused interventions aim to disarm the patient's efforts to avoid internal experiences.

Guiding Principles

Four principles guide the selection of treatment based on patient level of impairment and coping style:

1. Benefit corresponds with treatment intensity among *functionally impaired* patients.

The flexibility of this principle can be illustrated by considering the variety of ways in which treatment intensity might be increased. Changing the setting to be more or less restrictive, increasing the frequency of sessions, increasing the length of sessions, altering the intensity by using group or individually focused treatments, and supplementing therapy with homework assignments, collateral contact, or supplementary phone call contacts are examples of the latitude available to the therapist's discretion.

The three remaining principles apply to the determination of patient coping style and the decision to direct efforts toward insight or symptom presentations.

2. Therapeutic change is most likely when the patient is exposed to objects or targets of behavioral and emotional avoidance.
3. Therapeutic change is greatest when the relative balance of interventions either favors the use of skill building and symptom removal procedures among externalizing patients or favors the use of insight and relationship-focused procedures among internalizing patients.
4. Therapeutic change is most likely if the initial focus of change efforts is to build new skills and alter disruptive symptoms.

Prescriptive therapy is designed to reduce the positive consequences of unwanted behaviors while bringing the patient into repeated confrontation with the external consequences or internal processes that evoke fear, unhappiness, and avoidance. These internal and external experiences constitute life stressors that evoke discomfort. As a general rule, one avoids two kinds of experience, either by directly avoiding the external circumstances that evoke distress or by internally constricting one's personal, sense of distress, discomfort, and fear.

The principles that guide the effort to fit treatment strategies to patient coping styles emphasize, respectively, the importance of exposure to feared events in the extinction and resolution of avoidant responses, the value of using the patient's coping style to identify the particular experiences that are being avoided, and the desirability of addressing disruptive symptoms and deficient skills first in the sequence of interventions. Collectively, these principles emphasize the importance of exposing individuals who use an external coping style to external cues that are avoided by direct action and impulsive behavior, while increasing coping skill, and of exposing individuals who use an internal coping style to internal sources of distress that are avoided through internal processes of minimization and constraint. It should be noted, however, that compared to externalizing patients, those who avoid internal experiences by the use of emotional constriction and cognitive reconstruction are more complex. Developing and managing a way of exposing individuals to feared impulses, thoughts, sensations, or feelings is more difficult than exposing them to external events. Both because of this relative difference and because external symptoms are often disruptive to one's life, maximal change is likely to occur when any external symptoms that are present are addressed first in treatment.

Indexing Cues

Functional Impairment

Beutler, Clarkin, and Bongar (in press) revealed that patient level of impairment could be reduced to three indices. The first of these is the presence of family problems, in either the nuclear or the contemporary family. The second index was the presence of social isolation and withdrawal. The third index was identified by the presence of supportive relationships. Thus, the presence of family, the availability of friendships, and involvement of the patient in social activities are all indications of having relatively low levels of impairment.

A global measure of functional impairment is obtained from the Global Assessment of Functioning (GAF) scale used in the DSM-IV. Table 5.1 presents

TABLE 5.1. Indicators of Level of Impairment

Abbreviated/Modified Global Assessment of Functioning (GAF)
1. *Absent or Minimal Symptoms*—At least average social functioning in interpersonal, social, intimate, work, and other (e.g., school and legal) relationships. Ratings should be based on performance in social roles rather than subjective report because the patient's distress may lead them to overestimate their level of impairment.
2. *Mild Impairment*—Some difficulty in social, work, interpersonal, intimate, or other relationship activities but meets most of his/her social responsibilities and is able to maintain interpersonal relationships.
3. *Moderate Impairment*—Experiences a good deal of difficulty in meeting personal responsibilities, or maintaining interpersonal relationships. Significant impairments or disruptions to work, intimate, and social relationships.
4. *Severe Symptoms*—Unable to care for self and to carry out important role responsibilities. Symptoms seriously interfere with ability to carry on work or school duties, to relate to other people, to establish intimate relationships, etc.

Indicators of Disturbed Family/Household Functioning
1. Expresses substantial mounts of anger directly to family/household members.
2. Feels a lot of anger at family/household members, whether or not it is expressed.
3. Estranged from one or more family/household members.
4. Avoids being around one or more family/household members.
5. Has been kicked out of his/her home.
6. Would like more closeness with his/her parents, siblings, or other household members.
7. Becomes distressed during or following contact with one or more family/household members.
8. Has little contact with most family/household members.

Indicators of Social Isolation
1. Seeks to be alone.
2. Is more avoidant of groups than usual.
3. Avoids social gatherings.
4. More distant from friends than usual.
5. Not comfortable with others.
6. Recently withdrawn from family or friends.
7. Actively avoids confrontation with others.

Indicators of Lacking Social Suport
1. Has no more than one friend with whom he/she shares common interests.
2. Does not feel trusted and respected by any other people in his/her life.
3. Has no family member in whom he/she can confide.
4. Feels abandoned or rejected by family and relatives.
5. Feels lonely most of the time, even when with others.
6. Does not feel like an accepted member of a current family unit.
7. Does not feel valued by most family members.
8. Does not have a social group of people with whom he/she feels comfortable and safe.
9. Does not seek the help of others during times of crisis.

a simplified and adapted version of this measure. Generally, mild and moderate impairment suggest limited treatment needs, with the former raising a question about the need for treatment and the latter being suggestive of time limited interventions.

More specific and refined indications of one's level of impairment, with reference to the areas of functioning found by Beutler, Clarkin, and Bongar (in press) to be related to the level of social impairment, can be obtained from their descriptions of current and past relationships. The clinician can gather such information by observing the patient's interactions and asking the patient to describe his or her close friendships, relationships with family members, and current intimate involvments. All these dimensions are captured in various subscales of the STS Clinician Rating Form. Table 5.1 identifies some of the ratings that are made from this latter form, by the clinician, with reference to social withdrawal, social support, and the presence of family problems.

As a general rule, the level of treatment intensity is selected to correspond with the number of items on which a problem is indicated. Intensity may be maintained by increasing the variety of treatments, the length of treatment, or the spacing of treatment sessions.

Coping Style

The second set of indicators that one must use relates to patient coping style. Externalizing and internalizing coping styles are used to reduce uncomfortable experience, from wherever it arises. People cope by activating behaviors that range from and combine those that allow direct escape or avoidance of the feared environment (externalization) and those that allow one to passively and indirectly control internal experience such as anxiety (internalization). To effectively confront and expose the patient to the experiences that are being avoided, the effective therapist must learn to distinguish between external and internal coping styles.

The cues that distinguish these two coping styles can be inferred both by patterns of responses on omnibus measures of personality and psychopathology and by reviewing the patient's past and current history of reactions to problems. We discuss examples of each of these methods in the following pages. In all cases it should be noted that it is easier to identify externalizing coping styles than internalizing ones. For most purposes, one is forced to assume the presence of internalized coping styles by the relative absence of externalized patterns.

Patients may be administered the MMPI-2 both as a general measure of personality and as a specific measure of coping. A statistically derived ratio is used to determine whether patients tends toward externalization or internalization as their dominant coping style. The therapist and supervisor are given this information and should use it in designing the nature of treatment, following the strategies and principles outlined here.

There are several MMPI-2 subscales that constitute this equation, each being entered as a standard T score, extrapolated directly from the computer- or hand-generated profile. The formula that we have used is:

$$IR = \frac{Hy + Pd + Pa + Ma}{Hs + D + Pt + Si}$$

If the internalizing ratio (IR) is high (i.e., is greater that 1.0), it suggests an externalizing coping style that includes such attributes as projecting one's own feelings and motives on to others (Pa), active dependent behaviors (Hy), and high levels of unfocused energy (Ma). These patients tend to be more impulsive and undercontrolled than the average mental health patient.

In contrast, a score that is less than 1.0 indicates that the patient is less impulsive and more self-inspecting than the average patient, on a relative basis. Such patients are acutely sensitive to their internal states (Hs), are self-critical (D), emotioanlly distressed (Pt), and socially restrictive (Si).

The problems associated with an externalized style of coping result from excessive and disruptive behavior. He is "too impulsive," "too needy," too aggressive," "too loud," and so on. If the patient's problem angers other people, or is a behavior that is defined as being "too much," one may expect it to represent an externalized coping style. These people are typically seen as extroverted, unthinking, undercontrolled, gregarious, impulsive, or insensitive to social expectations; they act in poorly socialized ways, engage in behaviors that are disruptive to social order, or seen as annoying to others. They tend to be judged by clinical raters as relying on such defense mechanisms as projection, acting out, minimization, denial, and displacement.

In contrast, those with scores favoring internalization tend to inhibit impulses and feelings and have a relatively low need to seek stimulation in their environments. Often, such individuals tend to be dominated by contemplative, self-reflective, fearful ruminations. A therapist may find it helpful to add their own theoretical understandings to revealing the more specific aspects of these internalizing processes, conflicts, and experiences that characterize these individuals.

Internalizing individuals are these whose problems are usually characterized by the absence of certain activities. While these individuals also may be described as being "too" something (e.g., "shy," "withdrawn," "quiet," or "inactive"), a close inspection of these descriptors reveals that they refer to the absence or insufficiency of some behavior rather than its presence. A better description of these patients' problems is that they have difficulty doing something. Thus, being "too shy" may be more accurately described as having "difficulty making intimate contact"; "too withdrawn" may refer to, "difficulty socializing." Similarly, being "too quiet" or "too inactive" refers to insufficient vocalizations and difficulty being assertive or active.

Compared to externalizers, internalizers are more insightful and self-reflective. While an externalizing person may be judged to be gregarious, impulsive, and undercontrolled, an internalizing one is socially reclusive, constrained, and overcontrolled. Those who are internal copers tend to look to their own acts and potential failings as the causes of stressors whereas the active externalizers tend either to see the source of stress as external or to view stress fatalistically. These latter individuals deny personal responsibility for either the cause or the solution of problems.

The list of characteristics and interpersonal patterns identified in Table 5.2 is adapted from the STS Clinician Rating Form for rating patient coping style. Observing and noting how many characteristics a patient presents of externalizing and internalizing coping styles helps therapists identify a patient's dominant pattern of response.

Frequently, a patient exhibits both internalizing and externalizing patterns, at different points in time or with different conflicts. The designations of coping styles are more accurate reflections of the balance between both internalizing and externalizing tendencies. Most people tend to favor one or the other coping style in most treatment-relevant events. In the STS Clinician Rating Form, separate ratings are made to identify how many characteristics the patient presents, both on internalizing and externalizing dimensions. The dominant coping style is represented in decision making, by a ratio of these two coping types, similar to that employed by the MMPI-2. That is, the separate scales are translated to standard scores and then constructed as a ratio between the external and internalizing scale. The ratio score, based on standardized scores is helpful because they allow one to employ a normative comparison.

The clinician-based observations (STS) and the patient self-reports (MMPI-2) result in slightly different predictions. For the most part, indicators derived from patient self-reports are more closely related to treatment outcomes than those derived from clinician reports (STS). Of course, the best index may be when both self-report and clinician impression are used and they are consistent. When they are not consistent, or when the clinician must choose between the two, patient self-report provides a better basis of decisions related to patient coping style than other methods.

It is important to maintain a consistent focus of treatment, based on objective findings, and not be led prematurely by fallible personal opinions. An alteration of the identified coping style should only be made following a consensual and cross-validated confirmation. Barring such a consensual change, the patient's initial designation as an internalizer or externalizer establishes the nature of the treatment focus to be used throughout treatment.

TABLE 5.2. Characteristics of Internalizing and Externalizing Patients

An Externalizing Patient:
1. Is socially gregarious and outgoing
2. Seeks to impress others
3. Seeks novelty, activity, or stimulation to avoid being bored or inactive
4. Seeks to have social status
5. Is insensitive to other's feelings
6. Has an inflated sense of importance
7. Is impulsive
8. Is bossy with others
9. Often speaks without thinking of the consequences
10. Reacts to frustation with overt anger
11. Is probably not very concerned with what others think about him/her
12. Has sometimes gotten in trouble because of a short temper
13. Gets frustrated easily
14. Gets bored easily
15. Enjoys loud parties and festive occasions
16. Is immature in feelings and behavior
17. Insists on having things his/her way
18. Doesn't take responsibility for problems that occur
19. Disregards others' feelings
20. Has little empathy for others
21. Quite often gets in trouble because of his/her behavior

An Internalizing Patient:
1. Is more likely to feel hurt than anger
2. Is quiet in social gatherings
3. Worries or ruminates a lot before taking action
4. Feels more than passing guilt, remorse, or shame about minor things
5. Lets things "get to" him or her
6. Lacks self-confidence
7. Likes to be alone
8. Is timid
9. Is reluctant to express anger directly
10. Is an introvert
11. Does not often go to parties
12. Doesn't let feelings show

Adapting Treatment to Patient Impairment Level

A central principle of PT is that it works with the existent levels of experience and skills that characterize the therapists. By this means, therapists are encouraged to institute the treatment procedures that have been found to be useful in their own experiences, given certain contingencies. The only requirement is that therapists work within the empirically informed principles that constitute the bases of PT.

In the case of patient impairment, the guiding principle emphasizes the importance of altering the intensity of treatment. Therapists have several options from which to choose in complying with this principle. Their selection of options depends on their own judgment and skill with different procedures. These options include increasing the frequency or length of sessions, increasing the length of therapy, altering the setting of treatment to include a more intensive and protected form, or combining interventions (drugs and psychotherapy, group and individual therapy, family and group therapy, etc.). The most usual strategy is to increase the frequency of sessions to two or more times per week. This is especially desirable when the problem includes a significant habit component, such as chemical dependency or compulsions, over which the patient has limited control. If the patient is willing and receptive, a concomitant 12-Step program is also useful in cases of chemical dependency.

In the case of anxiety and depression symptoms, increasing the frequency and spacing of sessions is often helpful. When suicidal or other physically desctructive behaviors are considered to be a high risk, instituting a medication regimen along with the psychotherapy should be considered seriously.

Strategies for Adapting Treatment to Patient Coping Style

In the guiding principles articulated earlier in this chapter, we can see the foundation for exposure and response prevention treatments. These treatments are widely used for addressing problems that are observed through external symptoms and avoidance of certain environments. Phobias, obsessive–compulsive disorders, posttraumatic stress disorder, acute stress reaction, and situational stress disorders all fall within this domain. These disorders all include direct avoidance of certain environments and the preferred strategy in treatment is to introduce the avoided events, feelings, and environments, either through imaginal stimulation or *in vivo*, until the resulting distress diminishes. An additional component of these treatments, however, is the development of skills for interacting with people and for controlling distress.

This same principle of exposure and skill building can be applied more generally than indicated by broad, diagnostic labels. We believe that they can be applied both to other externalized conditions, such as impulse disorders, and to a variety of internalizing patterns as well. The difficulty in treating these latter cases, however, is that the evoking cues, stressor events, and experiences being avoided are entirely subjective. An excessively impulsive person may be avoiding lack of stimulation—they may be stimulation seekers, they may be seeking power or status—avoiding impotence or lack of status, or they may be responding avoidantly to the expected consequences of social contact. The preferred treatment may be learning the skills that will allow them to tolerate bland and unstimulating environments, accepting the loss of power and status, or confronting interpersonal attack.

The issues of reinforcement, exposure, and extinction are no less important for internalizing individuals. Those who avoid uncomfortable feelings—that is, those who are emotionally avoidant—may have a low tolerance for emotional intensity of any kind. They may seek to reduce stimulation. Others may attempt to avoid specific unwanted feelings, such as anger or even love and intimacy; they may fear the rejections of others, or they may fear environmental stimulation and activity. Treatment may focus on teaching the patient to allow the experience of anger, to tolerate distress, or to accept the expression of love and intimacy. The principles of treatment are the same, but the complexity of treating internalizing individuals requires that the treatments take quite different forms. Among internalizers, the cues to which treatment endeavors to expose a patient are often buried within that individual's unique history of conflict and feeling development. For these individuals, the therapist must seek a way to expose the patient to cues that are only indirectly associated with overt symptoms. Insight and emotional awareness become relevant goals in this case. To expose one to avoided knowledge (insight) or feelings (awareness) requires creative flexibility on the part of the therapist.

The nature of the interventions used to confront the patient with feared knowledge and feelings may present problems because it is difficult to reconstruct past history and create feelings when these are the objects of avoidance and because the indirect treatment of these complex problems may delay the remission of disruptive symptoms. The first principle emphasizes the importance of beginning treatment by focusing on the symptoms that are most easily altered with direct treatment methods. The principle can be reduced to the following strategy of change:

1. Efforts to directly modify symptomatic problems should be initiated early in treatment, preceding the application of procedures that seek to indirectly influence symptoms, through insight and understanding.

This strategy is critical in the treatment of patients who have both complex coping styles (a combination of internalizing and externalizing styles) and who have specific, external symptoms such as drug abuse, that limit their levels of personal control. Only after some initial progress has been made in reducing the influence of drug use can the strategies of insight and awareness be expected to be valuable. Two strategic rules can then be used to define how one might deal, differentially, with patients who present the two contrasting coping styles:

2. If a patient's most typical method of coping is characterized by active avoidance of blame or responsibility, impulsivity, aggression, or other

externally observed symptoms, the preferred treatment strategy is to confront the patient with the feared consequences of failing to engage in these avoided acts and instituting a program of skill development to facilitate alternative behaviors.

Motivational interviewing (Miller & Rollnick, 1991) is a procedure that can be incorporated into most therapeutic interventions, for example. This or other procedures that help the patient to identify positive goals whose acquisition is limited or halted because of their current addictive behaviors or skill deficits often helps patients develop focus and motivation for change. Analyses of costs and benefits of one's behavior, long-and short-term objectives or goals, and structured behavioral contracts are alternatives that provide both confrontation and positive objectives that are progresive and in reach. Confrontation of this sort among externalizing patients will work to establish increased impulse control and will directly change symptomatic presentations.

3. If the patient's most typical method of coping emphasizes self-reflection and criticism, social withdrawal, emotional avoidance, and control of internal reactions, the preferred treatment strategy is to facilitate awareness of how these events have and do affect an individual.

Emotional intensity, anger, fear, and loss of approval are among the most obvious experiences being avoided by internalizing coping styles. This strategy implies heightening patients' awareness of these unwanted emotions through the use of insight-oriented (e.g., reflections and interpretations) and experiential treatment procedures (The reader interested in a volume devoted to experiential treatment is referred to Daldrup et al., 1988). The value of using these strategies among internalizing patients is established in empirical research, but the basis of the differential effectiveness of behaviorally focused and insight-focused procedures for externalizing and internalizing patients may not be clearly apparent.

Simplistically, the task of adjusting the intervention to fit variations in a patient's coping style is one of selecting among the focus and objectives of treatments. It would improve the efficiency of treating both internalizing and externalizing patients if one were able to reduce the infinite possible targets of avoidance to a finite number of internal and external experiences. For example, if one could conclude that most of the symptoms of distress among externalizing/impulsive patients arise in response to lack of interpersonal skill or efforts to avoid a sense of personal helplessness and stagnation, one's efforts could be restricted to these issues, identifying impulsive acts as efforts to reaffirm power and to obtain the reassurance of living through self-stimulation.

Similarly, one could increase the specificity of focus among internalizing/self-reflective patients if it could be concluded that these patients' energy is devoted to reducing the strength of fear, sadness, and anger. Under these conditions, we would be able to help externalizers to extinguish these fears by directly exposing them to environments that are unstimulating and in which they lack personal power until such environments failed to evoke avoidant responses and fear. By the same token, we would be able to help internalizers by exposing them to very stimulating and emotionally arousing environments until such environments failed to evoke fear and avoidance.

In the absence of such clear-cut objects of avoidance, however, we are restricted to identifying external environments that are avoided by the externalizing patient and inferring the thoughts, wishes, feelings, and impulses that govern the avoidance patterns of internalizers. Thus, PT for externalizing patients is designed to focus on changing behavioral symptoms—excessive behaviors—independently of whether one acquires greater personal knowledge and self-understanding. On the other hand, PT treatment for internalizing patients is designed to facilitate insight and awareness as a means of confronting the patient with feared experiences and altering problems.

Because many conditions, especially depression and substance abuse, include external symptoms that are socially destructive or dangerous, guiding principle 3 emphasizes the importance of beginning treatment with direct interventions of these external symptoms. Because a description of the various uses of insight-oriented and symptomatic interventions is relatively complex, we have separated this discussion into two chapters. The next chapter presents a discussion of the techniques and procedures attendant on patient coping style.

Chapter 6

Adapting Treatment to Patient Level of Impairment and Coping Style: Part II

Techniques and Procedures

Direct Change of External Symptoms

Direct change procedures are the treatments of choice for all patients in the early phases and stages of treatment. They are especially advantageous for externalizing patients. Among these patients, the entire treatment program is devoted to directly affecting external symptoms and skill deficits. In contrast, among internalizing patients, direct symptomatic change procedures continue until the immediate danger of self-destructive and violent behaviors are judged to be past and a significant change in symptoms has been observed. Operationally, PT has established a rule of thumb, establishing a 1-week period during which the patient is free of destructive, external symptoms such as drug abuse, aggressive attack, and parasuicidal impulses before shifting the focus of treatment to the use of interventions whose effects are indirect (i.e., operate through awareness and insight).

Direct treatment of symptoms focuses either on the problematic symptoms themselves (e.g., drug abuse) or the behaviors that place the patient at risk for continuing the symptoms (e.g., social pressures and automatic thoughts associated with or preceding drug abuse). In either case, symptomatic change and the development of new skills are the primary goals of direct treatment. Accordingly, the therapist seeks either to change the reinforcement schedules and cognitive patterns that are associated with these symptoms or to change the events in the environment that evoke the symptoms and problems (i.e., those environmental or cognitive cues that evoke problems). As dictated by the principles of change, the therapist attempts to reduce the positive consequences of engaging in the identified behaviors, constructs ways of confronting the patient with feared but unrealistic consequences of changing behaviors, and explores positive behaviors and goals, continuing this process until the old behaviors are extinguished and replaced by new ones.

Within these guidelines, there are two important steps in formulating the treatment goals that guide the implementation of direct, symptomatic treatment. The first step is to organize and prioritize the symptoms that are targeted for change (i.e., destructive impulses, drug use, cravings, and risk behaviors), and the second step is to identify skills that are lacking for tolerating stress or interacting with others. Most of the techniques used for symptomatic change include the following three aspects:

1. Self-monitoring problematic behavior is used to track the positive consequences of the symptomatic behavior, the feared consequences of initiating desirable behavior, and the effects of interventions.
2. Patients are encouraged to try new behaviors but to take change as it comes—they are not coerced; nor are they encouraged to change at a rate that is faster than the rate they can willingly accept.
3. Skill building and symptom change procedures are generally followed by opportunities for self-evaluation and feedback.

In this chapter, we describe some representative techniques that illustrate these various steps, but we do so with the understanding that the way that various procedures are used and implemented must be adapted to other relevant dimensions of the patient's presentation. For example, the manner in which particular techniques are employed will change as a function of the patient's level of resistance (chapter 7, this volume) and distress (chapter 8, this volume). The therapist should be selective about the use of the procedures described here, reserving the use of the most highly therapist-guided procedures for the least resistant patients.

Effective psychotherapy will provide structure, support, and focus. As a general rule, the larger portion of early sessions (sessions 1–4) should be given both to developing a relationship that is sufficiently strong to support confrontation and to the direct interventions designed to reduce level of risk. The symptoms that place the patient at risk for continued drug use and for suicidal or homicidal behavior are the first points of focus, and direct treatment of these symptoms should be implemented as soon as a suitably solid therapeutic relationship has been established. When risk of destructive or self-destructive behavior is high, the focus should be drawn to these symptoms in the first session, even employing risk-control procedures to change behavior, if necessary. If self-injurious behaviors and violence are not immediate risks, the therapist should begin to focus the interventions on drug abuse and depressive symptoms by the second session of treatment.

Not all patient symptoms have the same importance. The following priority is given to therapeutic focus in PT:

1. Destructive potential
2. Drug use
3. Cravings
4. Intolerance for stress and withdrawal
5. Risk situations
6. Social withdrawal
7. Dysfunctional (e.g., depressogenic) thoughts
8. Vegetative signs (disturbance in sleep, sex, and appetite).

The first three of these foci should be addressed among all patients, regardless of their coping styles. Among externalizers, treatment will progress down the list, increasingly incorporating cognitive and environmental events associated with risk situations and evoking events. For these individuals, symptom reduction and skill development go hand in hand. Thus, treatment goals will include skills for increasing the patient's tolerance for drug withdrawal, altering the reinforcing power of a variety of risk situations, activating skills for social interactions, altering dysfunctional thoughts, and modifying the environments that support the patient's vegetative signs of depression. The use of direct, symptomatic interventions, in this case, will continue throughout the sessions of planned treatment.

Among internalizing patients, relatively less direct attention is given to specific symptoms beyond those associated with personal and drug abuse risk. In these cases, the therapist attempts to transition from direct to indirect procedures within the first six sessions. A 1-week period of control over self-defeating and destructive impulses is used as a marker for moving the focus to internal experience and indirect procedures.

In the following paragraphs, we describe some of the procedures and techniques that have been successful in directly altering each of the eight symptom areas identified in the foregoing paragraphs.

DESTRUCTIVE POTENTIAL   The therapist's first concern should be with safety, both of the patient and of others. In the case of threats to others, legal mandates to report and prevent are followed. Explorations of destructive urges should be continued until the therapist is assured that the patient is in reasonable control of these impulses, having either resolved the urge for suicide and violence or having made a believable commitment to refrain from destructive acts.

The therapist's interventions when destructive thoughts are present should include the following elements (Bongar, 1991):

1. *Ask about the presence of suicidal and homicidal ideation.* This should be a detailed check on the significance of suicidal impulses and frequency of thoughts.

2. *Consider psychiatric hospitalization.* The patient should be referred for independent consultation if the therapist considers the risk to be significant and the patient declines voluntary admission.

3. *Reduce the potential lethality of the patient's probable method of self-harm.* This means that one should persuade the patient to give up firearms or medications to a third party for security for the duration of treatment.

4. *Develop a "no-suicide" or "no-harm" contract.* This injunction is most applicable if a therapeutic relationship has been established. A contract against harm is then useful as a part of that relationship.

5. *Warn potential targets of violence.* If a specific person is targeted as the object of intended violence, the therapist has a duty to warn that individual of his or her potential danger.

6. *Involve family support systems.* If possible, contact the patient's family to ensure that social support is available and active during times of crisis. Note that prior patient consent is required to make such contact, whereas it is not required for notifying the potential victim.

7. *Provide emergency procedures to patients.* Ensure that the patient is familiar with the procedures and has the necessary phone numbers available.

Assessing suicide potential is an important and ongoing aspect of working with people who are self-destructive, either by way of drug abuse or by more active behaviors. The FAST, described in chapter 3, is a convenient method of gaining information on the presence of certain thought patterns that are associated with suicidal risk and violence (Firestone, 1986). The FAST assesses both state and trait qualities of thought.

In assessing destructive symptoms, it is especially important for the therapist to attend to the frequency ratings that the patient applies to self-destructive and destructive thoughts on the FAST. Responses reflect ratings that range from *Never* to *Most of the time*, with the time frame being the previous 2-week period. The critical responses indicate:

1. *Self-contempt* (Vicious self-abusive thoughts are frequently present in states of agitated depression or where depression is coexistent with anxiety disorder.)

2. *Injunctions to inflict self-harm* (Responses to this set of items is prominent in the thoughts of clients with agitated depression as well as those with suicidal ideation.)

3. *Thoughts associated with isolation, hopelessness, and despair* (Such thoughts are present both among those who abuse substances and those who are depressed.)

Some responses and items appear to reflect thoughts that occur with a relatively higher frequency during a depressed state than during remission. For example, such items as the following might be informative in assessing behavior associated with a low self-concept.

- "You're worthless. The things you believe about yourself are really true. Other people put themselves down, but in your case, the bad things are real."

Other items such as the following might indicate a sense of hopelessness and despair:

- "You thought you mattered, but you don't. You don't matter to anyone. You don't matter. Who would care if you weren't around?"

The FAST can be used as a screening instrument for identifying clients at risk for suicide, and the associated thoughts that can be explored in the course of treatment. In addition, composite scores have been empirically derived to indicate the level of global risk. For example, a score between 43 and 48 indicates a mild level of concern on the Suicide Intent Composite score; moderate levels of risk are indexed by scores between 49 and 59 and serious risk is indicated by a score that is 60 or above.

The client's composite risk score on the FAST can be used with a subjective assessment of the patient's individual responses and with information gathered from other instruments. At all times, the therapist should be alert to signs to indicate the degree to which suicidal ideation, hopelessness, and homicidal impulses are present. Assessment of these impulses always call for a high level of clinical judgment and expertise. The therapist must form impressions regarding the presence of impulses, plans, and means to be destructive and of when to raise and when to delay discussion of the patient's suicidal plans.

A therapist must understand that most depressed patients will have some suicidal ideation and therapists who work with them must learn to be tolerant of these thoughts without overreacting. Consultation with a supervisor and, if necessary, with a staff psychiatrist, will help determine whether one's concerns are justified. In addition, therapists must keep a perspective that their own power is limited. The therapist is not and cannot presume to be responsible for protecting the patient from all the potential events and choices that represent a potential for danger. Thus, acknowledging that as a therapist one cannot prevent the patient from self-injury and emphasizing the importance of both time and faith in the patient's judgment may be helpful.

Stress inoculation and structured problem solving are skill-building techniques borrowed from cognitive therapy and are often helpful for combating self-destructive as well as drug use impulses. The therapist teaches the patient a process for recognizing and solving problems while managing anxiety levels. This process involves the following steps: (1) identifying fearful and panic reactions, (2) practicing relaxation and cognitive-control of anxious thoughts, (3) defining the problem in clear specific terms, (4) brainstorming a number of possible solutions, (5) examining the pros and cons of each brainstorming solution (for the present, future, and significant others), (6) choosing the best hypothesized solution, (7) implementing the behavior after some planning, preparation, and practice, and (8) evaluating the outcome and assessing for additional problems to solve. This process is typically long and difficult and requires that the therapist provide support and encouragement if the patient is to persist in learning these skills.

Periodic reevaluation will allow both tracking and modification of the intervention to accommodate observed changes in risk levels.

DRUG USE AND CRAVINGS   Both the FAST and the STS Clinician Rating Form pinpoint risk of drug abuse. In particular, the FAST taps current thought states that are self-destructive and that may point to substance abuse as a way of coping.

- "Have another drink/hit. You need to relax."
- "You need something that's relaxing, a place to go where you can just relax and sleep."

The endorsement of avoidant thoughts such as these reveals a pattern of isolated and escapist drug or alcohol use. When combined with other indicators of functioning, the intensity and clinical importance of these concerns with substance abuse become more salient. A clinician may particularly attend to indications of agitation in a patient who is experiencing self-injurious impulses. Self-destructive thoughts may become more obvious and prevalent as drug use increases and impulse control erodes among such patients.

At some point in the first six sessions, if substance use is problematic, the patient should be asked to make a commitment to remain drug free. There are procedures that have been used to help the patient explore this decision. For example, a therapist can use the *advantages–disadvantages analytic* procedure to explore the patient's beliefs, enhancing motivation, and identifying goals to support new skills. Drug abusers often operate from the assumption that drug use has more advantages than disadvantages or selective attention prevents them from acknowledging the numerous disadvantages of drug abuse. A 2-×-2 matrix is used in this procedure to illuminate and then compare advantages and disadvantages for the drug-free and drug-using lifestyles. In this analysis, the patient and therapist work collaboratively to identify and record the consequences of using and not using drugs.

To supplement and extend this process, the therapist may use guided *imagery* to help patients visualize what they would be like if they were drug free. Similar imagery to enhance the image of "self-control" can be used to control cravings. Imagery techniques are often combined with thought insertion and self-control techniques. Several variations may be used to reduce drug use or cravings. For example, Beck, Wright, Newman, and Liese (1993) discuss the uses and advantages of three imagery techniques that can be used for controlling cravings and drug use:

1. *Image refocusing* is a distraction technique in which patients refocus attention from internal cravings to imagined external events. This is accomplished by "thought stopping" (patients can use the image of a stop sign, a police officer, a brick wall, etc.) and then describing to themselves what is going on around them.
2. *Negative image replacement* is a procedure in which the patient is asked to replace the positive but distorted image of drug use with an accurate negative image of the many unfortunate consequences that have and do accompany drug use.
3. *Positive image replacement* is a procedure in which the patient inserts and practices positive thoughts associated with staying drug free. It is used to cope with cravings and feelings of hopelessness.

In using these procedures, the patient may be asked to imagine living a drug-free life, developing imagery about health conscious and productive activities, and imagining engaging in non–drug-related activities that have been pleasant in the past. He can be asked to use these images as replacements for negative images and as distractions during times of craving.

Cravings and impulses can be addressed in other ways, as well. The patient may be encouraged to participate in a 12-step program and to track regularity of attendance. Other skill-building interventions include the following:

1. *Identifying and correcting dysfunctional thought patterns.* The therapist begins by identifying unrealistic thoughts associated with the cravings (e.g., I can't go on without it"; "Just one more time, won't hurt." Suggesting the use of alternative thoughts that more realistically identify the presence of risk may be helpful.
2. *Homework assignments.* The therapist assigns homework that is designed to encourage and train the patient to engage in alternative behaviors to replace use and abuse behaviors. The patient may be taught to identify early signs of craving and to practice relaxation, divert his or her focus to incompatible acts or experiences, and insert thoughts that reinforce self-control (e.g., "Relax and breathe"; "I can delay use for the next few minutes"; "I have control of this moment"). Redirecting passive behavior into active exercise or work can also be helpful.
3. *Provide supportive, emergency protection.* The therapist should make sure the patient has a safe place to go when the cravings are intense and knows how to alert people about his or her need. Family and nonusing friends provide such outlets as do drug abuse centers, hospital emergency rooms, and churches. The therapist must ensure that the patient knows the procedures and the relevant phone numbers.

TOLERANCE FOR STRESS AND WITHDRAWAL SYMPTOMS   Patients often feel unable to tolerate the acute symptoms of distress or of drug or alcohol withdrawal. During acute withdrawal, medications are helpful and the staff psychiatrist or the patient's physician may provide or may already have provided antianxiety agents to help the patient manage the feelings. Some stress management training should be offered to those patients who find the anxiety associated with cravings and withdrawal to reach the limits of tolerance. This usually includes practice in relaxation (described later) along with the cognitive management and redirection strategies outlined in previous paragraphs.

Relaxation Training.   Drug abusers may use substances to self-medicate for anxiety (or to "unwind" or relax). Drug-free methods to achieve relaxation may be useful because they may deactivate or decrease the urge to unwind with substances. Beck et al. (1993) suggests that a rationale for relaxation training be provided and that patients are to understand that relaxation is a skill anyone can learn. They make several points in preparing the patient for relaxation: (1) relaxation training is a method for reducing tension that, left unchecked, might trigger cravings, (2) relaxation training helps one to develop an improved general sense of well-being and lowers one's subjective sense of stress in everyday activities, and (3) when relaxed, individuals are less likely to act or react impulsively.

Thought Substitution.   Systematic relaxation can be used to help insert self-control thoughts in the acute treatment of these patients. The patient may be provided with self-enhancing thoughts while relaxed and asked to practice these thoughts during homework activities. The thoughts invoked at this time may include reassuring self-statements that remind the patient that the symptoms will pass with time: "The feelings will go away if I just give them a little time."

Social Support.   Another ingredient of the successful management of withdrawal symptoms is the presence of supportive family and friends. Patients should identify and provide therapists with the names of individuals who may provide emotional support for the patient. The therapist may contact these people (with signed consent from the patient) when patients are going through withdrawal or when they are experiencing particularly strong cravings, in order to arrange a place for the patient to find safety and time while the symptoms pass.

RISK SITUATIONS   Substance abuse does not take place in a vacuum. It takes place in particular environments, social groups, and relationships. The level of risk is learned through previous associations with drug use. The degree of risk to which one is exposed is a direct function of the similarity of the current environments to those environments in which the person has previously purchased, stashed, and used drugs in the past.

Reducing risk is a function of both addressing the thoughts and behaviors associated with drug use and avoiding situations that have been associated with drug use in the past. Assessment of risk is a natural extension of the assessment and treatment of cravings and withdrawal. In the course of treating these symptoms, the therapist should identify the places and associated cognitive processes associated with drug use (Marlatt & Gordon, 1985). From there, a number of interventions can help reduce the influence of these stimuli.

The *Daily Thought Record* (DTR) is an effective tool for helping patients identify the nature of impulses that arise in different situations. They can be used in the construction of "drinking chains" (Wakefield et al., 1996) (i.e., events, thoughts, and actions that lead to substance abuse). Keeping track of thoughts that encourage drinking or depression is a fundamental strategy that may be used in conjunction with other techniques (e.g., advantages–disadvantages analysis). The DTR (Beck et al., 1993) has five columns (Figure 6.1) in which the patient tracks situations that evoke drug abuse, automatic and associated thoughts, related emotion, an alternative or replacement thought, and a rating of the outcome of practicing and replacing the automatic thought with the alternative one. This form helps teach patients to identify and monitor automatic thoughts and to construct more productive replacements for them.

The DTR allows the patient and therapist to examine beliefs about drug use in a systematic and reasonably objective fashion. Places, persons, and times that have characterized one's previous use can be listed and the relative level of risk assessed by a combination of patient rating and by imaginal reenactment of being in that place and time. The thoughts of use, including anticipated positive effects, should also be catalogued. The timely (i.e., immediate in the moment) completion of the DTR may also provide a distraction that defuses the intensity of the existent craving/urge. The DTR allows an individual to identify triggering events and thoughts that are associated with increased risk and to cope with these evoking mood states, situations, and thoughts. Beck et al. (1993) have provided some questions at the bottom of the DTR form to help patients promote the generation and application of rational responses to urge-related automatic thoughts.

Stimulus control procedures help address the second level of the problem, replacing the behaviors associated with purchasing and using drugs. This procedure is a logical extension to the assessment of daily, evoking thoughts. In managing evoking stimuli, the therapist helps the patient identify both external and internal drug use stimuli (e.g., drug paraphernalia, time of day, anxiety, and boredom). Developing explicit plans and practicing the skills

FIGURE 6.1. Daily Thought Record

Directions: When you notice your mood getting worse, ask yourself, "What's going through my mind right now?" and as soon as possible jot down the thought or mental image in the Automatic Thought column. Be sure to record the date and time in the situation column.

Situation (w/ date & time) Describe: 1) Actual event leading to unpleasant emotion, or 2) Stream of thoughts, daydreams or recollection, leading to unpleasant emotion, or 3) Distressing physical sensations.	Automatic thought(s) 1) Write automatic thought(s) that preceded emotion(s). 2) Rate belief in automatic thought 0–100%.	Emotion(s) 1) Specify sad, angry, anxious, etc. 2) Rate degree of emotion 0–100%.	Rational Response 1) Write rational response to automatic thought(s). 2) Rate belief in rational response 0–100%.	Outcome 1) Re-rate belief in automatic thought(s) 0–100%. 2) Specify and rate subsequent emotions 0–100%.

Questions to help formulate the rational response: (1) What is the evidence that the automatic thought is true? (2) Is there an alternative explanation? (3) What's the worst that could happen? Could I live through it? What's the best that could happen? What's the most realistic outcome? (4) What should I do about it? (5) What's the effect of my believing the automatic thought? What could be the effect of changing my thinking? (6) What constructive action might solve this problem? (7) If (friend's name) was in this situation and had this thought, what would I tell him/her?

needed to avoid these situations and to cope with or deal with these situations may aid patients in achieving the goal of abstinence. Flashcards may be useful for enhancing the effectiveness of coping statements when cravings become particularly strong. Beck et al. (1993) suggest using flashcards that contain either a list of advantages associated with not using substances or a list of desirable objects that could be purchased with the money intended for drugs.

Beck et al. (1993) suggest the use of imagery techniques to reduce the risk of situations that have been associated with drug use. *Imagery rehearsal* is used to build skills in patients who know that they are going to be in a high-risk (cue laden) situation. This technique can be combined with role-playing techniques to further encourage new skills. For example, the patient may be asked to envision a high-risk situation in which he exercises assertiveness by saying "no." This procedure may be varied to address several related issues also used in combination with role-playing exercises that are aimed at identifying thoughts associated with craving and risk. The therapist may wish to incorporate material from the thoughts and/or situations column of the DTR in the imagery rehearsal exercise.

Mastery imaging is a related procedure in which patients imagine themselves as strong and powerful individuals with mastery over their drug cravings. Mastery images may be used along with thought-insertion procedures. The patient's flagging self-image may be bolstered by images of success and competence in refusing drugs or accomplishing feared tasks.

Graded task assignment may help the patient correct faulty behaviors, develop new skills, and avoid high-risk environments. Self-instruction (Meichenbaum, 1979) can be used to help patients guide themselves through identified steps for avoiding situations and keeping impulses from escalating. Alternative environments with which one can replace the risk-filled environments can be identified and a contract can be established for the patient to seek out these environments.

To employ the graded task procedure, the various risk environments should first be ordered by level of risk they pose to the patient. The most risk-filled situations should be the target of concerted effort to develop self-instructional controls, relaxation, and alternative activities to support and help them avoid these situations. Once again, social support from family and nonusing friends can provide a buffer against drug use.

Dramatic changes may be made via successive approximations of the desired behaviors. Patients choose increasingly challenging assignments that are directed toward the desired goal/behavior of abstinence and risk avoidance. This may be most useful in developing a drug-free social support network, replacing old associations with new social relationships. This is an important procedure to keep in mind throughout therapy but is most important in the early and middle stages of treatment.

SOCIAL WITHDRAWAL   Depressed patients frequently withdraw from social contact and even reduce their engagement in activities that once were pleasant and pleasurable. Social involvement is an important part of the treatment for depression, anxiety, and drug abuse. Thus, one of the early tasks of therapy is to target ways to become and remain involved with other people.

If the patient has family and nonusing friends, these resources can be used to help prevent drug use. Both depressed and drug-abusing patients frequently need new sources of support and friendship. Thus, one of the early tasks of therapy is to identify potential groups wherein one might find relationships. A list of churches, recreational groups, and weekly activities of a recreational and educational nature can be found in the daily newspaper. The therapist can help the patient define which of these places and organizations may be most compatible with his or her efforts to become active and involved.

Activity scheduling can help patients overcome some of the lethargy that prevents them from becoming socially active. For example, a Daily Activity Schedule can be used for the patient to record the number and type of social activities per week. The pleasure and value of these activities can then serve as the basis of discussion with the view to selecting and using those that are most helpful. If the recordings are to be done as homework, the patient should be provided with written instructions in the use of the Daily Activity Schedule. The dimensions to be rated should be clearly specified, and a copy of the rating scale should be included in the materials given the patient as homework. Even if the ratings are done in the therapy session, one should not rely totally on verbal instructions. Written materials can be used and sent home with the patient for ongoing reference.

An assigned schedule of activities may be especially helpful when depressed, anxious, and/or drug-abusing individuals have a restricted repertoire of activities in which they engage. Many abusers engage virtually solely in activities that center on drug use or procurement. These drug-abuse ''lifestyle'' activities are problematic/high-risk situations especially at the beginning of therapy and they must be avoided. Unfortunately, simply avoiding problematic situations may be boring for the patient and may be problematic to abstinence. Therefore, safe alternative substitute activities should be identified and their implementation encouraged. Activity schedules can be utilized for a variety of purposes, including (1) gathering baseline data on how patients actually spend their time, (2) helping structure time in a constructive way, and (3) creating a stable basis of social support by increasing acquaintances and friends.

Activity records can be combined with an assessment of the pleasant events to which the patient is exposed in order to identify forgotten activities that can then be scheduled and employed as rewards for abstinence. A patient's social support network may also combine with these techniques to enhance the effectiveness of all three.

Interpersonal skills training is another procedure that can help overcome social withdrawal. Wakefield et al. (1996) describe useful procedures for improving communication. Because many patients may be in relationships and because problematic relationships are likely (and the resultant stress may be a precursor to depression, anxiety or a trigger for drug use), these exercises may be useful in achieving positive mood states and/or abstinence from drugs. They generally consist of (1) measuring the level of social skill, (2) identifying and defining the skills to be trained, (3) role playing appropriate social skills such as assertiveness or communication, and (4) extending this practice to daily activities.

As in most direct methods of intervention, recordkeeping is important in the facilitation of social involvement. The records should record the time of various activities, the pleasure, the risk, the number of people involved, and the degree that such activities affect mood, impulses, and cravings. These records can be used to monitor the success of various procedures. Chief among the direct interventions for altering social behaviors are skill training procedures.

DYSFUNCTIONAL DEPRESSOGENIC THOUGHTS   The correction of thoughts that are thought to be dysfunctional or depressogenic is central to many of the symptomatic changes we have identified. Doing so, of course, hinges on having first identified the presence of such thoughts and having conceptualized the A-B-C response chain. This chain defines the relationship between evoking or antecedent environments (A), dysfunctional thoughts and beliefs (B), and consequential behaviors and feelings (C).

Beck, Rush, Shaw, and Emery (1979) emphasizes that these depressive thoughts distort the features of objective reality, leaving an individual with an exaggerated, negative view of the present situation and past events and with an unrealistically negative expectation of future consequences of one's acts. Distortions in the past, present, and future are referred to as the "cognitive triad." Such distortions are thought to arise both from habitual and situation-specific thoughts—automatic thoughts—and schematic assumptions. Focus on symptomatic change, however, need only focus on the nature of automatic thoughts.

Classifying the nature of depressogenic automatic thoughts helps the therapist identify when an analysis of the A-B-C response chain may be productive as a basis for therapeutic work. Accordingly, Beck et al. (1979) identified six basic forms that depressogenic automatic thoughts might take. This list has proven to be somewhat cumbersome and overlapping, leading Lefebvre (1981) to factorially reduce it to four categories:

1. *Catastrophizing*: exaggerated, negative interpretation of present or antic- ipated events. Catastrophizing thought patterns usually can be recog- nized by the presence, in one's descriptive language, of such words as "awful," "terrible," and "critical."

2. *Overgeneralization*: an exaggerated estimate of how often or how many people are affected by a given event. This type of automatic thought can be recognized in one's language by the use of such terms as "always," "never," "everyone," "no one."

3. *Personalization*: the tendency to see one's self as the object of unrelated events or of being unrealistically responsible for events that occur. Per- sonalization appears in one's language in several ways, all of which reflect assigning an inordinate amount of importance to the personal meaning of events. Such language may include an excessive reliance on the use of "me"—the object or victim of events, by the presence of "must," "should," "have to," and other demand language and by self- directed criticisms such as name calling.

4. *Selective abstraction*: an unbalanced weighing of the importance and con- sequences of negative events over positive ones. Thus, positive attributes of self, others, or events are ignored and instead one exaggerates the likelihood of future negative events, the importance of negative attri- butes, and/or the likelihood of negative consequences.

Working with these automatic and depressogenic thoughts begins with the patient learning to identify their presence. Only when they can be rec- ognized does the therapist attempt to instigate methods of change. Discussion in psychotherapy sessions, in which examples of these thoughts are solicited in common activities, is a good place to start. Any situation during or follow- ing which the patient becomes upset, distressed, or depressed can illustrate and begin the process of identification. Homework assignments in which the patient is asked to keep track of and tabulate the nature of the distortions of thought may follow this in-therapy work.

Reattribution of responsibility is often a central concern in the treatment of substance abusers and those with depression. For those who externalize blame, there is value in assigning the cause of one's behavior to one's self rather than to external situations and events. In contrast, those who inter- nalize responsibility for bad events may be helped to reassess one's role and to begin looking to external rather than personal causes of problems. Through the Socratic method (guided discovery), patients are led to see (in a nonjudg- mental fashion) that they are responsible for their drug use and that external factors (e.g., a problematic relationship, difficult job, or social pressure) do not cause them to use drugs. Others who exaggerate self-blame may come to see that they are not the sole source of responsibility for bad things in the world. The goal is to shift from external factors to internal responsibility for destruc- tive choices while shifting from internal to external in perceptions of events over which one has no control.

Downward-arrow techniques may also be used to help patients decatastrophize (reevaluate and modify catastrophic thoughts) and see distortions in thinking. Therapists probe the patient's thinking and record the beliefs that accompany/underlie automatic thoughts with each successive thought leading downward to the next until a final underlying belief is identified. For example, a therapist may inquire about a patient's belief and then ask variations of the question, "What does that mean to you?," or "What would happen then?," as the patient explores deeper and deeper assumptions about his or her behavior. Core beliefs may occasionally be elicited in this fashion and the procedure may be useful to use in conjunction with other procedures such as advantages–disadvantages analyses or the DTR to bring the nature of distorted beliefs into higher relief.

Evidence analysis procedures are a collection of techniques that are used to help the patient evaluate the validity of their guiding assumptions. These procedures are used in conjunction with the DTR, beginning with a simple procedure of identifying events and associated thoughts to be tabulated in various activities. One can often identify one or two particular types of thoughts that characterize a person (misattributions or arbitrary inference) and these can be identified to help the patient develop a short-hand method for identifying when they are engaging in problematic thinking.

After ensuring that the patient can identify the problematic thoughts and the situations in which they arise, the second step is to help the patient recognize the feelings and behaviors that are associated with the thoughts. Again, the DTR is used to help define the relationship between the characteristic thoughts of the patient and the resulting and recurring feelings. Using the DTR, the patient may be asked to identify the antecedent situations (A), thoughts and beliefs (B), and their consequences (C) that form the chain of behavior. Making ratings (usually from 1 to 10) of the intensity and negativity of these thoughts, at this point, can serve as a baseline against which to assess subsequent changes. The third step involves assessing the validity of negative thoughts and implementing new and more adaptive ones. This step typically proceeds by first identifying a situation in which depression or drug use has occurred. It is helpful if this is a situation that has given rise to strong feelings and that was very recent in the patient's memory; this ensures that there is strong emotional attachment to the events.

Immediately after identifying the situation (A), the therapist can begin to define and identify the problematic assumptions and beliefs that accompanied it (B), and then the nature of the consequential depression, anxiety, and/or drug use itself (C). Sometimes it is easier to access the beliefs and assumptions that are problematic, and the situations in which they occur, by first inquiring about the troublesome feelings and behaviors (C). Usually, the strength of these feelings, as well as the strength of the beliefs, are rated on a simple scale to serve as a reference against which to assess the impact of change efforts.

Once two or more A-B-C sequences have been identified, the therapist initiates a dialogue about their relative importance. They are prioritized for consideration, based on which of the sequences seems to be most productive (usually identified by the degree of distortion that the therapist judges may be present by the patient's use of language). The therapist can then initiate a discussion of the bases for the distorted thoughts themselves. This discussion can take several courses but generally is aimed at first identifying the evidence that the patient believes support the identified beliefs. Once this evidence is identified, countermeasures are inserted to challenge the validity or uniformity of this evidence. These interventions range from (1) raising questions about the uniformity of the patient's evidence ("What evidence might there be that your belief may not be true or at least not always true?"), (2) raising consciousness about alternative viewpoints ("Is there any other way that you could view this situation?"), (3) inspecting how realistically the patient assesses the importance of the events ("Would others consider this as important as you do?"), (4) evaluating the patient's assumptions about attribution ("Is it possible that you didn't cause all of the problems?"), (5) raising questions about the patient's assumptions about frequency of events ("Is it true that everyone thinks this?" or "Is it true that this always happens?"), or (6) challenging the patient's criteria of what is adequate, worthwhile, expected, or necessary ("Is it possible that your standards are unrealistic?").

Once the thought has been convincingly identified as not true, not always true, or not true of everyone, the therapist can begin to suggest alternative thoughts for practice. The patient may be asked to draw conclusions from his or her analysis of the evidence and to construct a thought that would be more true or more often true than the one that has accompanied their problematic behavior. This thought may then be modified by the therapist and the patient can be asked to practice it or try it on a few times before assessing what changes have taken place in the strength of belief in the original thought and the strength of feelings that were originally present. Again, a simple rating of the strength of current beliefs and feelings is usually sufficient to demonstrate that changes in thoughts produce changes in feelings. Practice in the use of the rational alternatives constructed might be carried over into homework activities and new situations.

VEGETATIVE SIGNS   Ordinarily, sleep disturbances, appetite changes, and reduction of sexual desire pass as depression dissipates. Therefore, these symptoms are often treated as secondary signs of depression. However, when working with externalizing patients, it is often found that one or more of the symptoms are of primary importance. The therapist should start working with symptoms that are primary and more common to depression. Careful monitoring of subjective depression is important to make the distinction between what symptoms are primary and secondary. The therapist should initially define and later return to and question the patient about associated vegetative signs of depression. If the symptoms remain problematic after subjective depression has declined, one may elect to direct specific intervention efforts to these symptoms. Behavioral methods to increase activity, alter sleep, increase sexual arousal, and alter weight may be implemented. The various procedures used for these multiple purposes vary somewhat, but all have the following principles in common:

1. Identify the nature and frequency of occurrence of the specific symptoms.
2. Implement a change in the consequences of these symptoms or in the antecedents.
3. Continue to monitor the symptoms, looking for change.
4. Proceed by systematically altering either the events that follow the behavior or that precede it until some positive change is noticed in the frequency or nature of the symptoms. This contingency is then repeated until the behavior is extinguished.

Exercise is a general method that has rather broad effects and can be used to address many of the secondary symptoms of depression and anxiety. In addition, the energy and focus needed for exercise are generally incompatible with the effects on the body of chronic substance abuse. Thus, exercise may a particularly helpful abstinence supporting activity for the patient as well as a method for addressing the vegetative signs of depression. It may also heighten the patient's awareness of the physical advantages and disadvantages of substance abuse.

Although it is important to have medical approval before patients are given the go-ahead to embark on a physical fitness program, one can usually find some physical activity that is appropriate for the patient. Even the act of walking or rolling a wheelchair can be a place to start with a nonambulatory patient. The patient is asked to engage in the exercise at a level that is not strenuous. Indeed, exercise may never need to become strenuous to be effective. Mild exercise on a regular basis will provide the basis for increasing the amount of activity without increasing exercise load or stress, as the body acclimates and becomes stronger.

Activity regulation is also a general procedure that can be applied to correcting a variety of secondary symptoms, ranging from sleep disturbance to sexual disturbance and weight loss. The essential ingredients are to establish a program of regularity and predictability that is coupled with recordkeeping of progress and change.

Sleep disturbances, for example, can be effectively treated by first monitoring when a patient initiates and terminates bedtime; tabulating behaviors associated with eating, sex, and sleeping; and beginning to alter some of the precipitators or consequences of not sleeping. Following the initial record-keeping, the therapist may ask the patient to initiate several changes while continuing to track sleep time. These changes in sleep hygiene include getting up at a certain time, adjusting the temperature and sound in the room, discontinuing the use of alcohol and stimulants during the day, eliminating naps, restricting the amount of time in bed without sleep, and eliminating the practice of reading and watching television in bed. Most sleep problems will be correctable over a period of 2 to 3 weeks with these changes. There are a variety of self-help materials to assist the therapist in initiating these changes.

Likewise, the specifics of sex problems can be addressed both by scheduling time for discussion and practice and by implementing self-help procedures that are specific to making sexual activity changes (e.g., Kaplan, 1987). Various sexual problems associated with depression can be altered successfully by systematically exposing the patient to arousing stimuli, introducing non-demand pleasuring, introducing relaxation and stress tolerance procedures, and encouraging greater intimacy with one's significant other.

Indirect Procedures and Techniques

Beyond the point at which the patient has experienced symptom reduction for at least a week and does not evidence active destructive intent, treatment of the internalizing patients is more indirect and complex than that applied to externalizing patients. In part, this is because the treatment must blend a symptomatic and a broader thematic focus. As we have emphasized, treatment of complex problems must first offer direct assistance in the alleviation of dangerous and self-destructive behaviors associated with drug abuse and suicidal risk before implementing indirect treatment procedures. For example, an initial treatment contract could specify that the goals of treatment are both reduction of drug abuse and depression and the alteration of recurrent, self-destructive cycles of interpersonal behavior.

As risk behaviors come under control, the nature of internalized coping styles requires a shift of focus from symptom change to insight and awareness. Somewhere between the fourth and tenth session, the therapist can usually have successfully made this shift and is ready to address the hidden motives and fears that a patient presents. This shift is associated with the use of procedures that support the strategic objective of increasing emotional awareness and understanding of schematic processes. The treatment will shift to enduring thoughts and expectations that transcend the problems presented.

There are three tasks that form the basis of indirect treatment: (1) developing and following a problematic theme, (2) applying techniques and procedures that exert a direct influence on symptoms, and (3) transferring the focus from the use of direct to indirect interventions.

DEVELOPING AND FOLLOWING A THERAPEUTIC FOCUS   A central task of the early phases of treating an internalizing patient is developing a formulation of the schematic thoughts and assumptions that characterize a recurrent difficulty or theme in the patient's problems. This formulation must then serve as the focus and guiding thread of treatment. Maintaining this focus helps keep the therapist and patient oriented to the tasks and objectives they are trying to accomplish. The formulation identifies the problematic aspect of the patient's experience and the changes that are to be achieved.

A guiding focus can generally be defined by reference to the therapist's preferred theoretical viewpoint. However, research informs us that most of the time, therapists who develop such formulations do so implicitly rather than explicitly. Therapists frequently depart from such implicit formulations, being guided more by the pressures of whatever the patient brings to the particular session than by the coherent theme that binds session material together. Consistently following an explicitly defined theme ensures a level of consistency across treatment sessions that is frequently found lacking in conventional treatment.

Relevant themes tend to be more obvious during times of problems than during times of quiescence. Miranda and Persons (1988), for example, found that while dysfunctional schemas could be identified among depressed patients during asymptomatic periods, these themes were more difficult to identify and occurred with less pervasiveness than they did when depression was present. As these findings suggest, themes are enduring and in-dwelling characteristics of people, but they gain ascendency during periods of client depression and stress.

There are a number of ways that guiding themes can be developed, including a systematic analysis of the dynamic needs expressed in interpersonal relationships (Strupp & Binder, 1984; Luborsky, 1984). There is no inherent value or truth that we know of that would indicate that one of these methods should be selected over another. Thus, the thematic formulations we recommend for the purposes of PT are selected because of their ease of use and because their theoretical ties permit broad applicability and use. Therefore, we bring together two related, empirically derived methods for identifying thematic patterns for use in PT. One of these methods identifies schematic patterns associated with enduring responses and the other identifies the state-like thoughts that are provoked by acute stress and that arise from early experience.

The FAST provides a view of problem-provoking thoughts, focusing on those that take the form of an internal dialogue. The level of intensity and anger that is present within this dialogue has been associated with depression, anxiety, drug use, and self-defeating behaviors. The durability and generality of the identified themes can often be identified by examining the FAST. Some items are indicative of long-term patterns, character traits, or core beliefs of the client; for example, a client may acknowledge having such thoughts as, the following:

"You're too shy to make any new friends." (Rationalizations for self-denial)
"Don't be loud, don't be conspicuous, keep quiet."
"Just stay in the background." (Isolation)

Endorsements of such items are taken as indicative of a long-standing *trait* of introversion, self-consciousness, and shyness. If the particular client indicates that he or she had experienced these thoughts throughout life, it is taken as an index of a corresponding pattern of core beliefs.

The Early Maladaptive Schemas (EMS) form (Young, 1995) was developed to assist therapists in identifying the enduring cognitive schemas that underlie personality disturbances. In contrast to the FAST, the EMS (Young, 1995) provides a general description of the patient's assumptive world. It requires that the therapist identify which of five general groups provide the best description of the guiding schemas and rules that direct the patient's activities. Five basic schemas are identified (disconnection and rejection, impaired autonomy and performance, impaired limits, other-directedness, and overvigilance and inhibition). Within each of these categories, there are a variety of more specific cognitive processes, totaling 18, that describe a patient's perceptions and concerns.

Therapists should review the most recent administration of the FAST and EMS and then develop a coherent, explicit formulation of the forces that characterize the patient's behavior. At a minimum, an effective focal theme for an internalizing patient identifies (1) the internal experiences—ideas and emotions—that cause fear and struggle for the patient when aroused, (2) the expected negative consequences of expressing or allowing one's self to experience these things, and (3) the compromise behaviors (coping styles) that are used to avoid or reduce the power of these internal experiences.

Uncovering a consistent and integrated focal pattern can be accomplished with the EMS by exploring, in detail, the interpersonal relationships in which the patient has had problems, attempting with each relationship to identify the three elements of a focal theme. It is helpful to identify specific points of struggle and difficulty in each of these relationships and to record each of the three elements that were present during the struggle. Looking at the descriptors, a clinician then seeks to find one or two common and pervasive themes that cut across these relationships. These themes are then written down as a general formulation for ongoing reference.

SYMPTOMATIC FOCI   The initial symptomatic focus of treatment for an internalizing patient, ordinarily, is directed to addressing the patient's destructive potential and/or gaining a commitment to remain drug free or refrain from other discrete and problematic behaviors. The methods for dealing with these symptomatic areas have been described in the preceding section. They can be applied in the treatment of internalizing patients with only minor modifications. The goal is to transition out of the use of direct interventions to indirect intervention by the sixth session, but it may take a bit longer than this before a drug-abusing patient is able to remain drug free for a week.

In initially addressing the patient's symptoms, the specific procedures used may vary but generally incorporate four elements: (1) self-monitoring of thoughts and destructive actions, (2) facilitating the development of a cognitive connection between the patient's symptoms and the identified theme and schema that characterize the patient, (3) encouraging the patient to change at a rate for which he or she is ready, and (4) providing opportunities for self-evaluation and feedback.

DESTRUCTIVE POTENTIAL   In working with internalizing patients, the first priority is to modify self-destructive and aggressive behaviors and develop skills in stress tolerance. It is helpful if the therapist establishes a clear understanding of the nature of thoughts that accompany destructive impulses. This will establish a foundation by which to establish a contract to structure and limit the expression of destructive acts. It will also allow the therapist to work with the patient to develop a system for self-monitoring and tracking change in these thoughts. Specific procedures may include encouraging social activities to ensure the presence of a supportive structure in the patient's environment (e.g., family and friends) and offering a no-suicide contract. These and other techniques were described earlier and should be reviewed as readers attempt to organize a treatment program for the internalizing patient.

In the case of the suicidal, internalizing patient, the therapist should work to move the patient past the state-like suicidal thoughts addressed in treating the externalizing patient, to include those that are identified as trait-like as well. The EMS and FAST, as previously discussed, may provide some information that will help develop a thematic focus for dealing with such problems.

Once identified, the therapist employs the procedures outlined in the earlier section to directly modify suicidal impulses, develop new social skills, and provide protection for the patient. Attention to destructive impulses will continue after the therapist shifts to the use of indirect influence procedures. However, at this point, the objectives of the interventions will also change, shifting from symptom change and skill development to the exploration and disclosure of the origin of the destructive thoughts and their consequences. The therapist's own theoretical position will guide the nature of these interventions, but they generally consist of a combination of reflection of feelings, interpretation, and directed activities designed to enhance awareness and understandings of etiological events.

DRUG USE   In a similar way, during the direct treatment phase, the therapist should raise questions about the patient's drug use and, if applicable, eventually encourage a commitment to become drug free. Involvement in a 12-step program is often helpful for the patient and can be recommended by the therapist. Such treatments are particularly helpful for patients who are distrustful of and uncooperative with professional therapists. Identifying the patient's thoughts—both state- and trait-like—that are associated with drug use, monitoring use, seeking alternatives, and bolstering available support systems should be included in the treatment until the patient will agree and is able to remain drug free.

TRANSFERRING TO INDIRECT INTERVENTIONS   The third and primary step in the use of indirect interventions is to shift to the use of procedures that facilitate insight and emotional awareness. As soon as destructive and addictive symptoms are reduced, the preponderance of interventions should shift to those that are selected in order to (1) facilitate insight into developmental origins of the problem, (2) enhance exposure to feared emotions and events, and (3) increase anticipated, positive consequences of non–drug use. After the therapist initiates this insight-oriented phase of treatment, he or she may still have to return to the use of a direct, symptomatic focus from time to time; however, one should not lose sight of the importance of indirect procedures and should ensure that at least half of the therapeutic hour is devoted to procedures that are designed to facilitate insight and emotional awareness among internalizing patients. The indirect procedures selected should be those that will expose the patient to feared ideas and feelings, especially of those arising from early experience and learning. Thus, the therapist should encourage the patient to discuss and review the origins of these fears, evoking arousal until their emotional impact is altered. Insight facilitated by the therapist's interpretations provide a new way for patients to conceptualize their problems, to understand the nature of their reactions, and to find alternatives.

Research informs us that there are qualities of indirect interventions that tend to improve their effectiveness at relieving patient distress. These include (1) restricting one's focus to a finite number of thematic patterns, (2) following and staying with the patient's affect, and (3) maintaining a safe and protected environment while the patient engages in the process of making changes.

FOLLOWING RELEVANT THEMES   Once a theme or set of relevant themes has been identified, it is critical that the therapist organize all interventions around the theme or themes that have been defined as characteristic and problematic. The therapist constructs questions, interpretations, reflections, and directed work to illustrate and alter these themes. The major procedures that are designed to induce insight are questions and interpretations. The judicious use of *questions*, for example, can help a person identify the anticipated consequences of expressing unwanted feelings—the second component of the theme. Questions can also help a patient explore the genesis of the thematic components and identify how their efforts to cope have been a compromise between their fears and feeling or impulse states. This understanding can lead to an exploration of the rationality of the fears and a reconceptualization of the meaning of early experiences.

Interpretations are complex interventions that are designed to facilitate a reconceptualization of one's problems in terms of a recurrent theme. Interpretations combine elements of reflection, questioning, and restatement. Research is clear that the value of interpretations is a function of the accuracy of the interpretation. Accuracy is identified by how closely the interpretation coincides with the theme that the therapist uses to organize his or her responses. The effectiveness of an interpretation is also enhanced when it incorporates several component parts of the theme at once. Thus, an interpretation that identifies both the feared internal experience and the anticipated consequences of experiencing, or a summary of the patient's efforts to cope with, this feared event is likely to be more effective than an intervention that just includes one component, such as the avoided feelings.

The impact and value of an interpretation is also improved if it incorporates a discussion of the patient–therapist relationship. These need not be only transference interpretations but may also include discussions of the patient's reactions to therapy, feelings about the therapist, and concerns with progress.

A therapist has a choice of what elements to incorporate in an interpretation, and these are likely to have different consequences. For example, saying, "It sounds like you become afraid of feeling such strong anger and try to avoid it by secluding yourself," has quite a different impact than saying, "It sounds like when you experience such strong anger, you become afraid that it will overcome you. You fear that you may become unable to control these murderous feelings." The first interpretation identifies the feared experience and the patient's efforts to cope; the second identifies the feared experience and its anticipated (worst) consequence. Both may be true, and the therapist must select which aspect of the theme he or she wants to highlight. This decision may be based on what level of arousal the therapist seeks to initiate with the intervention. This aspect of therapy is described in a later chapter.

In addition to those procedures that are designed to induce insight, the therapist also uses a variety of procedures to enhance emotional sensitivity or awareness. These often lead to important insights and the therapist should become skilled at both tasks when working with the internalizing patient.

We have already discussed the use of *reflections* as a method of enhancing the quality of the working relationship. However, reflections can also be used to enhance patient emotional awareness, as well, because they identify feeling states that exist, at least momentarily, in the patient's phenomenological experience. However, patients frequently minimize or suppress the intensity of their emotions because of the discomfort or fear that these emotions evoke. They do this by misidentifying or labeling these unwanted feelings, denying the thoughts and feelings, or immediately suppressing their expression when they begin to emerge. A well-timed reflection can highlight those moments in which the patient is experiencing the avoided and feared emotions. A comment such as "You feel angry when you think of that" draws attention to an avoided feeling state before this feeling activates the patient's avoidant response. It can, thus, become conceptualized as "anger." By identifying inner experiences as "anger" or "fear," the patient comes to recognize the cues for such feelings, becomes cognizant that these feelings are not always dangerous, and can begin to extinguish urges to avoid them. The safety of the therapeutic environment allows further exploration in the absence of the feared consequence defined by the focal theme. The therapist can take advantage of this process to help the patient reconfigure the expectation of danger in this feeling.

Directed activities are also aimed at enhancing awareness. A wide variety of these have been used in successful behavior and experiential therapies. Some of them deserve special attention here.

Role playing is a procedure that can be used to develop new behaviors directly; however, it may also be used to increase one's awareness of the feelings that are present and important in different relationships. Feelings may become clearer and more intense during enactment than during the more removed discussions typically characteristic of psychotherapy sessions. By having the patient role-play aspects of a problematic relationship, the unwanted and feared feelings may become intensified enough that either the patient or therapist can identify his or her presence.

By the same token, *directed fantasy* can be used to identify aspects of a relationship or interchange that produces discomfort. Directed fantasy is similar to role playing but has more flexibility in how it is constructed. It also allows the patient to avoid becoming distracted by the therapist's or the patient's own ineptitude in enacting the roles, inducing instead a realistic picture of the relationship in his or her own mind.

In directed fantasy, the therapist can ask the patient to identify with and describe the physical sensations and cognitive processes associated with certain emotions that might be avoided and threatening. These can be exaggerated and intensified by encouragement and description that may then involve a fantasized or *in vivo* role-playing exercise. The patient's fears of expression and coping styles can then be observed directly or through patient self-report to fill in the blanks that comprise the thematic focus and facilitate emotional awareness and insight.

FOLLOWING PATIENT AFFECT   The principle of extinction emphasizes that the power of a therapeutic intervention is closely related to the emotional significance attributed by the patient to the material addressed. Extinction comes through exposure to feared and avoided experience. By presenting feared topics and experiences within therapy, the therapist is able to prevent the activation of whatever means the patient usually uses to escape or avoid these experiences. One can allow the patient to bring material up as it evolves or take more active steps to identify the points of anxiety. In either case, to maximize exposure to feared mental content, it is necessary for the therapist not only to tolerate patient distress but to encourage movement toward the source of the patient's anxiety or fear.

The nature of events and thoughts that evoke anxiety and fear identify the experiences that the patient is motivated to avoid. By approaching these experiences rather than avoiding them, the anxiety is reduced. Sometimes engaging in procedures that give rise to these fears will also stimulate fear on the part of the therapist. Therapists may become fearful that their patient's strong emotions will produce deterioration or that, as therapists, they will not have the skill to help control and protect the patient. A therapist must approach a patient's fears and anxiety with confidence that it will dissipate and diminish if both patient and therapist are willing to stay with the feelings without avoidance and escape. This is a principle of faith—that anxiety and fear will undergo a natural course of decline when the objects of fear and anxiety are faced rather than avoided. Therapists who become fearful of a patient's intense feelings are likely to increase this intensity rather than reduce it. Therapists must be calm, confident, and permissive of the full range of emotions. Indeed, they must seek to identify and expose the things that produce discomfort for the patient, allowing them to run their course and then subjecting them to the light of rational analysis. This process of exposure and reprocessing allows these feelings to become less influential.

Aside from the possibility that a therapist may attempt to abort the patient's expression of strong emotions, there is another difficulty that therapists may experience that will diminish the process of extinction. Specifically, therapists must be able to identify what experiences are being avoided by the patient when the content of these experiences are ignored, discounted, or denied. It is here that the therapist's knowledge and skill are critical. To identify the avoided emotions, the therapist must be able and willing to encourage patients to move toward and allow the presence of their own negative and avoided feelings.

Following the patient's feeling is most easily accomplished if the therapist narrows the scope of focus to the most immediate and present situations and examples of when that feeling has been evident. Central to this process is the desirability of creating a moment in which there is the experience of fear and the impulse to avoid an experience. As one follows the fear, it is then possible to inquire about the content of thought that is associated with these feelings. This often draws the patient and therapist to an exploration of the origins of these strong feelings.

As implied by the principles we enumerated earlier, reduction of anxiety and fear is accomplished more readily by exposing a patient to an environment that actually stimulates fear and anxiety than by simply talking about what might frighten someone. Thus, the use of techniques such as directed fantasy and discussing feelings that are roused by the therapeutic relationship itself are ways of identifying patient emotions. As we note in later chapters, these procedures not only allow us to identify the nature of feared emotions but can also be used to increase one's level of emotional arousal and motivation to change. But, for the current purposes, it is sufficient to know that using such procedures can help a therapist identify a thread of emotional experiences that can be followed and used as a guide to identifying relevant topics for productive discussion.

THERAPY PROVIDES SAFETY FOR RECONCEPTUALIZATION AND CHANGE
As a therapist follows a person's emotions through a history of interpersonal relationships, raises strong feelings, and confronts patients with feared experiences, it is to be expected that patients may develop a feeling of vulnerability and lack of safety in the therapeutic environment. Maintaining a patient's sense of safety is a preeminent concern to the therapist. To facilitate an environment that encourages experimentation and change, it is imperative that the therapy relationship be safe and protected. Although tears and repairs in the relationship are the norm, it is important that a therapist periodically return to the process of relationship development to reinforce and encourage the assurance that the relationship is safe and comforting. Acceptance, understanding, and collaboration are important attributes of a healing relationship capable of supporting change.

Keeping contractual commitments cannot be underestimated as a means of ensuring that the relationship has the perception of being safe. That is, it must be safe from external intrusion, not just be perceived as safe. The therapist should exert considerable care to ensure that confidences are protected and that authentic understanding is achieved. Collaboration in defining goals and pursuing efforts to identifying and selecting the thematic focus of treatment also facilitates the sense of safety by reinforcing patient self-control.

Prescriptive therapy encourages the explicit and collaborative specification of the goals for treatment. For example, a therapist might use the EMS to encourage the patient to identify the two or three clusters that seem to be the most true or relevant to the presenting problems. Treatment may then explore the development of relevant schema and the associated beliefs that are associated with the patient's problems.

Assessing Therapist Skill in Adapting Treatment to Coping Style

The skill of the psychotherapist is manifest in three ways: (1) the accuracy with which he or she can determine what is being avoided by the symptomatic behavior, (2) how well the procedures developed and used bring the patient into contact with these avoided experiences, and (3) how well the therapeutic environment is able to maintain a supportive and safe environment in which the patient can develop adaptive and healthy ways of coping.

The STS Therapy Process Rating Scale assesses aspects of therapist activity related to the differential selection of psychotherapy techniques within each of the areas defined by this manual. It is completed by trained clinicians and within the domain of adapting treatment to patient coping style, the following items are rated on a 5-point scale, ranging from "Never" or "Not at all" to "A lot."

1. Therapist focuses on client's identifiable, problematic behavior.
2. Therapist seeks to identify the rewards or payoffs for problematic behavior(s).
3. Therapist seeks to identify relationship between client's pattern of thoughts and actions.
4. Therapist employs techniques such as relaxation, contracting, systematic desensitization, and self-control methods to change behavior.
5. Therapist evaluates client's progress in terms of behavioral change.
6. Therapist seeks to identify recurring conflicts in interpersonal relationships.
7. Therapist employs techniques to increase client's self-understanding.

The sum of those items that reflect on the use of focused and direct efforts to alter behavior (items 1, 2, 4, and 5) are cross-tabulated against measures of patient externalization. The sum of ratings on those items that reflect on the use of indirect and insight-oriented techniques (items 3, 6, and 7) to facilitate understanding and awareness are cross-tabulated against measures of patient internalization. Together, these indices are taken to suggest the level of compatibility that exists between the treatment implemented by a therapist and patient coping style.

Chapter 7
Adapting Therapy to Patient Resistance Levels

R esistance occurs when a patient's sense of freedom, image of self, safety, psychological integrity, or power is threatened. Such resistance in an interpersonal relationship indicates that a patient is trying to prevent or restore these threatened losses. Variations in a patient's resistant behaviors are the result of enduring traits and situation induced reactions. Resistant *traits* are expressed as stable, cross-situational dispositions that order patients along a dimension of vulnerability to threat. Resistant *states*, on the other hand, are a function of the particular constraints imposed by the therapeutic environment itself.

A mental health clinician must adapt treatment both to enduring traits and the treatment-induced reactions that reduce a patient's compliance. Conceptually, the development of differential treatment plans for high- and low-resistant behaviors are easily done and specified; however, it is quite a different thing to implement interventions that the resistant patient accepts. There are no more difficult adjustments for a therapist to make than those designed to overcome patient resistance to the clinician's efforts to provide help.

Psychotherapy gives rise to many expressions of resistance, sometimes by accident and occasionally by design. Patient behaviors that are identified as indicating high and low resistance to therapeutic influence are indicators for the differential use of patient-directed and therapist-directed activities, respectively. That is, high-resistance behaviors indicate the need for few, or no, therapist-directed interventions; however, if directiveness is unavoidable, the level of directiveness should be as low as possible, even to the point of en-

The authors wish to thank Lisa Firestone, Ph.D., Robert Romanelli, Lynnette Glasman, Ph.D., and Oscar Goncalves, Ph.D. for their assistance with sections of this chapter.

couraging patient-directed activities. On the other hand, low-resistance behaviors indicate the patient's ability to accept and benefit from external direction and guidance from the therapist.

Recognizing overt resistance is usually quite easy. Recognizing more passive and covert resistance is much more difficult. But for however difficult it is to recognize subtle resistance patterns among patients, implementing the prescribed nondirective procedures and avoiding proscribed directive and confrontive interventions when treating patients who are overtly angry and rebellious are even more difficult for most therapists. The timely insertion of nondirective interventions in the midst of aggressive expressions by patients requires the therapist to set aside his or her own resistance and acknowledge that the patient's oppositional behavior may be the direct result of therapeutic intervention—-even therapeutic errors on the part of the therapist. The idea that resistance may be caused by the treatment itself is difficult for most therapists to accept, but such recognition opens one to the possibility that it can also be overcome by therapeutic interventions.

Strupp and Binder (in press) reported that none of the highly trained and experienced therapists that were used in the well-known Vanderbilt study of psychodynamic psychotherapy were able to deal effectively with patient resistance. They observe that resistance is especially difficult for a therapist to treat when it is manifest as overt anger directed at the therapist. They note that therapists tend to respond to such anger in kind (i.e., they become angry and defend themselves) even when they believe such therapist responses are inappropriate. Therapists are likely to become angry, critical, and rejecting, all of which reduce the communication value and willingness of patients to explore problems.

Prescriptive therapy emphasizes the necessity of educating therapists to effectively work with patient resistance and to adapt the treatment used to the presence of both characteristic resistant traits and transitory states of resistance.

Guiding Principles

The therapist's ability to adjust his or her stance and adopt the role of either an authority or a peer with the patient, while remaining nondefensive when challenged, is central to working with resistant patients. The principles that guide a therapist's interventions with regard to resistance are as follows:

1. Therapeutic change is most likely when the therapeutic procedures do not evoke patient resistance.
2. Therapeutic change is greatest when the directiveness of the intervention is either inversely correspondent with the patient's current level of resis-

tance or authoritatively prescribes a continuation of the symptomatic behavior.

Within all theoretical frameworks, there are suggestions for handling and minimizing patient resistance. In a behavioral tradition, these may include patient-generated behavioral contracts or behavioral exchange programs, whereas in a systems framework they may involve prescribing the symptoms and reframing, and in the tradition of relationship therapy they may involve acceptance, approach and retreat, and evocative support.

Indexing Cues

Patient resistance is expressed both as an enduring aspect of one's personality and as a situational reaction to threatened loss of control or power. In the first case, resistance is a frequent and dominant aspect of one's relationship with others. In the second instance, resistance may be observed only in interactions with those who have power or authority and are generally confined to situations that limit freedom or exert power over the patient. Accordingly, clinicians must be able to both adapt the overall treatment plan and the moment-to-moment interventions in order to accommodate these two manifestations of resistance. To adequately do so, it is necessary that therapists learn to identify and distinguish between temporary and enduring propensities to become defensive and resistant. Therapists must also identify those aspects of their own interventions that may precipitate resistant patterns and behaviors.

We think it is important for the therapist to formally assess both the trait-like and state-like manifestations of defensiveness. Trait-like patterns can be assessed by standardized, omnibus personality tests such as the MMPI-2. There are several MMPI-2 subscales that seem to identify a common trait of interpersonal defensiveness. The most obvious subscales include Dominance (Do), Needs for Control (Cn), Conflict with Authorities (Aut), and Readiness for Treatment (TRT). The advantage of using the MMPI over simpler procedures is the presence of good normative data. A simplistic discrimination between high and low resistance can be based on whether the sacle or the mean of several scales is above or below the normative mean.

In our own work, we have come to rely heavily on the TRT subscale of the MMPI as a single score measure. It correlates well with the other identified subscales and has the advantage of being readily available from standard, computerized scoring procedures.

Attendant on an assessment of trait-like resistance, the therapist should plan to adjust the nature of the activities assigned as homework and the level of directiveness expressed within the therapy session. Resistance level should be reassessed every few sessions (approximately every fifth session) and the interventions adjusted accordingly.

The STS Clinician Rating Form is a second method of assessing resistance that has been found to be valuable. The following items are extrapolated from the STS and identify behaviors that are associated with various levels of resistance. They are identified by reviewing the patient's history and behavior during recent, stressful events or during the process of treatment, itself. A patient with low levels of resistance potential:

1. Usually follows the advice of those in authority.
2. Avoids confrontation with others.
3. Has a history of accepting and following the directions of those in authority.

Patients with high levels of trait-like resistance respond in the opposite fashion. High levels of trait-like resistance may be indicated by the nature of the patient's description of events and people in his or her life. A patient that has a high level of (trait) resistance potential:

1. Frequently expresses resentment of others.
2. Seems to expect that others will take advantage of him/her.
3. Tends to be controlling and demanding in intimate relationships.
4. Is distrustful and suspicious of others' motives.
5. Expresses resentment about not having the advantages and opportunities that others have had.
6. Often has broken "the rules."
7. Enjoys competition.
8. Has been oppositional (does the opposite) when others try to control him or her.
9. Is often dominating in relationships.
10. Resents those who make the rules.
11. Is happiest when he or she is in charge.
12. Often feels blamed for other peoples' mistakes or faults.
13. Has tried to "get even" when provoked.
14. Frequently avoids being the "loser" in disagreements.

State-like patterns of resistance, in contrast to trait-like patterns, require the therapist to adapt to momentary changes within therapy sessions in order to reduce the negative effects that might arise from interpersonal confrontation. Because high levels of resistance are often masked by words of cooperation and attentiveness, the level of state-like resistance within the therapy session can be best assessed by nonverbal and vocal behaviors that suggest the presence of anger and withdrawal. Frequently, it is how one speaks rather than what one says that identifies the patient's level of defensiveness. Thus, vocal tones, facial expressions, and body movements are used to index patient defensiveness within sessions. To use some of these nonverbal cues effectively, a therapist must learn to ignore (momentarily) the content of what a patient is saying to attend to the quality of expression. This is not to discount the importance of more obvious behaviors such as angry words, failure to comply with homework assignments, and discounting therapeutic interventions; the occurrence of these behaviors should be noted by therapists. The specific signs of state-like resistance are a *change* of behavior in which the patient begins to evidence the following:

1. Trouble understanding or following directions
2. Stubbornness in accepting something that is obvious to the therapist
3. Being closed to new experiences
4. Responding to suggestions in a passive–aggressive way;
5. Lateness or avoiding appointments;
6. Expression of fear that the therapist is trying to take advantage of him or her
7. Holding on to a point of view and being unable to be argued out of a position once it is set
8. Arguing with the therapist or others
9. Holding a grudge
10. Becoming overtly angry at the therapist

Strategies for Adapting Treatment to Patient Resistance

Among patients who have a high propensity to react with resistance or who exhibit recurrent patterns of resistance, the treatment strategy should ordinarily emphasize low therapist directiveness. The therapist may "suggest" rather than assign homework and the work itself should be self-directed. In cases of persistent and extreme resistance, the therapist might consider using a paradoxical intervention in which the symptom is prescribed or in which the patient is encouraged to avoid changing for a short period.

In contrast, among those who manifest few indices of resistance, the therapist can feel comfortable most of the time with making direct suggestions and assignments. Guidance, interpretations, suggestions, and assignments are usually well received by such patients. For example, the therapist might "assign" specific, therapist-selected, and active homework tasks. Because a patient may change rapidly in level of manifest resistance, it is important to reassess each patient's level of trait-like resistance every few sessions. We recommend reassessing patients every fourth or fifth session with corresponding adaptations being made to the nature of homework and directive interventions.

The general strategies of change can be summarized as follows:

1. Therapists should avoid disagreement with the resistant patient and attempt to increase their levels of perceived freedom and capacity for self-direction.
2. Therapists should reserve the provision of direction and guidance to those patients who are nonresistant.

As these strategies indicate, the therapist has much more freedom in working with compliant patients than in working with defensive ones. Whether state-like or trait-like, the presence of resistance introduces a number of proscriptions—the therapist should *not* be authoritative, should *not* be directive, should *not* be confrontive, and so on. A compliant patient can tolerate all of these roles and activities; in fact, nonresistant patients may even do better with such authoritative and directive roles than they do with nondirective ones (Beutler, Engle et al., 1991).

Techniques and Procedures

Some general guidelines define some of the types of techniques and procedures that are likely to be effective for working with patient resistance.

1. Patients with high resistance should be provided with opportunities for self-directed improvement.
2. Therapists should increase the relative reliance on nondirective interventions.
3. Patients with high resistance are likely to respond better than most patients to paradoxical interventions.
4. Therapists can adapt by de-emphasizing both the use of confrontive procedures and those that invoke the therapist's authority.
5. Patients with low levels of resistance respond to the therapist's role of authority and to direct guidance.

Treating the Low-Resistant Patient

Patients who are not resistant-prone and not currently resisting are good candidates for therapist suggestions and interpretations, for receiving homework assignments that are guided and "corrected" by the therapist, and for behavioral strategies that provide structure and monitor therapeutic activities.

STRUCTURED HOMEWORK   We recommend that low levels of trait-like re-sistance be used to cue the initiation of a series of highly structured homework assignments (e.g., a series of tasks from standard self-help books and manu-als). In applying structured homework assignments, therapists should review and monitor progress. A therapist ordinarily assigns readings and the com-pletion of associated forms that allow the patient to self-monitor changes on a weekly basis. The therapist can also provide direct suggestions regarding change in depressive, anxiety, and drug-abuse patterns. The assignments should be checked and the therapist should note whether or not the patient completed the work.

The books that will be used for assigning homework assignments should either focus on specific symptoms of depression (*Feeling Good*; Burns, 1992), as appropriate for externalizing patients, or increasing personal understanding (*A Road Less Traveled*; Peck, 1985), as appropriate for the treatment of inter-nalizing patients. The homework assignments will complement the self-evaluation of mood and drug use that is initiated before each session. This information will be collected each week, for future reference, and the content of the assignments will be available for discussion in the ensuing session, depending on whether the therapist sees it as important to do so.

DIRECTED TECHNIQUES   Therapists who work with patients who present low levels of resistance are encouraged to implement a variety of directive procedures within the session. These techniques can be selected and modified from among those described in chapter 6. The particular procedures selected should depend on whether the patient manifests externalized or internalized coping strategies.

For patients who have both low levels of resistance and who present with externalizing coping styles, the most compatible strategy includes both the use of therapist guidance and direct instruction. The objective of these inter-ventions should be constructed with the objective in mind of directly changing patient symptoms and behaviors. Cognitive or cognitive–behavioral interven-tions such as those outlined by Beck et al. (1979) for treating depression and by Beck et al. (1993) for treating substance abuse, are ideal for these circum-stances. Procedures of cognitive therapy can be applied quite directly by the therapist.

Identifying automatic thoughts is a first step in applying cognitive–behavioral procedures. The therapist first teaches patients about the component chain of relationships that is associated with behavior and feelings, within an A (antecedent)-B (belief)-C (consequence) framework. Patients are then engaged in a process of discussing these components and identifying these elements within the context of their particular presenting problems. Structured home-work assignments complement these efforts and are designed to facilitate this process of identifying the chain of reactions. Patients may be asked to record thoughts associated with particular urges or dysphoric feelings throughout the week. Once patients are able to recognize the relations between thoughts and feelings, they are systematically taught a method of processing and assessing the validity of their assumptive thoughts.

Evidence gathering and analysis is a problem-solving procedure in which patients are taught to systematically inspect and question their assumptions. Thus, they are asked to identify the evidence for the validity of their depressogenic thoughts (e.g., "I should be a better person") or for the self-defeating assumptions that give permission for continued drug use (e.g., "one little hit won't hurt—I deserve it after what I've been through"). The therapist then encourages the patient to question this evidence and to explore the possibility that these beliefs are invalid. Terms such as "should," "shouldn't," "have to," "can't," "always," and "never" are questioned and changes in terminology are considered. Excuses that justify continued drug use are also questioned and the general validity of these internal dialogues is questioned.

Monitoring and recordkeeping are other procedures that focus on symptom change and patient responsibility. The general guidelines emphasize that externalizing patients with substance-abuse problems or other high-risk problematic behaviors be provided with interventions that are focused on the specific behaviors associated with these problems and are constructed and overseen by the therapist. Monitoring and recordkeeping are typical of various forms of cognitive therapy (Beck et al., 1993), though the nature of monitoring and the level of therapist control by the level of additional information available to the therapist. The various procedures emphasize an ongoing record and graph of drug use that the patient and therapist can use for quick visual reference of progress. Patients may also be given a DTR as discussed in chapter 6, and asked to record the urges and rationalizations that occur within the context of drug abuse or other problematic behavior(s).

Activity schedules, such as those described in chapter 6, can also be useful to encourage patients to increase the level of prosocial participation. The therapist may prescribe certain social activities that are contrary to problematic activities (e.g., drug use) and that distract the patient from depression. The patient may be asked to record the intensity of depressed and anxious moods, keeping ongoing records of automatic thoughts, and practicing alternative thoughts and problem-solving tactics.

Directed, evocative procedures may be inserted by the therapist for treating low-resistant patients who rely on internalizing coping strategies. The focus of such interventions, because of the patient's coping style, will be on the facilitation of insight and personal awareness. Here, the therapist should consider it relatively safe to provide direct interpretation of the patient's motives and intentions and to implement directed fantasy, two-chair dialogues, work with internal splits or voices, and other activities that bring the patient into direct contact with avoided, internal experiences. In this case, the therapist's strategies can incorporate procedures that are both authoritative/directive and insight-oriented.

INTERPERSONAL TECHNIQUES   The therapist who is working with a patient who is low on both resistance and internalization may usefully borrow procedures from interpersonal psychotherapy (IPT; Klerman, Weissman, Rounsaville, & Chevron, 1984). These procedures first provide education about the nature of the problem and then reinforce the patient's tendency to assume a patient role in which rest and reliance on an authority are seen as necessary steps in healing. A patient's problems are described as an illness in this framework, and the therapist emphasizes that treatment of such illnesses requires both a period of recovery and the need to follow the doctor's orders.

The therapist using these procedures then assesses the patient's problems and provides feedback about the nature and expected course of the problem. In depression, for example, the therapist attributes the problems to chemical imbalances that may be present and reveals that the normal course of depression is cyclical. This pattern consists of periods of depression followed by periods of recovery. The therapist also introduces one of four basic interpersonal themes that may be at the basis of the patient's problems: deficits in skill, unresolved grief, role transitions, and interpersonal disputes. The patient's history and current situation is then discussed in terms of this theme. Historical events are explored in this same context, as revealing how one came to be sensitized to events that include loss, external requirements and demands, life change, and interpersonal conflict.

DIRECTED EXPERIENTIAL TECHNIQUES   Directed procedures that emphasize awareness and insight also include a variety of experiential interventions. Daldrup et al. (1988) and Elliott (1996) describe the use of these procedures for facilitating emotional awareness. In using these procedures, the patient is led by the therapist to focus on current feelings, sensations, and fearful or angry thoughts and then to imagine events that might increase the intensity of the negative experiences they can identify. Often, the therapist draws the patient's attention either to the presence of contradictory impulses, wishes, and feelings (splits) or to a current or past interpersonal struggle that is still unsettled (unfinished business). In both instances, the therapist is directive in drawing attention to the conflicting emotional experiences, particularly attending to those wishes and sensations that have been ignored, suppressed, or denied. The opposing sides of the intra- or interpersonal struggle is then separated by requiring the patient to play different roles or voices that are present in the struggle. The patient is asked to role-play each of the opinions and feelings represented, paying attention to the internal processes that arise while engaging in the role-playing activities. The therapist may give the patient words to use that are designed to exaggerate the intensity of the feelings being portrayed, and in this way he or she attempts to keep the conflict uppermost in the patient's thoughts for as long as the emotional intensity can be sustained.

In carrying out these procedures, the origin of unfinished business and emotional conflicts is often sought by suggesting that the patient follow the emotional thread (see chapter 6) that is highlighted and foremost in the conflict. The therapist asks the patient to identify the time in his or her life that such feelings were first noted, the responses that significant others had to the enactment of these feelings, and the events that preceded and followed the revelation of these feelings. Unconscious and/or conscious decisions that the patient may have made about the expression and experiencing of intense feelings are identified and applied to current problems.

Thus, the therapist helps the patient understand how parents and other significant people in the patient's early life who addressed issues related to anger, sex, happiness, and fear set a standard for the patient's own expression. The patient is guided to reconstruct interactions with parents and parental figures who set the original ground rules, using two-chair and role-playing exercises, and to explore alternative ways of resolving and expressing feelings.

VOICE WORK   In a procedure that blends cognitive, interpersonal, and experiential themes, Voice Therapy (Firestone, 1986) seeks to gain access to the internalizing patient's inner life by identifying the angry and rejecting dialogues that people hold with themselves when they make mistakes or have trouble. These voices are usually within easy reach of one's awareness when they are engaging conflictual behavior, are failing in efforts to achieve goals, or have made a mistake. Although this type of work is flexible in the degree of therapist directiveness required, it is the therapist who must construct the framework and direct the patient's experience. Therapist guidance is organized around three tasks. The patient is first asked to identify the nature of internal voices, with particular attention to those that are heard to be speaking from the second person ("you're stupid," "you always act inappropriate," "you never learn," etc.). In the second step, the patient is asked to express these voices as they are heard in the patient's own head and even to exaggerate the emotional intensity associated with their content and expression. This process continues as long as the patient is able to access a level of emotional intensity associated with the inner voices.

As the voices become articulated and clear, and as they lose some of the intensity originally associated with them, the therapist then suggests that the patient begin responding and answering the voices. The aim of this step is to help patients develop an understanding of their primal source with therapist encouragement and guidance. Patients are usually able to identify a parent from whom these voices derive and the process of answering and responding to the voices assists in the development of cognitive resources for combating them.

Treating the High-Resistant Patient

The resistant patient presents a major challenge to psychotherapists; however, this is not because they lack the necessary therapeutic tools and techniques. Most of the technical procedures that a therapist uses for treating the compliant and nonresistant patient can be adapted to work with the resistant patient by minimizing confrontation and eliminating direct therapist demand. However, the flexibility of which the techniques are capable is not paralleled in the therapist's skill in adapting and using the techniques. In chapter 1 we emphasized that skill requires a facilitative attitude, sound knowledge of change principles, tools, and techniques. The conducive attitude includes one of nondefensiveness; sound knowledge includes an understanding of how patients are likely to respond to confrontation and structure; tools include environments that maximize choice and offer support; effective techniques are those that avoid rousing defensiveness. The therapist is challenged to find creative ways of helping the defensive patient stay open and receptive. In working with resistant patients, the effective and skillful therapist must avoid confrontation and antagonism and must resist becoming defensive in the face of a patient's subtle or not so subtle attack. The selection of specific techniques and procedures should aid, not impede, this process.

Among the interventions of choice to use in treating defensive and resistant patients are nondirective and evocative interventions, paradoxical interventions, and reading assignments that make few direct demands on patients. The cognitive, behavioral, interpersonal, relationship, and experiential procedures that we have described in previous chapters can all be useful, but only if the therapist can successfully transfer responsibility for their initiation and progress to the patient.

SELF-MONITORED HOMEWORK   Homework is a helpful aspect of treatment for the resistant patient, as it is for the nonresistant patient, especially as applied to drug abuse. Ordinarily, in the hands of a skillful therapist, two differences will distinguish the homework tasks used for resistant patients from those given to patients with low resistance: (1) the assignments should be derived from and accompanied by self-help workbooks that can be used by the patient and selected from a predetermined list (e.g. Burns, 1992), and (2) patients should self-monitor their success in drug and depression control, with little effort made on the part of the therapist to check or collect homework assignments. To show continuing interest, therapists will probably want to check on homework completion, but in most instances will make no effort to check patient's work or to collect homework material. Thus, successful treatment will allow resistant patients to pace their own work and they will be invited to seek help and assistance as they feel it is needed.

SELF-DIRECTED WORK   Bibliotherapy is another useful adjunct to psychotherapy sessions among resistant patients. Such patients may be encouraged to select and read one of the many self-help books that are available. It may be advantageous to add books to the lists that are of special interest to the therapist and to select the books to be specific to the response dispositions of patients who use externalizing and internalizing coping styles. Two different lists might be constructed and presented, the particular one depending on whether the books focus on altering daily behaviors and problems (externalizers) or whether they focus on altering one's awareness and understanding (internalizers). If therapists use the same books for working with high-resistance patients as they use for low-resistance patients, they will need to exercise care to emphasize patient control and self-initiation in the selection of books and in the designation of homework assignments.

The self-help focus that characterizes the homework suggestions that are given to resistant patients should be paralleled within the therapy hours themselves. For patients who are high in trait-like resistance, therapists should take care to employ relatively few directive interventions and can rely on the use of self-monitoring, personal narratives to evoke self-exploration and exploration of the patient's important relationships. Throughout, in the treatment of these patients, the therapist should avoid making direct and therapist-controlled efforts to modify patient drug use or depression and to follow the patient's lead in defining the topics of treatment focus.

To further the aims of the patient's need for self-direction, the therapist might encourage patients to become involved in self-help groups. Such groups as Alcoholics Anonymous, Adult Children of Alcoholics, ALANON, or Narcotics Anonymous are well developed for chemical abusers, and similar programs are available for other types of problems and symptoms. In suggesting such involvement, however, the therapist should place no specific demands or requirements for becoming active in these programs. Supportive counseling and the provision of reflective acknowledgement are verbal techniques that are expected to work well with this type of patient. Interpretations, directives, and role-playing activities should be avoided.

NONDIRECTIVE INTERVENTIONS   Addressing high state-like resistance requires more sensitivity to momentary changes than that required for treating trait-like resistant patterns. Treating patients with momentary resistant states requires the therapist to employ procedures that avoid confrontation, are nondirective, and that deemphasize status differences. Thus, therapists may begin by using informal titles and names and by adopting a peer-like rather than an authority-like relationship.

Nondirective interventions in which the therapist relies on reflection and questions have been found to be highly effective with resistant patients. The power of clarifications, acknowledgements of feelings, and reflecting the presence of unhappy and even resistant feelings are seldom recognized among psychotherapists. The therapist who gives the patient time and who is calm while remaining active and involved may avoid a significant amount of conflict and struggle. Therapists seldom get into trouble because they say too little. Although such temerity may be seen as disinterest or ineffectiveness, it is also apparently empowering and often may force the patient to take a stand and to act in his or her own behalf.

Nondirective interventions that are expected to be successful during periods of high resistance are reflection and support, and an approach–retreat method in which difficult topics (e.g., drug-use status) are raised but are followed by therapist withdrawal into relative silence, allowing the patient to struggle with the problems presented. In these interventions, the therapist *must not* become argumentative, should place no investment in how, or if, the patient succeeds in resolving anger, and should be willing to be challenged. The effective therapist in these circumstances is one who is willing to be wrong and who remains calm and reflective in the midst of turmoil.

PARADOXICAL INTERVENTIONS   The therapist may provide a way of reframing a patients' problem that activates their resistance tendencies in the service of positive ends. Paradoxical interventions, for example, may be used to get the patient to resist by becoming less symptomatic or by giving up rigid interpersonal themes. For example, the therapist may encourage the resistant patient to go slowly. Therapists may even prescribe a period in which there is no change in order to "make adequate preparations," or he or she may ask the patient to enact or exaggerate the symptoms in order to "get a better perspective on what it does."

To place such suggestions within a framework that encourages the use of resistance to positive ends, the therapist usually gives a rationale. A therapist, for example, may offer the aggressively narcissistic patient the following advice: "You're not ready to make a lot of changes yet. You should wait until you are stronger and more sure of yourself." Another suggestion may take the following form: "You still don't have the maturity to handle change yet, so you will not be likely to change until you gain a little more ground in that area." Still another may suggest the following: "You should try ignoring your wife's requests just a little bit more than you are now, at least during the first few weeks of our treatment, so that both you and I can see what she does when she's pushed like that." And still another may suggest: "It is important that we get a clear picture of what happens when you use drugs around your parents. I expect that it makes them angry and gives you more reasons to be angry with them. So, I'd like to suggest that you notice very closely what they do when you are using. Also notice all the ways that you tell yourself that you deserve to get away from them."

Such procedures undermine patients' struggle to ensure their personal sense of autonomy. Although the usual efforts of helpers tend to drive resistant patients to defend their autonomy by being stridently against any changes, the imposition of a suggestion that they are unable to change, or should not change, directs their efforts to assert autonomy in the act of changing. Their motivation for defiance shifts from staying the same to making changes. Oppositional adolescents and resistant patients with characterological problems have all been shown to benefit from such interventions.

EVOCATIVE, NARRATIVE WORK   The use of narratives may be especially helpful with high-resistant patients. The use of narratives is designed to evoke self-exploration and to help patients understand the personal meanings they assign to important events in their lives. The use of narratives is founded in the observation that a narrative imposes order on the way in which people describe their lives and that a change in the nature of this story can have significant power for changing a person's feelings about his or her life.

Narrative work is founded in the observation that people intentionally and often frantically search for meaning in their lives when they are faced with the ambiguity and uncertainty of crisis. These meanings ordinarily take the form of a story that assigns a meaning to the events and predicts an outcome. As patients find such meaning, the stories they tell conventionally become better organized, more complex, and more integrated. At the same time, patients themselves often come to feel better and to experience correspondingly less distress. The use of narratives in psychotherapy provides a way of facilitating the struggle to find meaning in the problems one faces.

To facilitate narrative development, the therapist may simply ask patients to tell the story of their problem and subsequently encourages them to expand the elements of the stories until they contribute to an understanding of life purpose. More simply, the therapist asks patients to define a problem and to construct a story about that problem relative to their own lives. Patients should be encouraged to incorporate each of the foregoing elements:

1. The setting or background information for the establishment of the narrative
2. The initiating event or conflict that triggers the narrative—usually this is a description of a problem or event
3. The internal responses that arise from the triggering event and efforts to resolve it
4. The goal or objective of the characters portrayed in one's personal narrative
5. The actions and movements of the different players in the narrative

6. The outcomes or results of efforts to resolve the problem
7. The ending or close of the narrative—how it turns out

There are some prescriptive guidelines that can facilitate the process of narrative review. These employ the following general procedures:

1. Therapists focus their questions on different elements of the narrative structure, including background information for the story, a description of the subjective experience of the characters, the goals and objectives of the main characters, the activities of the various protagonists, the results of these actions, and the ending to the story.
2. Therapists raise questions about how different narrative stories are related to one another.
3. Therapists seek clarification about the causal connections and relationships that might be present within and between stories.

As the process of story development and explication continues, the therapist should help patients increase the complexity of their stories. Movies or books can be recommended as ways of stimulating thoughts and ideas to help in this process. As stories become enriched and complex, patients are likely to change the perceptions of these problems in their own lives beyond the black–white perceptions of right and wrong, good and bad, that often justify impulsive acts and substance abuse. Thus, the therapist encourages the patient to explore alternative explanations for the events that happen in the story and to discuss the other possible outcomes and variations of possible experience portrayed by the principal players.

Narratives that include the foregoing elements and structure provide room for making interconnections that lend coherent meaning to one's personal stories. Abundant research demonstrates that simply talking or writing about emotionally loaded events in this way results in the efficient accumulation of knowledge and understanding. Following the development of the stories, the therapist encourages patients to elaborate on the stories, to produce other stories that might be related, and even to construct stories to explain their struggles and their lots in life. As these stories become more personal and complex, the therapist should seek to move patients toward using these stories to define ways to give their own lives enhanced meaning.

Assessing Therapist Skill in Adapting Treatment to Patient Resistance

Therapist compliance with the guidelines for treating low-and high-resistant patients will be assessed following each therapy session. The following items are paraphrased and extracted from the STS Therapist Rating Scale. Rating how frequently the therapist uses these procedures is a way of identifying the relative use of directive and nondirective interventions.

Directive Interventions

1. Asking closed questions during the session
2. Making interpretations during the session
3. Being confrontation during the session
4. Interrupting client's speech or behavior during the session
5. Giving information or instructions to the client
6. Assigning structured homework
7. Analyzing A-B-C relationships
8. Evidence gathering and analysis
9. Monitoring and recordkeeping
10. Activity scheduling
11. Interpersonal analysis
12. Directed experiential techniques
13. Voice work

Non-Directive Interventions

1. Asking open-ended questions during the session
2. Passive acceptance of the client's feelings and thoughts
3. Reflecting the client's emotional states during the session
4. High percentage of time following the client's lead
5. Low percentage of incidences in which the therapist introduced topics
6. High percentage of incidences in which patient introduced topics
7. Self-monitored homework
8. Self-directed therapy work
9. Nondirective and paradoxical work
10. Evocative, narrative work.

A directive therapist is one who asks closed questions, interprets, interrupts to maintain the topic, and confronts patient behavior. The nondirective therapist asks open question, is accepting of patient expressions, is patient, reflects emotions, follows the patient's lead, does not introduce new material, and allows the patient to generate the topics for discussion. This therapist may use paradoxical and evocative interventions, but time and patience are devoted to allowing patients to let their stories unfold.

The proficient and flexible therapist is one who can engage in either directive or nondirective interventions, depending on which is called for, and can move smoothly and seamlessly between the extremes of being an authority and being a peer. The proficient therapist is skilled in assessing patient needs and in creating an environment that evokes rather than makes changes occur. Accordingly, each of the foregoing items may be rated for frequency, skill, smoothness, and flexibility by external raters. Moreover, the level of directiveness can be cross-tabulated against measures of patient resistance to derive an index of treatment compatibility.

Chapter 8

Adapting Therapy to Patient Level of Distress and Impairment

Strong emotions have motivational properties. As we have noted previously, some people are stimulation seekers, attempting to induce certain emotional states either out of boredom or out of a need to affirm their existence, whereas others attempt to reduce these states, finding them undesirable and uncomfortable. Psychotherapy patients usually seek treatment to reduce the intensity of painful emotional states. Yet, if emotional levels are too low, one loses the incentive to change and work in treatment to make things different. Thus, the management of emotional intensity or distress is a central process in most psychotherapeutic endeavors (Orlinsky et al., 1994; Frank & Frank, 1991).

Because of the importance of emotions both to the development of human problems and to their resolution, theorists make fine distinctions among varieties of experience. They distinguish among such feelings as rage, anger, frustration, and irritation, as well as among depression, dysphoria, unhappiness, and distress. But, in spite of the efforts made to distinguish among these experiences, the nature of emotions and the procedures used for their management in psychotherapy and even the issue of whether emotions should be the targets for direct or indirect change remain points of controversy and confusion.

The therapist works with emotions from three different perspectives. First, the therapist distinguishes among emotions of different types and identifies the particular emotion or emotions that are most problematic for a given patient. Second, the therapist identifies how distressing or intense the problematic emotions are and determines whether they are contributing to the patients efforts to change or, alternatively, interfering with the concentra-

The authors wish to thank Lisa Firestone, Ph.D. for her assistance on parts of this chapter.

tion and focus the patient needs to change. Third, the therapist identifies whether the problematic emotions are situational reactions or enduring traits.

The specific identity of the problematic emotions are used to assess outcomes of treatment. Thus, the questions asked at the end of treatment are how much change has occurred in the patient's feelings of being sad, depressed, angry, or fearful. The intensity of the emotions are compared to that present at the beginning of treatment in order to assess change, and a determination is made as to whether the emotions are now within the range expected to be characteristic of nonpatient populations (i.e., whether the feelings are of normal intensity).

In one way, the decisions arising from an assessment of emotional experiences overlap with those made on the basis of an assessment of the patient's coping style. If an emotion is a momentary reaction that coincides to a definable external situation, the therapist knows to work with procedures that alter the situation or environment. If the emotion is enduring and cuts across situations, the therapist knows to work with the internal processes of the patient, such as expectations, schematic constructs, and the like. However, the role of emotional intensity goes beyond this consideration to address the problem of treatment motivation. Accordingly, it directs the therapist in the selection of strategies that either increase or decrease affective arousal in order to maintain a level that motivates change but is not so intense as to disrupt perception and judgment.

Varieties of Emotional Experience

It is conventional to distinguish among different types of emotions. Research suggests that six (love, joy, fear, sadness, surprise, and anger) primary emotions can be reliably differentiated even in young children and across cultures (Fridlund, 1994; Greenberg & Korman, 1993; Greenberg & Safran, 1987). Both positive and negative emotions are represented in this catalogue of emotional qualities. Complex emotions arise both from combining these primary emotions and applying culture-specific labels and expectations to describe and direct their expression. Together, these forces result in a variety of differences in how emotions of any type are expressed and described (frustration, hurt, resentment, depression, anxiety, etc.). Because complex emotions are more difficult than primary ones to identify reliably, it is helpful first to identify the primary emotions that most often and most characteristically are expressed in problematic ways in the patient's interpersonal life.

In psychopathological descriptions, the classical diagnostic system relies heavily on the assumption that emotions are qualitatively distinct from one another. For example, the diagnostic distinctions between mood and anxiety disorders illustrate the assumption that there are qualitative distinctions in these emotional experiences. In addition, the diagnostic system also recognizes distinctions in severity or intensity of various emotional states. Thus, not only are anxiety and depression differentiated from one another, qualitatively, but each is seen as varying along a continuum of severity and disruption.

Most standardized psychological tests attempt to tap differences in intensity and disturbance associated with the level of emotions being expressed. The assessment of intensity in psychological tests is generally a more reliable measure than are qualitative distinctions among complex emotions. Differentiations among types of emotions are usually weak and inaccurate, even though clinicians frequently believe in these distinctions quite firmly. The fuzziness of these distinctions, especially between anxiety and depression, persists even when standard psychological tests are used as the basis for their definition. While self-reports can differentiate among global, primary emotions, such as depression, anxiety, and anger, there is a high degree of overlap among these emotions and even more so when the emotions being assessed are complex composites of a variety of primary emotions. Research indicates that the most reliable and valid distinctions are made between positive and negative affectivity. There is less agreement in the distinctions made within each of these categories, such as sadness, fear, and anger, and still less agreement when one attempts to distinguish among varieties of fear, anger, and so on. When negative emotionality is high, the ability of a clinician to differentiate among specific emotional qualities is generally lost altogether (Coyne, 1994; Gotlib, 1993).

The determination of whether an emotion is state-like or trait-like is related to how pathological and disturbed the patient will be judged to be. Emotions that are judged to be enduring or trait-like are generally seen as more indicative of psychopathology than those that are seen as situational or reactive. Trait-like emotions are seen as chronic, enduring aspects of one's behavior, and as being less easily changed than state-like emotions. Thus, chronic depression (dysthymic disorder or depression with melancholia) is seen as more serious and less treatable than reactive or situational depressions; pathological grief is distinguished from normal, situationally induced grief by its durability; and a prolonged reaction to traumatic events is accorded a more serious diagnosis (e.g., posttraumatic stress disorder) and more negative prognosis than the immediate affectivity noted in acute stress disorder. Thus, the persistence of intense distress (dysphoria) and the chronic absence of emotions (i.e., anhedonia or apathy) are associated with severe anxiety disorders, personality disorders, and thought disorders—those conditions that are most difficult to treat.

In contrast to the pathognomic nature ascribed to persistent emotional traits, acute negative emotions are seen as indicating that one has a good prognosis. These situationally acute emotional reactions are thought to signal the presence of patient motivation to undergo therapeutic change (e.g., Frank & Frank, 1991). Thus, state-like emotional reactions are particularly important in treatment planning. Their level may serve as indicators for the use of specific interventions that either raise or lower emotional discomfort and for procedures that increase one's motivation for change.

Ultimately, the presence of emotional pain (intense fear, sadness, and anger) that brings and holds people in treatment and the quality or type of emotional experience may direct the topic of psychotherapy interviews. The way to address emotions in psychotherapy is a frequent point of disagreement among theorists and even between therapists and patients. If one keeps in mind the different roles played by chronic and acute emotions, respectively defining the level of psychological impairment and signaling the presence of motivation for change, a therapist can make differential decisions about treatment. Patients are generally most highly motivated to change persistent and intense emotions, whereas therapists often seek to ensure the presence of at least some acute distress in order to maintain patient motivation for change. The therapist is often loath to remove distress too quickly for fear of negatively affecting the patient's investment in treatment. It is commonly assumed, though usually implicitly rather than explicitly stated, that there is a window of optimal distress or tone that must be maintained for treatment to progress well (Frank & Frank, 1991).

Guiding Principles

Qualitative distinctions among emotions are necessary for directing the focus of interventions. In PT, the intensity of trait-like emotions is used in assessing outcomes and determining the intensity of the prescribed treatment. Emotional states, on the other hand, are used to determine whether the treatment sessions themselves will address emotional control or will attempt to facilitate emotional discharge and abreaction. To do this, the PT practitioner must be attentive both to the moderately reactive emotional pain that characterizes the patient's activities outside the therapy hour and to the moment-to-moment variations in emotional state that characterize the patient's response within the therapy hour. The guiding principles governing therapist decisions are as follows:

1. The likelihood of therapeutic change is greatest when the patient§ level of emotional stress is moderate, neither being excessively high nor excessively low.

All therapeutic schools identify procedures that confront and procedures that support or structure. Providing structure and support as well as behavioral and cognitive stress management procedures can reduce immediate levels of disruptive emotion, whereas confrontational, experiential, and open-ended or unstructured procedures tend to increase arousal.

2. Therapeutic change is greatest when a patient is stimulated to emotional arousal in a safe environment until problematic responses diminish or extinguish.

This latter principle is the simple principle of exposure and extinction. Its activation can be through repeated interpretation of a consistent dynamic theme or through in vivo exposure training, again depending on a therapist's proclivities and the way that the other principles are being addressed.

These principles must be taken within the context of the previously discussed principles, particularly the principle of exposure. Principle 2, in this chapter, reiterates the view that therapeutic change is greatest when a patient is exposed to distressing events in the absence of expected negative consequences. Reiterating the importance of this principle is meant to emphasize the multiple roles of exposure in the process of initiating corrective change and underlies the different roles played by state-like (motivational) and trait-like (pathology) markers of distress.

Indexing Cues

The level of patient distress is both a state-like quality that arises within sessions and a trait-like quality that characterizes and impairs patient functioning. Therefore, the therapist must be able to recognize the nature of the emotion as well as the signs of distress and negative affectivity that are indicative of at least three positions along the trait-to-state dimension. At the most trait-like extreme, the initial evaluation provides information about diagnosis, severity of impairment, and chronicity of emotional distress. These indices are available for therapist review, and the measures of diagnostic symptoms and impairment serve as measures of change and improvement.

Moderately reactive distress can be assessed both by standard psychological tests and by observing interpersonal behaviors. The State-Trait Anxiety Scale (STAI-State; Spielberger et al., 1983), for example, provides an estimate of reactive distress and can be administered before each treatment session. In our research, and because we have not yet developed a precise, predictive value statistically, we use one standard deviation on either side of the normative mean of the STAI to identify the point at which patient distress should be a focus of efforts to increase or decrease it.

In addition, it is important that the therapist learn to recognize verbal tone and nonverbal behaviors as indicating level of distress and unhappiness. The

TABLE 8.1. Ratings of Distress

Clinician Ratings

1. Has a low energy level
2. Is apathetic
3. Affect is flat or blunted
4. Has many symptoms of emotional distress
5. Is anxious
6. Worries a lot
7. Overreacts to disappointments and discouragement
8. Usually expects the worst
9. Is often fearful or frightened
10. Worries about little decisions
11. Is content and satisfied
12. Has difficulty concentrating
13. Has an unsteady or shaky voice
14. Conveys strong or intense feelings
15. Seems to take things very seriously
17. Is stoic and unexpressive
18. Reacts to stressful events with little indication of feeling distress

Estimated Patient Reports

1. I feel anxious or unhappy a lot of the time
2. The future seems very uncertain to me.
3. I don't expect things to get much better in the future.
4. I worry more than most people.
5. I am as likely to achieve my goals in life as most people are.
6. I often feel nervous or anxious even when things are going okay.
7. I have more headaches or stomach pains than most people.
8. I feel faint and dizzy more often than most people.
9. I seem to have more problems than most people.
10. I get distressed more often or easier than most people.
11. I find it harder to make decisions than other people do.
12. I often feel like crying.

Self-esteem

1. Overly self-critical
2. Feels guilty or unworthy most of the time
3. Feels self-dislike or self-hatred
4. Feels inadequate most of the time
5. Has little energy to do things
6. Feels unhappy or sad
7. Feels hopeless and ineffective

8. Believes he or she is worthless or "bad"
9. Has trouble trusting his or her own decisions
10. Has excessive expectations of personal performance
11. Does not feel able to master new tasks

STS Clinician Rating Form provides a means of summarizing clinician impressions about patient behaviors that indicate level of distress. This information is summarized at the end of each treatment session by way of a series of questionnaires (Table 8.1) that allow the therapist to make a qualitative judgment of whether it is "too high" to "too low." The questions require the therapist to rate the presence of distress cues in each of three areas: (1) clinical indicators, (2) estimated patient self-report, and (3) self-esteem.

At the most state-like or reactive level, momentary changes in emotional tone can be assessed directly by asking the patient to attend to internal states and behavioral cues of distress and discomfort. The recognition of variations in these emotional qualities among patients is important for defining the content of therapeutic interventions, associated with the major themes that arise in psychotherapy. The pervasiveness of basic or primary emotions in the psychotherapy session can be identified with reasonable reliability. The revised Client Emotional Arousal Scale (CEAS-R; Daldrup et al., 1988; Machado, Beutler, & Greenberg, 1999) is included in Appendix C and is a rating scale for helping therapists identify (1) the major emotions issue for the patient in psychotherapy, (2) their modal intensity during psychotherapy, and (3) their maximal or peak intensities during the session. Like the STS Clinician Rating Form, this instrument may serve as an aid to the therapist in identifying the dominant expression of emotions within the treatment session.

At this level of emotional recognition, the therapist must often ignore the more enduring aspects of depression and anxiety in order to attend to the intensity of state-like indicators of emotional experience. Movement, facial expression, vocal dysfluency (e.g., stuttering), and verbal speed all serve as indices of the level of immediate states of distress. Level of subjective distress affects a patient's speed and frequency of hand, leg, and upper-body movements; the tightness of facial muscles; stuttering and disjointed speech; and rapid, pressured, or unusual speech patterns. Table 8.2 provides a nonverbal behavior rating scale from which level of distress has been reliably rated (Burgoon, Le Poire, Beutler, Bergans & Engle, 1989). This form can be used to help identify and cross-check patient estimates of immediate distress provided by the patient.

At times prosaic and vocal (nonverbal) cues are inconsistent with the content of patient verbal reports of subjective distress. When such inconsistencies occur, the nonverbal patterns of behavior are thought to be more accurate and valid indices of internal states than verbal acknowledgments because they are less susceptible to conscious efforts to deny and distort them. Thus, to note such discrepancies, the therapist must be able to separately observe speech content and nonverbal behaviors from time to time in order to determine whether the communication is reliable and valid.

Strategies for Adapting Treatment to Patient Level of Emotional Arousal

While stated in different ways, the principles of change that are reliant on level of patient distress are translated into a strategy of selecting and managing the use of supportive structure and confrontation/exposure. Specifically, we may state these strategies as follows:

1. The peak intensity of emotions expressed by the patient during therapy sessions should be moderately high, with some expressions of both moderately intense arousal and relaxation.

TABLE 8.2. Nonverbal Rating Scale

Subject # _____

Subject position on monitor: top/bottom/full screen
(Left side of screen) 1 2 3 4 5 6 7 8 (Right side)

1   OVERALL AROUSAL

Still	7	6	5	4	3	2	1	Restless
Cool	7	6	5	4	3	2	1	Bothered
Calm	7	6	5	4	3	2	1	Anxious
Composed	7	6	5	4	3	2	1	Uncomposed

NONVERBAL AND VERBAL MEASURES

Congruent	7	6	5	4	3	2	1	Incongruent
Synchronized	7	6	5	4	3	2	1	Nonsynchronized

2   KINESIC BEHAVIORS

Nodding

Frequent	7	6	5	4	3	2	1	None

Smiling

Frequent	7	6	5	4	3	2	1	None
Appropriate	7	6	5	4	3	2	1	Inappropriate

Facial Expression

Frequent	7	6	5	4	3	2	1	None

Random Head Movement

Frequent	7	6	5	4	3	2	1	None

Random Trunk and Limb Movements

Frequent	7	6	5	4	3	2	1	None

Random Trunk and Limb Movements

Frequent	7	6	5	4	3	2	1	None

Self Adaptors

Frequent	7	6	5	4	3	2	1	None

VOCALIC BEHAVIORS

Relaxed	7	6	5	4	3	2	1	Tense
Cool	7	6	5	4	3	2	1	Bothered
Rhythmic	7	6	5	4	3	2	1	Jerky
Composed	7	6	5	4	3	2	1	Uncomposed
Resonant	7	6	5	4	3	2	1	Flat

Nervous Vocalizations and Nervous Laughter

Frequent	7	6	5	4	3	2	1	None

Relaxed Laughter

Frequent	7	6	5	4	3	2	1	None

Fluency

Frequent	7	6	5	4	3	2	1	None

2. Among apathetic patients, the therapist attempts to induce arousal and raise levels of distress to a sufficient level as to provoke motivation to seek a change in one§ behvior.
3. Among patients whose emotions are consistently high, the therapist attempts to reduce levels of present and current distress and arousal to levels that do not interfere with concentration and planning.

The direct alleviation of distress is fostered by the application of the principle of exposure. Among patients whose motivation is not so excessive as to interfere with the acquisition of new understandings or behaviors, the therapist may attempt to repeatedly expose the patient to one of two basic kinds of experiences, depending on their preferred coping style. For patients who present internalizing coping styles, presenting and raising distressing thoughts, images of past events, or unwanted feelings are the strategies of choice. In contrast, among patients who present with external coping styles, the strategy of choice is to present them with unwanted external consequences (e.g., external control, feared events) or avoided behavior (e.g., phobic objects), and holding the intensity of the resulting affect at a level of moderate discomfort until dissipation occurs.

In determining whether to attempt to increase or decrease the patient's emotional state, we recommend that the therapist keep in mind the three levels of emotional reactivity discussed in the preceding section: chronic, moderately reactive, and immediately reactive. The therapist should attempt to identify the levels of distress suggested in each of these domains. Patients with dominantly high-intensity, trait-like emotions should be considered for longer-term treatment. Recommendations for further treatment may hinge on the assessment of these dominant, negative (sadness/depression, fear/anxiety, and anger/hostile), and enduring emotional traits.

Regardless of the importance of emotional traits for setting the intensity of planned treatment, work within the treatment session will rely more heavily on state-like reactions. For within-session work, a priority should be established with the most immediate state-like distress indices taking precedence over less reactive and less immediate indicators of discomfort in guiding these decisions. Thus, indications of either high levels of distress or of apathy that are evident within the immediate session will be given precedence in determining whether to confront the patient or to provide support. If one cannot gain a clear picture of these immediate, in-session reactions, the therapist should rely on the formal tests of distressed state, using established psychological measures such as the STAI. When immediate behavioral cues or formal state measures of presession distress are not available, the therapist should look to indications of more trait-like measures to determine how treatment should be managed.

The essential strategies for managing subjective distress in psychotherapy are to implement procedures that confront patients with avoided experience when their state-like levels of distress are low and to provide support and structure when these levels are high. The challenge is to keep the level of immediate or state-like distress within a range that will move the patient toward the treatment goals, neither so high as to drive them out of treatment nor so low as to induce disengagement. Usually this means using an approach-and-retreat procedure in which confrontation is alternated with support and ample assurance that the end of the session is sufficiently imbued with supportive care, enabling the patient to leave the session with a sense of comfort and relative peace.

Techniques and Procedures

To implement the strategy of lowering the discomfort of highly distressed individuals and raising the motivational distress of apathetic individuals, the therapist must have a range of techniques available. As a general rule, the procedures for reducing distress are better developed in psychotherapy than are the procedures for raising emotional tone and overcoming apathy. Thus, it is quite easy to work with people who are highly motivated for change but who may be unable to concentrate and attend to therapeutic material. In contrast, it is relatively more difficult to work with those whose distress is low, leaving them feeling no particular need either to change or to find value in a psychotherapeutic experience. Distress is lowered by instituting structure, offering reassurance, and using specific procedures for relaxing and reducing cognitive or muscular tension. Systematic relaxation, hypnosis, and self-instruction, for example, have been used successfully in behavioral management programs for individuals with high levels of discomfort.

Working with the Distressed Patient

When presession assessment and in-session observations reveal that state-like distress levels are high, the therapist should implement supportive, structuring, or relaxation procedures to reduce discomfort. Distress, including that associated with intense drug cravings and fantasies, that interfere with one's ability to concentrate and focus on relevant material within the therapy session or within the days immediately preceding requires the introduction of procedures that structure and control autonomic and psychophysiological responses.

CATHARTIC METHODS   Reducing high levels of reactive distress can be achieved by initially allowing the patient to ventilate. That is, many patients tend to feel better when allowed to express and unload the burden of unhappiness. Offering comforting and supportive comments, especially acknowledgments of the validity and worth of one's feelings and reflections of intense but often hidden feelings are usually helpful in providing immediate relief. One should be careful that ventilation is not taken to the point that the patient begins to become less organized and planful. Sometimes patients become overwhelmed by the intensity of their own emotions when ventilation becomes a goal in its own right. Thus, ventilation and cathartic methods should be accompanied by procedures that offer structure, support, and direction.

COGNITIVE VOICE WORK   Among the directed procedures for altering levels of distress, Firestone (1988) describes two uses of voice work. In the cathartic method, the patient is encouraged to intensify the internal voices. Sometimes these voices become intensely critical, hostile, and disorganized. Indeed, when this occurs, the procedure is often dramatic and induces abreactive experience. Because it produces more emotional intensity, this use of voice work will not be of great advantage for reducing distress among those patients who already feel out of control. The analytic or cognitive method of voice therapy is more appropriate (and therefore effective) for the task of reducing intense emotions among clients presenting with a high level of distress and/or low ego strength. The cognitive method of invoking the internal dialogue is an analytical approach in which the focus of work is on identifying tasks and changes that could be accomplished.

In this procedure, the therapist encourages the patient to select an area of needed change, plan a behavioral change procedure, and identify the tasks required to accomplish the behavioral goals. All these procedures require direct action on the part of the patient and may serve as both distractions and methods for training skills. The activity and structure provided by the therapist who is implementing these procedures offers support and structure that will allow the intensity of emotions to dissipate. For example, a client who is in an agitated state might find relief of the immediate symptoms of anxiety by using the cognitive method of unburdening and identifying voice alternatives together with some supportive, reassuring statements from the therapist.

COGNITIVE–BEHAVIORAL PROCEDURES   Behavioral procedures may be inserted to further the aims of providing structure to intensely distressed patients. For example, following a period of emotional release and expression, the patient might be invited to engage in a moment of directed relaxation. This relaxation exercise might be highly structured (in the case of compliant patients) or patient guided (in the case of highly resistant patients). Typically, such exercises involve focusing on breathing, with suggestions to breathe smoothly, deeply, and evenly while increasing one's sense of relaxation. Suggestions that a patient let go of fear and anticipatory, fearful thoughts may also be inserted, perhaps along with a pleasant visual image that is associated with relaxation. Further suggestions to lower muscle tension and become limp and relaxed may follow, again varying from the procedures of systematic tightening and releasing muscles to simply focusing on points of muscular or psychophysiological stress and then to relax. The selection among these procedures depends on the level of therapist-initiated structure that the patient is able to tolerate.

As the patient is able to relax, suggestions are often given to increase relaxation and to insert thoughts that emphasize and reinforce the patient's ability to cope ("I am relaxed and comfortable"; "I can control how I feel", "All I have to do is get through the moment", etc.). Formal hypnotic induction may or may not be used, but in either case, postrelaxation suggestions are often helpful (e.g., "You will find yourself able to use the tension associated with your anxiety as a cue for stopping, breathing, and becoming relaxed and comfortable").

Self-instruction is an additional aid to help the patient deal with distress. One method of activating such procedures is to help the patient identify external and internal cues that can be ordered to reflect escalating levels of distress. A stress control or escape behavior, ranging from taking a moment for relaxation to instituting self-seclusion to seeking help and contact from others (e.g., a sponsor) can then be identified for use at different points in this escalation process. Self-instructions may be inserted and practiced to script a method for patients to identify where in the escalation process they are and to talk themselves through the use of the various control strategies.

When the patient's level of distress is not (or is no longer) disrupting the focus and flow of the therapy session, the more extended cognitive assessment and correction procedures that we described in chapter 6 can be used to identify and correct the automatic thoughts and assumptions that underlie the excessive arousal. When disruptive thoughts are identified, new, rational alternatives can be elicited by questions and these new thoughts can be inserted and practiced to further reduce one's vulnerability outside of the therapy session.

The basic structure of using these procedures is first to identify the A-B-C relationship that precipitates or accompanies excessive arousal, to rate the extent of arousal and the extent of belief in the automatic thought, and then to question the assumptive beliefs. When these beliefs are analyzed and after they have been accepted as unrealistic or invalid by the patient, new and more realistic thoughts can be solicited for use in practice. These beliefs can be identified by a process of questioning that directs patients to consider what they might say or want said to them at these times of crisis, to provide correction. These alternatives are then rehearsed and practiced, with the therapist checking on the patient's state of distress as the thought is practiced. As the distress diminishes, it reinforces the use of these corrected thoughts. The thoughts may then be written down, taken home, and practiced by the patient as distressing situations arise.

Working with the Unmotivated Patient

The therapist who works with patients who have little emotional arousal or expression is faced with the problem of raising the level of distress, keeping it focused, and using it to mobilize the patient to action and change. Patient arousal is stimulated by procedures that confront and induce cognitive dissonance. Confrontational procedures, group interventions, and abreactive interventions are among the most frequently used procedures for overcoming patient apathy. The motivational interviewing techniques (Miller & Rollnick, 1991) used in substance abuse programs use group confrontation and feedback to stimulate distress and motivate change. The two-chair procedures used in experiential therapies (Daldrup et al., 1988), in contrast, are applied in either group or individual therapy and are designed to induce increased emotional sensitivity and awareness as a way of facilitating motivation and change.

If indices of presession anxiety/distress are below the point that sustains motivation and active work in the time between sessions, the therapist has to evoke emotions that can be used to motivate activity. The therapist can employ confrontation and other arousal induction procedures (experiential role-plays and imagery, etc.) to stimulate the patient. Among the procedures that are effective in raising distress are experiential techniques and cathartic voice procedures. The voice techniques both address schematic cognitive patterns and raise affective tone. These methods are appropriate to use with clients presenting with emotional distress ranging from low to moderate and who have sufficient ego strength to maintain their focus in the midst of strong emotions.

VOICE WORK   The cathartic voice procedures are aimed at encouraging critical inner voices to become strong and intense. Implementing cathartic expression requires that the patient become very active and involved with the internal voices that are self-defeating and abusive. It is important that patients are able to identify the critical internal voices that are present. With this ability, the therapist asks patients to state the voices aloud, as they hear them. Unlike the more cognitive and supportive methods of voice work, the therapist retracks patients and redirects their focus whenever they change the subject or fail to use second-person language. The therapist then allows the voice to unfold, periodically reminding patients to use the same words and intensity they hear when they engage in self-criticism.

To increase the intensity of the experience, the therapist may direct the patient to focus on a specific and highly loaded event of recent origin, construct a visual image that stimulates the voice's presence, and invite the patient to speak louder or more aggressively. More important, the therapist allows the patient to explore the voice or even to lapse into silence until the patient becomes more willing to express the voice in an intense manner.

EXPERIENTIAL PROCEDURES   Cathartic expression is often enhanced by the use of two-chair or one-chair procedures. In using these procedures, the therapist first asks the patient to engage in an experiment. Then the therapist and patient work together to identify either an internal conflict between the patient's wants or impulses or an external example of unfinished interpersonal business.

The two-chair procedure described and used in experiential therapies (e.g., Perls, 1969; Daldrup et al., 1988) is a particularly powerful tool for inducing awareness and facilitating emotional arousal. In this procedure, the patient identifies a person with whom he or she has struggled and talks to that person as if the person were in a chair opposite the patient. The dialogue is initiated and facilitated as the patient is asked to change roles several times while exploring things that he or she would like to say or fears saying to the other individual. A variant of the foregoing procedure is to identify two sides of an internal conflict experienced by the patient rather than two people in a relationship. The two sides of the conflict are engaged in a conversation or enticed into an argument. Again, the patient may be asked to change roles, from one side of the conflict to another, from time to time until there is some movement or resolution noted.

In all these procedures, the therapist attempts to facilitate and identify the content of those experiences and feelings that raise anxiety. These are interpreted or the patient is asked to provide his or her own interpretation. Usually, the interpretation and meaning assigned to the process are defined by working together with the patient so that both therapist and patient agree on its nature and relevance.

For example, the therapist may initiate a discussion between the warring parties by encouraging one party to express the feelings that have heretofore been hidden. Separate poles of the conflict are encouraged to respond and to conduct a dialogue about the tensions between them. Exaggeration of negative expression, frequent feedback on internal states, and imagination of feared events can intensify the emotional tone. The patient might be questioned about what occurrences would produce fear in a situation that has been identified as problematic, and then these events can be inserted into a fantasy presentation. Likewise, focusing on muscular sensations, urges, unexpressed feelings, and fears of the consequences, the therapist attempts to follow the thread of the patient's emotions through a chain of present and early memories that enhance arousal and activation.

GROUP METHODS   The use of group methods, including motivational interviewing interventions of Miller (Miller & Rollnick, 1991) and family confrontation, may also be helpful to arouse feelings of distress and overcome apathy. Group interventions can be particularly effective when the patient's self-view is different from the view that other people have of him or her. Group or family members are allowed to confront and provide feedback to the patient, identifying the fears and angry feelings that often serve as a barrier between the patient and significant others. The group confronts the patient with the significance of his or her problems and withdraws any activities that group members view as reinforcing or supporting the patient's behavior.

Even when treatment is conducted in an individual format, the therapist might suggest that the patient seek out information about how he or she is perceived by significant people in his or her life. If the patient is willing to talk about such perceptions to parents, friends, and other family members, it is likely that these perceptions will stimulate some confrontation and feedback that will rouse distress.

DIRECT EXPOSURE   Finally, the use of *in vivo* experience is frequently helpful in arousing emotions. Some patients with specific phobias manage to maintain surprising levels of apathy except when in a phobic situation. Direct exposure may be the only way to induce sufficient arousal to allow therapeutic progress for such patients. Similarly, patients with interpersonal or family problems, usually accompanied with denial and minimization of affect, may be observed and treated in situations that are known to cause the problems. By using such situations to confront the patient with how he or she is perceived by others, sufficient arousal may be obtained to advance the goals of treatment. One must be careful, however, because the use of such procedures may induce more arousal and distress than patients are willing to tolerate, driving them out of treatment. Again, the balance to be sought is a level of discomfort that supports movement but is not so extreme as to induce the patient to leave the situation.

Unfortunately, the task of raising arousal is often quite difficult and often requires a good deal of creative imagination in order to induce arousal. The therapist is encouraged to explore new methods and novel procedures for inducing arousal in these patients.

Assessing Therapist Skill in Adapting
Treatment to Patient Emotional Distress

Therapists are rated on a variety of scales to indicate their compliance with the principles and strategies of change. The STS Therapy Rating Form includes the following items that are completed by trained raters.

1. To what extent did the therapist attempt to deepen the client's contact with intense emotions?
2. Evaluate the extent to which the client's emotional state escalated during the session.
3. To what extent did the therapist encourage the client to discuss painful or emotionally charged material?
4. Rate the extent to which the therapist attempted to be supportive or reassuring.
5. How much did the therapist structure the session to reduce client's distress?
6. To what extent did the client's affect deescalate during the session?

Each of these items is rated for quantity or frequency. The level of therapist effort to induce emotional expression and intensity is cross-tabulated against therapist distress. A similar tabulation is made in a reciprocal fashion to indicate the use of emotional supportive and reassuring interventions. The cross-tabulation of these factors provides an indication of fit.

Chapter 9
Summary and Conclusions

Prescriptive therapy is an integrated intervention that adapts therapeutic procedures to fit specified patient qualities and characteristics. It is aimed at addressing complex problems such as comorbid substance abuse and depression, but the principles outlined are of general interest and application.

Prescriptive therapy training is a three-tiered system, beginning with the definition of general rules—what we define as treatment principles—and from these extrapolating differential treatment strategies and specific procedures and techniques. Accordingly, we began our description of PT with a review of the problems of applying single-theory formulations of mental health treatment to complex problems. We then reviewed findings that define patient qualities and characteristics that serve as moderators for the differential assignment of treatments. Systematic treatment selection (STS) is one of several models that extracts interventions from various approaches, integrates them, and applies them to patients based on fit. Prescriptive therapy derives from this type of selective process of decision making and cross-theory interventions.

The steps in applying PT began with the description of principles that guide the development and maintenance of the psychotherapy relationship and continued with the articulation of 10 general principles that guide the application of psychotherapy to specific patients, across theoretical orientation. We have focused on three particular matching dimensions and, accordingly, in each of the last four chapters we have identified a patient characteristic and a set of treatment strategies for adapting treatment to fit the status of a patient on one of these qualities. Specifically, we emphasized the role of patient impairment in orienting treatment intensity, the role of coping style in directing the focus of treatment, the role of resistance traits and states in determining the level of therapist directiveness and activity, and the role of patient distress in selecting interventions that increase activity and arousal levels or reduce subjective discomfort. In the case of patient distress, we emphasized the importance of selectively either reducing intense arousal through direct support and structure or increasing arousal by action, confrontation, and exposure.

Two of the ten overarching principles direct the development of the treatment relationship, one dictates the level of care, and seven of these cardinal principles of change can be used to guide the application of psychotherapeutic procedures. These principles facilitate the therapist's efforts to adapt each treatment plan to fit the unique pattern of characteristics of particular patients. These principles are as follows:

Relationship Principles

1. Therapeutic change is greatest when the therapist is skillful and provides trust, acceptance, acknowledgement, collaboration, and respect for the patient, within an environment that both supports risk and provides maximal safety.
2. Risk and retention are optimized if the patient is realistically informed about the probable length and effectiveness of the treatment, and has a clear understanding of the roles and activities that are expected of him or her during the course of treatment.

Principles of Level of Care

3. Benefit corresponds with treatment intensity among high functionally impaired patients.

Differential Treatment Principles

4. Therapeutic change is most likely when the patient is exposed to objects or targets of behavioral and emotional avoidance.
5. Therapeutic change is greatest when the relative balance of interventions either favors the use of skill building and symptom removal procedures among externalizing patients or favors the use of insight and relationship-focused procedures among internalizing patients.
6. Therapeutic change is most likely if the initial focus of change efforts is to build new skills and alter disruptive symptoms.
7. Therapeutic change is most likely when the therapeutic procedures do not evoke patient resistance.
8. Therapeutic change is greatest when the directiveness of the intervention is either inversely correspondent with the patient's current level of resistance or authoritatively prescribes a continuation of the symptomatic behavior.

9. The likelihood of therapeutic change is greatest when the patient's level of emotional stress is moderate, neither being excessively high nor excessively low.
10. Therapeutic change is greatest when a patient is stimulated to emotional arousal in a safe environment until problematic responses diminish or extinguish.

As a therapist attempts to apply these principles to real patients, it will be important to adapt and coordinate them with one another. The effective therapist must adapt not only to the patient's relationship expectations but to the patient's level of emotional intensity, defensiveness, and coping style as well.

Translated to the level of strategies, application of these 10 principles will (1) provide a safe and respectful environment; (2) expose the patient to a compatible balance of procedures that favor a focus either on the symptomatic expressions and skill deficits or to internal experiences that are avoided; (3) adopt either a predominantly directive or a nondirective role with the patient to lead him/her toward action and change; and (4) provide either support or confrontation and exposure to fit the patient's level of emotional distress. This is a complex process and requires that the therapist move flexibly among treatment procedures as the patient changes. For example, the therapist who adapts to the patient's emotional level must learn to differentiate among emotional traits that define the nature of patient problems or psychopathology and emotional states and those that define the focus and objectives of therapy. The therapist must also learn to differentiate among the qualitative differences that are associated with different emotions and to identify the level of emotional intensity or severity that is characteristic of the particular patient. This information is used to build a treatment program that is a complex interweaving of multiple responses to the many permutations that characterize patients.

A Case Example

B. K. is a 37-year-old white male. He reports having been depressed all of his life and has been using alcohol, cocaine, and heroine for the past 12 years. He currently uses heroine weekly and uses the other drugs on a daily basis. He has a college education and has been unsuccessfully employed in a variety of jobs. He is not married and has no close relationships. However, he does have a variety of rather superficial relationships with people with whom he does drugs. They provide him with most of his drugs and in return he does small jobs. He also plays music and begs for money.

B. K. has sought treatment on three other occasions but has never returned for a second treatment session. He has never been through detoxification, but on one occasion, he stopped taking heroine on his own for a period of nearly a year. He began using again after his girlfriend left him.

Recently, B. K. has become more involved with organized drug suppliers. These associations scare him, however. In the past few weeks he has had a persistent feeling that he was being followed and that undercover agents were watching him. He has also become very frightened that his drug supplier may be intending to do him harm. At the same time, he has some suicidal thoughts but no history of active suicidal behavior and no current intentions.

Functional Impairment

B. K. is currently living a marginal existence. He is isolated, has no contact with his family, and cannot identify a single individual to whom he can turn in case of serious trouble. He has been unable to sustain himself through independent work and he has lost friendships and resources because of his multiple impairments. He is seeking treatment because he has run out of other resources and his fears of being harmed have driven him to find some solution other than self-harm.

At intake, the clinician judges B. K. to have a moderate level of social impairment. This suggests the need to intensify treatment beyond the baseline expectation of once-a-week individual sessions. In consultation with the patient, a treatment plan is developed that includes three treatment sessions a week, supplemented by telephone calls, with the hope of decreasing the frequency of these sessions once drug abuse declines noticeably. The clinician also considers antidepressant medication and eventual group therapy to provide support. The patient is noncommittal about this form of treatment, as well as about the goal of becoming drug free. However, the therapist ultimately elects against using antidepressant medications, in fear that it will further weaken the patient's resolve to work toward developing a chemical-free lifestyle.

Coping Style

The patient has a history of both acting out, in the form of drug abuse and occasional brushes with the law, and depression and self-dejection. The MMPI-2 confirms the presence of mixed personality features. He has elevations on several internalizing scales, including the depression (D) subscale, social introversion (Si), and the anxiety (Pt) subscale. At the same time, he currently scores high on the paranoia (Pa) and impulse (Pd) scales. In general, the elevations favor an interpretation of externalization. The scores on the *STS Clinician Rating Form* confirmed this impression. Thus, the therapist directed attention throughout to the development of improved impulse control and social interaction skills, to the reduction of drug use, and to the minimization of exposure to high-risk situations.

The therapist elects to begin with a focus on the patient's medium- and long-term goals and initiates a discussion of how these goals are impeded by the specific behaviors of drug use and social withdrawal. As an effort to activate the patient toward longer-term, drug-free goals early in treatment, the therapist begins to encourage the patient to become involved in a 12-step program. The goal of this effort is as much to develop a social support network and to bring the patient to action as it is to control drug use.

The therapist also begins a process of weekly tracking the patients drug use (self-monitoring), cravings, and depression (using the BDI) and initiates procedures to inspect and alter the patient's unrealistic thoughts about his inability to overcome drug use. In this process, the therapist begins to identify social deficits, noting that the patient is seldom exposed to non–drug users. In the third session, social groups are identified in which the patient may find peers who do not use drugs. Role-playing exercises related to entering new groups and making acquantainces are initiated in the next session. Only when drug use declines to once a week and social contact has increased in non–drug-using contexts does the therapist begin to raise for consideration the patient's concerns that he is being followed and that others intend him harm. These beliefs are presented and approached in a cognitive framework, inspecting the automatic thoughts and evaluating the level of distortion. Only in the final stages of therapy does the therapist move to a consideration of the schemas represented in these automatic thoughts.

Resistance Level

From the beginning, B. K. seemed cooperative and motivated, even if only out of fear. This observation bodes well for the development of a good working relationship. Indeed, the therapist's efforts to provide reassurance and direction were well received and bolstered the quality of the working alliance.

The therapist was initially uncertain about how much to trust the initial and overt appearance of cooperation, fearing that the patient could not or would not sustain this initial level of cooperation. Thus, he provided a challenge to help assess the depth of this resolve. He provided the patient with a homework task, asking him to both track his drug use and to make one new friend who is not a drug user. The patient complied with the first part of the task and made an effort to introduce himself to a neighbor, only to find out that the latter individual was a heavy cocaine abuser. But, the patient's level of compliance with this difficult initial assignment convinced the therapist that the patient could be described as moderate to low resistant, an assessment that opened the door to the use of direct teaching and instructional techniques to help the patient to address his symptomatic problems.

Subjective Distress

The patient initially appeared anxious and acutely frightened. He scored a 28 on the BDI and earned a score more than 2 standard deviations above the mean on the state portion of the STAI, confirming his anxious state. The therapist used these scores to remind himself to provide some reassurance during each session, to acknowledge even small gains, and to reinforce all efforts that the patient made that showed the ability to make decisions and to control himself.

The therapist worked to provide some structure to reduce the patient's anxiety, and this helped to cement the treatment relationship. With a little time, the patient's distress subsided somewhat and allowed the therapist to devote more time to developing the relationship and urging a change in behaviors.

Assessing Therapist Compliance with PT Principles

Two methods were used in the foregoing case to help the therapist become self-observing in evaluating whether he was providing the most optimal balance of treatment ingredients. The therapist was encouraged to audiotape each session and to review it on his own, using the STS Therapy Process Scale to evaluate the frequency of using various classes of therapeutic strategies. He checked the relative levels of task/symptom-oriented procedures to insight and awareness-oriented ones, and rated his use of supportive versus confrontational procedures. The dimensions of treatment as reflected in scores on this scale have been presented throughout this manual, but the scale itself is reproduced in its entirety in appendix A to summarize the various treatment components. It assesses the degree of directiveness, task and symptomatic focus, insight focus, confrontation, and emotional intensity of the session. It also provides information on aspects of therapist behavior and engagement, including an evaluation of the quality of the therapeutic alliance.

The STS Therapy Process Scale is quite time-consuming, and it could not be completed after each session. Thus, in addition, a briefer measure, one that focuses on the level of compliance with the 10 principles around which PT is organized, was incorporated into the supervision process. Appedix B, following this chapter, presents the *PT Adherense Scale*, and it provides a series of Likert scales by which to summarize the degree to which the therapist was following the intended plan. Using this scale, a therapist can assure him or herself that he is in general compliance with the intended balance of interventions. In the foregoing example of B. K., it provided a reminder to (1) maintain a moderately intensive frequency of treatment sessions; (2) focus on changing symptoms of drug use and depression and enhancing skills to overcome social isolation; (3) provide structure and direction; and (4) continually monitor moment-to-moment distress levels in order to alter the interventions to either confront the patient with his reluctance to change or to provide support, structure, and acknowledgment.

Assessing General Therapist Skill

The therapist attempts to integrate the various aspects of intervention in a smooth and seamless way. The STS Therapy Process Scale includes assessments of overall as well as specific skill, in addition to the more specific dimensions of care embodied in the STS model. Thus, the following items (see appendix A) are designed to tap therapist skill and are rated by trained experts from direct observations. The rating scales themselves require the selection of responses along a continuum of agreement—strongly agree to strongly disagree.

1. The therapist makes accurate and/or meaningful interventions during the session.
2. The therapist accurately reflects the client's feelings during the session.
3. The therapist appropriately times techniques and interventions during the session.
4. The therapist smoothly and effectively employs techniques and/or interventions.
5. The therapist presents him- or herself in a professional and competent manner.
6. The therapist speaks clearly and concisely during the session.
7. The therapist presents him- or herself as being knowledgeable.
8. The therapist is able to attune to the patient's feelings.
9. The therapist effectively and smoothly facilitates closure of the session.

The results of these ratings should be considered along with the specific skill ratings that we have reviewed in chapters 4 through 8. These latter ratings indicate the degree to which the therapist adequately adapts treatment to patient needs. Measures of skill, together with the assessment of compliance derived from comparing responses to the STS Therapy Process Scale to the patient dimensions extracted from the STS Clinician Rating Form, or from the application of the more general PT Therapy Adherence Form, provide the therapist with a means of assessing his or her level of overall expertise.

Final Observations

We have seen in the foregoing example how the basic principles of treatment can be translated into a set of more specific strategies (activate social involvement, invoke the *in vivo* environment, etc.), and from there to the selection of particular techniques (behavioral charting, *in vivo* exposure, etc.). Although the level of this analysis is increasingly specific, in practice, it is important to maintain a high degree of flexibility in the use of specific techniques. Procedures and techniques have different properties depending on who is using them and how they are introduced. Thus, while the principles are sound and relatively inviolate, the selection of specific procedures will depend on the experience and familiarity of the therapist who uses them, as well as on the therapist's skill level with various procedures. The therapist should feel free to use the techniques that best fit his or her own preferences and backgrounds, wthin the constraints imposed by the guiding principles.

The therapist should remember that the level and frequency of using any set of principles is a dimension, not a simple, categorical, "do" or "don't do" decision. For example, a depressed patient who is moderately impaired, characterized by the use of externalizing coping styles, is highly resistant, and is highly distressed can be treated by a variety of procedures, but the preponderance of them should (1) provide close monitoring and frequent contact—this is favored over less frequent contact because of the patient's level of impairment; (2) be interventions that directly alter cognitions, build social activation skills, and confront social fears—these will be emphasized over insight-oriented procedures because the patient is impulsive and externalized; (3) be nondirective, self-directed, and evocative in nature—these will be emphasized over directive ones because of the resistant nature of the patient; and (4) be directed specifically to control and reduce in-session distress—these will be emphasized over abreactive interventions because the patient is highly distressed.

These strategic decisions may be activated in a variety of ways. The therapist might address specific symptoms of drug abuse by establishing contingent self-directed reporting and recording procedures, through collaborative behavioral contracting, or by a self-guided reading program. These nondirective and self-guided interventions may allow the patient to monitor emotions and keep the processes of emotional escalation in check. The creative skill of the therapist is the only limiting factor in the development of procedures that fit particular patient presentations and combinations of characteristics.

It is not only the patterning of interentions but the creative flexibility of the therapist's application that will both cement a strong working alliance and bring excitement to both parties with the prospect of change. We tend to believe that the therapist must be enthused and optimistic. Indeed, if the therapist is not enjoying him-or herself, the therapist may be doing something that is less than optimally helpful.

Appendix A: STS Therapy Process Rating Scale

Rater #1_____ Session#_____
Rater #2_____ Segment#_____
Subject # STS_____
Date_____

Watch videotaped session for 15 minutes and then make rating on these scales.

I. Directiveness

1. How often did the therapist ask closed questions during the session?

1	2	3	4	5
Never	A few times	Occasionally	Frequently	Very Frequently

2. How often did the therapist ask open-ended questions during the session?

1	2	3	4	5
Never	A few times	Occasionally	Frequently	Very Frequently

3. How often did the therapist make interpretations during the session?

1	2	3	4	5
Never	A few times	Occasionally	Frequently	Very Frequently

4. How often was the therapist confrontational during the session?

1	2	3	4	5
Never	A few times	Occasionally	Frequently	Very Frequently

5. How often did *the therapist* interpret the client's behavior towards him or herself and/or resistance during the session?

1	2	3	4	5
Never	A few times	Occasionally	Frequently	Very Frequently

6. The therapist passively accepts client's feelings and thoughts.

1	2	3	4	5
Strongly Disagree	Disagree	Marginally Agree	Agree	Agree Strongly

7. How often did the therapist provide reflections of the client's emotional states during the session?

1	2	3	4	5
Never	A few times	Occasionally	Frequently	Very Frequently

8. How often did the therapist provide information to or teach the client?

1	2	3	4	5
Never	A few times	Occasionally	Frequently	Very Frequently

9. What percentage of time did the therapist spend following the client?

1	2	3	4	5
Up to 20% of the time	Up to 40% of the time	Up to 60% of the time	Up to 80% of the time	Up to 100% of the time

10. What percentage of time were the topics discussed introduced by the therapist?

1	2	3	4	5
Up to 20% of the time	Up to 40% of the time	Up to 60% of the time	Up to 80% of the time	Up to 100% of the time

11. What percentage of time were the topics discussed introduced by the client?

1	2	3	4	5
Up to 20% of the time	Up to 40% of the time	Up to 60% of the time	Up to 80% of the time	Up to 100% of the time

II. Therapist Skill

12. The therapist makes accurate and/or meaningful interventions during the session.

1	2	3	4	5
Strongly Disagree	Disagree	Marginally Agree	Agree	Agree Strongly

13. The therapist accurately reflects the client's feelings during the session.

1	2	3	4	5
Strongly Disagree	Disagree	Marginally Agree	Agree	Agree Strongly

14. The therapist appropriately times techniques and interventions during the session.

1	2	3	4	5
Strongly Disagree	Disagree	Marginally Agree	Agree	Agree Strongly

15. The therapist smoothly and effectively employs techniques and/or interventions.

1	2	3	4	5
Strongly Disagree	Disagree	Marginally Agree	Agree	Agree Strongly

16. The therapist presents him/herself in a professional and competent manner.

1	2	3	4	5
Strongly Disagree	Disagree	Marginally Agree	Agree	Agree Strongly

17. The therapist speaks clearly and concisely during the session.

1	2	3	4	5
Strongly Disagree	Disagree	Marginally Agree	Agree	Agree Strongly

18. The therapist presents him/herself as being knowledgeable.

1	2	3	4	5
Strongly Disagree	Disagree	Marginally Agree	Agree	Agree Strongly

19. The therapist is able to attune to the patient's feelings.

1	2	3	4	5
Strongly Disagree	Disagree	Marginally Agree	Agree	Agree Strongly

20. The therapist effectively and smoothly facilitates closure of the session.

1	2	3	4	5
Strongly Disagree	Disagree	Marginally Agree	Agree	Agree Strongly

III. Emotional Arousal

21. To what extent did the therapist attempt to deepen the client's contact with intense emotions?

1	2	3	4	5
Not at all	A little	Some	Quite a bit	A lot

22. Evaluate the extent to which the client's emotional state escalated during the session.

1	2	3	4	5
Not at all	A little	Some	Quite a bit	A lot

23. To what extent did the therapist encourage the client to discuss painful or emotionally charged material?

1	2	3	4	5
Not at all	A little	Some	Quite a bit	A lot

24. Rate the extent to which the therapist attempted to be supportive or reassuring.

1	2	3	4	5
Not at all	A little	Some	Quite a bit	A lot

25. How much did the therapist structure the session to reduce client's distress?

1	2	3	4	5
Not at all	A little	Some	Quite a bit	A lot

26. To what extent did the client's affect de-escalate during the session?

1	2	3	4	5
Not at all	A little	Some	Quite a bit	A lot

27. The therapist redirected the client away from painful or emotionally charged material.

1	2	3	4	5
Not at all	A little	Some	Quite a bit	A lot

IV. Behavior vs. Insight Focus

28. Therapist focuses on client's identifiable, problematic behavior.

1	2	3	4	5
Not at all	A little	Some	Quite a bit	A lot

29. Therapist seeks to identify the rewards or payoffs for problematic behavior(s).

1	2	3	4	5
Not at all	A little	Some	Quite a bit	A lot

30. Therapist seeks to identify relationship between client's pattern of thoughts and actions.

1	2	3	4	5
Not at all	A little	Some	Quite a bit	A lot

31. Therapist employs techniques such as relaxation, contracting, systematic desensitization, and self-control methods to change behavior.

1	2	3	4	5
Not at all	A little	Some	Quite a bit	A lot

32. Therapist evaluates client's progress in terms of behavioral change.

1	2	3	4	5
Not at all	A little	Some	Quite a bit	A lot

33. Therapist seeks to identify recurring conflicts in interpersonal relationships.

1	2	3	4	5
Not at all	A little	Some	Quite a bit	A lot

34. Therapist employs techniques to increase client's self-understanding.

1	2	3	4	5
Not at all	A little	Some	Quite a bit	A lot

35. Therapist seeks to enhance client's understanding of his/her emotional experiences.

1	2	3	4	5
Not at all	A little	Some	Quite a bit	A lot

36. Therapist pursues discussion of early memories and/or events in the client's life.

1	2	3	4	5
Not at all	A little	Some	Quite a bit	A lot

37. Therapist tries to uncover early experiences and unconscious wishes.

1	2	3	4	5
Not at all	A little	Some	Quite a bit	A lot

38. Therapist Verbal Activity

1	2	3	4	5
Therapist Speaks up to 20% of the time	Therapist Speaks up to 40% of the time	Therapist Speaks up to 60% of the time	Therapist Speaks up to 80% of the time	Therapist Speaks up to 100% of the time

39. Degree of physical movement displayed by therapist:

1	2	3	4	5
Not at all	A little	Some	Quite a bit	A lot

40. Intensity of therapist verbal activity

1	2	3	4	5
Not at all	A little	Some	Quite a bit	A lot

41. Patient Verbal Activity

1	2	3	4	5
Patient Speaks up to 20% of the time	Patient Speaks up to 40% of the time	Patient Speaks up to 60% of the time	Patient Speaks up to 80% of the time	Patient Speaks up to 100% of the time

42. Degree of physical movement displayed by client:

1	2	3	4	5
Not at all	A little	Some	Quite a bit	A lot

43. Intensity of clients verbal activity

1	2	3	4	5
Not at all	A little	Some	Quite a bit	A lot

VII. Penn Therapist Facilitating Behaviors: Type 1 Alliance

44. The therapist is warm and supportive.

1	2	3	4	5	6	7	8	9	10
Very little or none		Some		Moderate amount			Much		Very much

45. The therapist conveys a sense of wanting the patient to achieve treatment goals.

1	2	3	4	5	6	7	8	9	10
Very little or none		Some		Moderate amount			Much		Very much

46. The therapist conveys a sense of hopefulness that treatment goals can be achieved.

1	2	3	4	5	6	7	8	9	10
Very little or none		Some		Moderate amount			Much		Very much

47. The therapist conveys a sense that he or she feels a rapport with the patient, that he or she understands the patient.

1	2	3	4	5	6	7	8	9	10
Very little or none		Some		Moderate amount			Much		Very much

48. The therapist conveys feelings of acceptance and respect for the patient as opposed to behavior in which the patient is put down (e.g., by jokes at the patient's expense).

1	2	3	4	5	6	7	8	9	10
Very little or none		Some		Moderate amount			Much		Very much

Type 2

Type 2 is working alliance based on the sense of working together in a joint struggle against what is impeding the patient. The emphasis is on shared responsibility for working out the treatment goals and on the patient's ability to do what the therapist does.

49. The therapist says things that show that he or she feels a "we" bond with the patient, that he or she feels a sense of alliance with the patient in the joint struggle against what is impeding the patient.

1	2	3	4	5	6	7	8	9	10
Very little or none		Some		Moderate amount			Much		Very much

50. The therapist conveys recognition of the patient's growing sense of being able to do what the therapist does (indicates needs to be done) in terms of the basic tools of the treatment (e.g., ability to introspect and analyze his or her own behavior).

1	2	3	4	5	6	7	8	9	10
Very little or none		Some		Moderate amount			Much		Very much

51. The therapist shows acceptance of the patient's increased ability to understand his or her own (the patient's) experiences.

1	2	3	4	5	6	7	8	9	10
Very little or none		Some		Moderate amount			Much		Very much

52. The therapist acknowledges and confirms the patient's accurate perceptions of him or her (the therapist).

1	2	3	4	5	6	7	8	9	10
Very little or none		Some		Moderate amount			Much		Very much

53. The therapist can accept the fact that the patient also can reflect on what the patient and he or she have through together, building up, as it were, a joint backlog of common experiences. (Referencs by the therapist to past patient-therapist exchanges sometimes may fit here).

1	2	3	4	5	6	7	8	9	10
Very little or none		Some		Moderate amount			Much		Very much

Appendix B: Prescriptive Therapy Adherence Scale

Patient ID#_____   Therapist_____   Rater_____
Session #_____   Date_____

Perscriptive Therapy Adherence Scale

Larry E. Beutler, Ph.D.

Prescriptive Therapy (PT) is governed by the application of 10 principles of effective treatment. Two of these Principles apply to establishing and maintaining a working and therapeutic relationship; one addresses the needed level of treatment intensity; and seven are designed to allow the therapist to tailor the in-session aspects of treatment to the individual patient. The first two principles should be rated in a general way, irrespective of the particular patient being seen. Adherence to many of the other principles, however, will require that one has certain information about the patient. Hence, completion of the PT Adherence Scale will require that there be an intake evaluation of some trait-like variables and that others be evaluated and considered before each session.

Thus, ratings of adherence require three steps: (1) identification of patient predisposing factors, (2) determining the phase of therapy, and (3) rating both the general and specific compliance of the therapist with the principles of PT.

Step 1: The *STS Clinician Rating Form* (STS) provides a means of assessing each of the four patient variables that determine how treatment will be conducted. This form will be completed after the first interview. The patient's status on the four variables should be summarized below here by reference to the relevant sections of the STS. Computation of scores on the STS are based on general patient norms.

Functional Impairment: (STS sum of sections I-A, I-B, I-C, & IV, Most recent rating)

High Impairment (Sum T $\geq$ 50)	Low Impairment (Sum T $<$ 50)

Coping Style: (STS ratio of sections V-A and V-B, At intake)

Internalizing (ratio $<$ 1)	Externalizing (ratio $\geq$ 1)

Resistance Traits: (STS weighted sum of section VI, Most recent rating)

High (T $\geq$ 68)	Moderate (T $<$ 68 & $>$ 32)	Mild or Low (T $<$ 32)

Subjective Distress: (STS sum of sections III-A, III-B, III-C or STAI This week)

Mild (Sum T $<$ 50)	High (Sum T $\geq$ 50)

Step 2: PT defines two stages of therapy. The first phase extends from the first treatment session until a clinically significant change has been made in the targeted symptoms. In order of priority, these are: (suicidal behavior, drug use, self-care functioning and work/school, overt symptoms of depression and anxiety, and subjective feelings). Change in the area defined as the highest relevant priority area indexes a movement to the second stage of treatment.

Stage of Treatment

Early Stage	Late Stage

Step 3: If the patient is still in the early stage of therapy, complete the ratings in both of the following sections. If the patient is in the late stage of therapy, complete only the portion pertaining to "General Ratings". Rate the compliance of the therapist to each of the principles by reference to the descriptors provided.

General Ratings

Relationship Principles

1. *Principle #1: Therapeutic change is greatest when the therapist successfully conveys trust, acceptance, acknowledgment, and respect for the patient and does so in an environment that both supports risk and provides maximal safety from criticism.*

Compliance with this principle requires that the therapist responds in a warm, accepting, and caring manner. The therapist should exhibit no defensiveness, should be able to listen, and should provide an atmosphere that is accepting and encouraging of expression.

How well did the therapist convey these attitudes during this session?

1	2	3	4	5	6	7
Very Poorly		Quite Poorly		Quite Well		Very Well

Principles of Level of Care

2. *Principle #3: Therapeutic change is most likely and maximal when the intensity of treatment is consistent with the patient's level of psychological and functional impairment.*

Generally patients with high impairment will be offered 25 sessions within a 20 week period. Patients with low impairment will be offered from 17 to 20 sessions in that 20 week period. Compliance with this principle requires that the therapist attend to the original contract which defined the number of treatment sessions offered and the period of time over which these sessions would occur. Now, there should be evidence that the therapist is working to keep the spacing and length of treatment within the agreed upon limits, and is spacing the sessions to meet the intensity requirements. The therapist should schedule appointments at a frequency that will ensure that the expected number of sessions will occur within the 20 week treatment period.

How well did the therapist schedule appointments to comply with the required degree of treatment intensity?

Level of Fit

1	2	3	4	5	6	7
Very Poorly		Quite Poorly		Quite Well		Very Well

Differential Treatment Principles

3. *Principle #5: Therapeutic change is most likely when the patient is exposed to the objects or targets of behavioral and emotional avoidance.*

Compliance with this principle in the early stage of treatment requires that the therapist help the patient identify *external* situations, people, places, or things that are avoided (e.g., avoiding social activities with non-drug users, avoiding stress associated with withdrawal, avoiding disapproval, etc.), and encouraging the patient to take risks by coming in contact with situations that are otherwise avoided (e.g., increasing social involvement, delaying drug use, applying for jobs, etc.). The therapist should help the patient plan small steps that gradually increase exposure and to evaluate the consequences of these graded efforts.

How well did the therapist keep the patient focused on becoming exposed to situations, places, people, or things that have been avoided?

1	2	3	4	5	6	7
Very Poorly		Quite Poorly		Quite Well		Very Well

4. *Principle #6: Therapeutic change is greatest when the internal or external focus of the selected interventions parallel the external or internal methods of avoidance that are characteristically used by the patient to cope with stressors.*

Internalizing patients should be confronted with internal experiences and feelings that are being avoided; externalizing patients should be confronted with external events and avoided behavior. The therapist's main efforts are to encourage the internalizing patient to *FEEL* and *BE AWARE* of their own anxiety, and to encourage the externalizing patient to *DO* things differently. The internalizing patient is also encouraged to discover the origin and conditions surrounding the feelings and symptoms.
Insight and awareness should be emphasized for this patient. In contrast, treatment of the externalizing patient emphasizes specific symptoms and

things to do and change. The preponderance of therapist work should be appropriate to these differential goals—Feeling versus Doing.

How well does the therapist behavior comply with this principle?

Level of Fit

1	2	3	4	5	6	7
Very Poorly		Quite Poorly		Quite Well		Very Well

5. *Principle #7: Therapeutic change is most likely when the therapeutic procedures do not evoke therapeutic resistance.*

Patient resistance is not always overt. Sometimes it is obvious through manner and voice, but other times it is only noticed by how he or she deals with the activities of therapy during the interceding week. Compliance with this principle is defined by how well the therapist either avoids resistance altogether or adapts to it when it occurs. It requires that the therapist remain calm, supportive, and objective, even if the patient becomes angry and defiant. Ideally, the patient will evidence no more than very mild levels of resistance and non-compliance with treatment demands, but if resistance does emerge, the therapist should not respond with anger, should not imply blame to the patient, and should avoid putting the patient on the defensive in any way. The therapist should be able to tolerate anger and being seen as wrong or ineffectual.

How well did the therapist avoid encountering patient resistance?

1	2	3	4	5	6	7
Very Poorly		Quite Poorly		Quite Well		Very Well

6. *Principle #8: Therapeutic change is greatest when the directiveness of the intervention is either inversely correspondent with the patient's current level of resistance or authoritatively prescribes a continuation of the symptomatic behavior.*

Compliance with this principle is defined by whether the therapist uses the procedures that best fit the level of defiance and resistance manifested by the patient. If the patient is oppositional and has very high levels of trait resistance, the therapist should demonstrate some effort to use paradoxical strategies such as prescribing the symptom, cautioning against change, or reframing the resistance as its opposite—cooperation. If the patient is not directly oppositional, though resistant, the therapist should respond with acceptance and with interventions that encourage the patient to feel more in control of what happens. The therapist should avoid direct guidance and making assignments. These things should be negotiated with the objective of getting the patient to set their own assignments and to find their own solutions. The patient's autonomy and power of self-direction should be reinforced and the therapist should avoid direct demands or generally, even direct suggestions. In contrast, for the low resistance patient, the therapist can provide guidance, set the agenda, and make homework assignments.

How well does the therapist adapt their level of directiveness to the patient's level of resistance?

Level of Fit

1	2	3	4	5	6	7
Very Poorly		Quite Poorly		Quite Well		Very Well

7. *Principle #9: The likelihood of therapeutic change is greatest when the patient's level of emotional stress is moderate, neither being excessively high nor excessively low.*

Compliance with this principle requires evidence that the therapist tries to adjust and maintain the patient in a state of mile to moderate anxiety during the session. If the patient becomes very anxious and distracted, unable to maintain a focus or chain of thought, or otherwise disjointed because of over-arousal, the therapist should provide support and reassurance. If the patient becomes apathetic, on the other hand, the therapist should rouse anxiety. Procedures such as confrontation, focusing on feelings, and experiments to arouse and engage the patient are examples of what might be done.

How well did the therapist keep the patient anxious enough to be motivated but not so anxious as to be inefficient?

1	2	3	4	5	6	7
Very Poorly		Quite Poorly		Quite Well		Very Well

8. *Principle #10: Therapeutic change is greatest when a patient is confronted with avoided behaviors and experiences to the point of raising emotional distress until problematic responses diminish or extinguish.*

Compliance with this principle requires that the therapist not only initiate a moderate level of arousal at key points during the session, but that the therapist work to maintain this level of arousal until it naturally dissipates. The therapist should not rescue the patient from his or her feelings prematurely and should tolerate and accept strong feelings expressed by the patient until they decline naturally.

How effectively did the therapist tolerate the patient's emotional expressions and allow it to dissipate without rescuing prematurely.

Level of Fit

1	2	3	4	5	6	7
Very Poorly		Quite Poorly		Quite Well		Very Well

Early Session Ratings (Before clinically meaningful change has been made)

Relationship Principles

1. *Principle #2: Therapeutic change is most likely when the patient is realistically informed about the probable length and effectiveness of the treatment and has a clear understanding of the roles and activities that are expected during the course of treatment.*

This principle emphasizes the importance of making and then keeping a contract with the patient. The therapist should show evidence of having made a contract or agreement with the patient about the length of treatment, the roles that each will assume, and the frequency and spacing of each session. The therapist should show evidence of keeping the patient appraised of the limits of confidentiality and the roles that are expected of both participants. This may include addressing homework, patient expectations, setting goals, or discussing blocks to achieving the patient's objectives. The therapist should answer questions related to the structure and nature of treatment, if asked and should not be evasive in doing so.

How well did the therapist keep the patient informed about what to expect?

1	2	3	4	5	6	7
Very		Quite		Quite		Very
Poorly		Poorly		Well		Well

Principles Applying to Level of Care

2. *Principel #3: Therapeutic change is most likely and maximal when the intensity of treatment is consistent with the patient's level of psychological and functional impairment.*

Generally patients with high impairment will be offered 25 sessions within a 20 week period. Patients with low impairment will be offered from 17 to 20 sessions in that 20 week period. Compliance with this principle requires that the therapist establish a contract that specifies how many sessions are to be offered and over what period of time. The therapist should schedule appointments at a frequency that will ensure that the expected number of sessions will occur within the 20 week treatment period.

How well did the therapist schedule appointments to comply with the required degree of treatment intensity

Level of Fit

1	2	3	4	5	6	7
Very		Quite		Quite		Very
Poorly		Poorly		Well		Well

Differential Treatment Principles

3. *Principle #4: Therapeutic change is most likely if the initial focus of change efforts is to alter disruptive symptoms.*

Compliance with this principle requires that the therapist address the patient's symptoms in each session. The therapist should not only inquire about the presence and frequency of the symptoms that have been targeted for change in the treatment contract, but should help the patient to identify specific ways that these symptoms can be changed. Homework assignments, in-session practice, and behavioral contracts are examples of ways that change may be changed, for example.

How effectively did the therapist address the symptoms of depression, suicidality, substance abuse, and other critical symptoms in this session?

1	2	3	4	5	6	7
Did Not Address		Quite Poorly		Quite Well		Very Well

Appendix C: Client's Emotional Arousal Scale

Client's Emotional Arousal Scale

Emotion:

Directions: Identify the emotion(s) presented by the client in the videotaped segment that you have just observed. If there is more than one emotion observed as present, please rank order them, e.g.: 1 for the primary or prevalent emotional state; 2, 3, for the others.

__fear   __joy/happiness   __sadness

__anger   __surprise   __disgust

__content   __hurt   __grief

Intensity:

Directions: For the following item make two ratings based only on the primary or prevalent emotion that you identified above:

1. Put an "M" above the number 1—7 indicating the client's response to the average or usual emotional experience as you observed it. This is the MODE rating.

2. Put a "P" above the number 1—7 indicating the client's response to the most intense expression of emotion as you observed it. This is the PEAK rating.

Do not use half numbers.

This is a measure of the intensity or strength of the emotional arousal. At one end, the rater can detect no emotional arousal in the voice body cues or verbal cues. At the other end of the scale, the voice, body, or language are intensely involved.

1............2............3............4............5............6............7

Client does not admit to any feelings. Voice, gestures or verbal content do not disclose any arousal	Client may admit to feelings but there is no overt emotional expression of emotion	Client expresses feelings but very little emotional arousal in voice, body or words	Client expresses feelings and sometimes allows the voice, body, gestures, or words to be involved	Client expresses feelings so that the voice, body or words are involved. Level of emotional arousal is moderately intense	Client expresses the feelings with fairly full arousal level. Still has a line that he/she will not cross	Arousal is full and intense. No sense of restriction. The person is focused, freely releasing, with voice, words, or physical movement an intense state of arousal

Client Emotional Arousal Scale—R

Segment #: _____

I.D.#: _____

Emotion:

Directions: Each of the six columns below is identified by a label—one of the primary or basic emotions: love, joy, surprise, anger, sadness, and fear. Below each of these basic emotions is a list of terms often used to describe them. This list is provided only to assist you in identifying which of the six primary emotions are presented by the patient in the videotaped segments of psychotherapy that you will be watching.

We would like you to identify the emotion(s) presented by the client in the videotaped segment that you have just observed. If there is more than one emotion observed as present, please rank order them, e.g.: 1 for the predominant or most prevalent emotional state, 2, 3, for the others. We are interested only in identifying the six basic emotions. However you can check as many words as you need to help you make your selection.

178

Love	Joy	Surprise	Anger	Sadness	Fear
adoration	amusement	amazement	aggravation	agony	alarm
affection	bliss	astonishment	irritation	suffering	shock
fondness	cheerfulness		agitation	hurt	fright
liking	gaiety		annoyance	anguish	horror
attraction	jolliness		grouchiness	depression	terror
caring	joviality		grumpiness	despair	panic
tenderness	delight		exasperation	hopelessness	hysteria
compassion	enjoyment		frustration	grief	anxiety
sentimentality	gladness		rage	sorrow	tenseness
desire	happiness		outrage	misery	uneasiness
lust	jubilation		fury	melancholy	apprehension
passion	satisfaction		wrath	dismay	worry
infatuation	ecstasy		hostility	disappointment	distress
longing	euphoria		ferocity	guilt	dread
	enthusiasm		bitterness	shame	
	excitement		hate	regret	
	thrill		dislike	remorse	
	exhilaration		resentment	loneliness	
	contentment		envy	homesickness	
	pleasure		jealousy	embarrassment	
	pride		torment	humilition	
	triumph			pity	
	eagerness				
	hope				
	optimism				
	relief				

Intensity:

Directions: For the following item make two ratings based only on the primary or prevalent emotion that you identified above:

  1. Put an "M" above the number 1—7 indicating the client's response to the average or usual emotional experience as you observed it. This is the MODE rating.

  2. Put a "P" above the number 1—7 indicating the client's response to the most intense expression of emotion as you observed it. This is the PEAK rating.

  Do not use half numbers.

This is a measure of the intensity or strength of the emotional arousal. At one end, the rater can detect no emotional arousal in the voice, body cues or verbal cues. At the other end of the scale, the voice, body, or language are intensely involved.

1..........2..........3..........4..........5..........6..........7

1	2	3	4	5	6	7
Client does not admit to any feelings. Voice, gestures or verbal content do not disclose any arousal	Client expresses feelings but there is no overt emotional arousal	Client expresses feelings but very little emotional arousal in voice, body or words	Client expresses feelings and sometimes allows the voice, body, gestures, or words to be involved	Client expresses feelings so that the voice, body or words are involved. Level of emotional arousal is moderately intense	Client expresses the feelings with fairly full arousal level. Still has a line that he/she will not cross	Arousal is full and intense. No sense of restriction. The person is focused, freely expressing, with voice, words, or physical movement an intense state of arousal

M _____
P _____

180

References

Abelson, H. I., & Miller, J. D. (1985). *A decade of truth of cocaine use in the household population* (National Institute on Drug Abuse Research Monograph No. 61). Washington, DC: U.S. Government Printing Office.

Almog, Y. J., Anglin, M. D., & Fisher, D. G. (1993). Alcohol and heroin use patterns of narcotic addicts: Gender and ethnic differences. *American Journal of Durg and Alcohol Abuse, 19,* 219–238.

Anderson, T., & Strupp, H. H. (1996). The ecology of psychotherapy research. *Journal of Consulting and Clinical Psychology, 64,* 776–782.

Barabander, C. S. (1993). Alcohol and drugs in the workplace. In S. L. A. Straussner (Ed.), *Clinical work with substance-abusing clients.* New York: Guilford Press.

Barrett-Lennard, G. T. (1972). Dimensions of therapist response as causal factors in therapeutic change. *Psychological Monographs, 76* (43, Whole No. 562).

Beck, A. T., Rush, A. J., Shaw, B. F., & Emery, G. (1979). *Cognitive therapy of depression.* New York: Guilford Press.

Beck, A. T., Steer, R. A., & Brown, G. K. (1996). *Manual for the Beck Depression Inventory—II.* San Antonio, TX: Psychological Corporation.

Beck, A. T., Wright, F. D., Newman, C. F., & Liese, B. S. (1993). *Cognitive therapy of substance abuse.* New York: Guilford Press.

Beitman, B. D. (1987). *The structure of individual psychotherapy.* New York: Guilford Press.

Beutler, L. E. (1979). Toward specific psychological therapies for specific conditions. *Journal of Consulting and Clinical Psychology, 47,* 882–897.

Beutler, L. E. (1989). Differential treatment selection: The role of diagnosis in psychotherapy. *Psychotherapy, 26,* 271–281.

Beutler, L. E. (1991). Have all won and must all have prizes? Revisiting Luborsky, et. al.'s verdict. *Journal of Consulting and Clinical Psychology, 59,* 226–232.

Beutler, L. E., & Berren, M. R. (1995). *Integrative assessment of adult personality.* New York: Guilford Press.

Beutler, L. E., Bongar, B., & Shurkin, J. C. (in press). *Am I crazy or is it my shrink?* New York: Oxford University Press.

Beutler, L. E., & Clarkin, J. F. (1990). *Systematic treatment selection: Toward targeted therapeutic interventions.* New York: Brunner/Mazel.

Beutler, L. E., Clarkin, J. F., & Bongar, B. (in press). *Systematic guidelines for treating the depressed patient.* New York: Oxford University Press.

Beutler, L. E., & Consoli, A. J. (1992). Systematic eclectic psychotherapy. In J. C. Norcross & M. R. Goldfried (Eds.), *Handbook of psychotherapy integration* (pp. 264–299). New York: Basic Books.

Beutler, L. E., Consoli, A. J., & Williams, R. E. (1995). Integrative and eclectic therapies in practice. In B. Bongar & L. E. Beutler (Eds.), *Comprehensive textbook of psychotherapy: Theory and practice* (pp. 274–292). New York: Oxford University Press.

Beutler, L. E., & Crago, M. (1983). Self-report instruments. In M. J. Lambert, E. R. Christensen, & S. DeJulio (Eds.), *The assessment of psychotherapy outcome* (pp. 453–497). New York: Wiley Interscience.

Beutler, L. E., Engle, D., Mohr, D., Daldrup, R. J., Bergan, J., Meredith, K., & Merry, W. (1991). Predictors of differential and self directed psychotherapeutic procedures. *Journal of Consulting and Clinical Psychology, 59,* 333–340.

Beutler, L. E., Goodrich, G., Fisher, D., & Williams, O. B. (1999). Use of psychological tests/instruments for treatment planning. In M. E. Maruish (Ed.), *The use of psychological tests for treatment planning and outcome assessment* (2nd ed.). (pp. 81–113). Hillsdale, NJ: Erlbaum.

Beutler, L. E., & Guest, P. D. (1989). The role of cognitive change in psychotherapy. In A. Freeman, K. M. Simon, L. E. Beutler, & H. Arkowitz (Eds.), *Comprehensive handbook of cognitive therapy,* (pp. 123–142), New York: Plenum.

Beutler, L. E., Machado, P. P. P., & Neufeldt, S. (1994). Therapist variables. In S. L. Garfield & A. E. Bergin (Eds.), *Handbook of psychotherapy and behavior change* (4th ed., pp. 259–269). New York: Wiley.

Beutler, L. E., & Mitchell, R. (1981). Psychotherapy outcome in depressed and impulsive patients as a function of analytic and experiential treatment procedures. *Psychiatry, 44,* 297–306.

Beutler, L. E., Mohr, D. C., Grawe, K., Engle, D., & MacDonald, R. (1991). Looking for differential effects: Cross-cultural predictors of differential psychotherapy efficacy. *Journal of Psychotherapy Integration, 1,* 121–142.

Beutler, L. E., & Williams, O. B. (1995, July/August). Computer applications for the selection of optimal psychosocial therapeutic interventions. *Behavioral Healthcare Tomorrow,* pp. 66–68.

Beutler, L. E., Williams, R. E., & Wakefield, P. J. (1993). Obstacles to disseminating applied psychological science. *Journal of Applied and Preventive Psychology, 2,* 53–58.

Beutler, L. E., Williams, R. E., Wakefield, P. J., & Entwistle, S. R. (1995). Bridging scientist and practitioner perspectives in clinical psychology. *American Psychologist, 50* (12), 984–994.

Browne, A. C. (1986). Drug and alcohol abuse among employees: Critical issues. *Employee Assistance Quarterly, 2,* 13–22.

Burgoon, J. K., Le Poire, B. A., Beutler, L. E., Bergan, J., & Engle, D. (1992). Nonverbal behaviors as indices to arousal: Extension to the psychotherapy context. *Journal of Nonverbal Behavior, 16,* 159–178.

Burns, D. D. (1992). *Feeling good: The new mood therapy.* New York: Avon Books.

Butcher, J. N. (1990). *The MMPI-2 in psychological treatment.* New York: Oxford University Press.

Calvert, S. J., Beutler, L. E., & Crago, M. (1988). Psychotherapy outcome as a function of therapist-patient matching on selected variables. *Journal of Social and Clinical Psychology, 6,* 104–117.

Carroll, K. M., Rounsaville, B. J., & Gawin, F. H. (1991). A comparative trial of psychotherapies for ambulatory cocaine abusers: Relapse prevention and interpersonal psychotherapy. *American Journal of Drug and Alcohol Abuse, 17,* 229–247.

Castro, J. (1993, May). What price mental health? *Time, 31,* 51–60

Chambless, D. L., Sanderson, W. C., Shoham, V., Johnson, S. B., Pope, K. S., Crits-Christoph, P., Baker, M., Johnson, B., Woody, S. R., Sue, S., Beutler, L. E., Williams, D. A., & McCurry, S. (1996). An update on empirically validated therapies. *The Clinical Psychologist, 49* (2), 5–14.

Christensen, A., & Jacobson, N. S. (1994). Who (or what) can do psychotherapy: The status and challenge of nonprofessional therapies. *Psychological Science, 5,* 8–14.

Costa, P. T., & Widiger, T. A. (1994). *Personality disorders: And the five factor model of personality.* Washington, DC: American Psychological Association.

Coyne, J. C. (1994). Self-reported distress: Analog or ersatz depression? *Psychological Bulletin, 116,* 29–45.

Dahlstrom, W. G., Welsh, G. S., & Dahlstrom, L. E. (1972). *An MMPI handbook: Vol 1. Clinical interpretation.* Minneapolis: University of Minnesota Press.

Daldrup, R. J., Beutler, L. E., Engle, D., & Greenberg, L. S. (1988). *Focused expressive psychotherapy: Freeing the overcontrolled patient.* New York: Guilford Press.

Derogatis, L. R. (1977). *The SCL-90 manual I: Scoring, administration, and procedures.* Johns Hopkins University School of Medicine, Clinical Psychometrics Unit.

Dobson, K. S., & Shaw, B. F. (1988). The use of treatment manuals in cognitive therapy: Experience and issues. *Journal of Consulting and Clinical Psychology, 56,* 673–680.

Dowd, E. T., Milne, C. R., & Wise, S. L. (1991). The Therapeutic Reactance Scale: A measure of psychological reactance. *Journal of Counseling and Development, 69,* 541–545.

Elkin, I. (1994). The NIMH treatment of depression collaboative research program: Where we began and where we are. In A. E. Bergin & S. L. Garfield (Eds.), *Handbook of psychotherapy and behavior change* (4th ed., pp. 114–139). New York: John Wiley & Sons.

Elkin, I., Shea, T., Watkins, J. T., Imber, S. D., Sotsky, S. M., Collins, J. F., Glass, D. R., Pilkonis, P. A., Leber, W. R., Docherty, J. P., Feister, S. J., & Parloff, M. B. (1989). National Institute of Mental Health treatment of depression collaborative research program. *Archives of General Psychiatry, 46,* 971–982.

Elliott, R. (1996, June). *Are client-centered/experiential therapies effective?* Paper presented at the annual meeting of the Society for Psychotherapy Research, Amelia Island, FL.

Firestone, R. W. (1986). The "inner voice" and suicide. *Psychotherapy, 23,* 439–447.

Firestone, R. W. (1988). *Voice therapy: A psychotherapeutic approach to self-destructive behavior.* New York: Human Sciences Press.

Forsyth, N. L., & Forsyth, D. R. (1982). Internality, controll ability, and the effectiveness of attributional interpretation in counseling. *Journal of Counseling Psychology, 29,* 140–150.

Frank, J. D., & Frank, J. B. (1991). *Persuasion and healing* (3rd ed). Baltimore: Johns Hopkins University Press.

Fridlund, A. J. (1994). *Human facial expression: An evolutionary view.* San Diego: Academic Press.

Garfield, S. L. (1980). *Psychotherapy: An eclectic approach.* New York: John Wiley & Sons.

Garfield, S. L. (1994). Research on client variables in psychotherapy. In A. E. Bergin & S. L. Garfield, (Eds.), *Handbook of psychotherapy and behavior change* (4th ed., pp. 190–228). New York: John Wiley & Sons.

Garfield, S. L., & Kurtz, R. (1977). A study of eclectic views. *Journal of Consulting and Clinical Psychology, 45,* 75–83.

Gaston, L. (1991). Reliability and criterion-related validity of the California Psychotherapy Alliance scales—Patient version. *Psychological Assessment, 3,* 68–74.

Gaston, L., Marmar, C., Thompson, L., & Gallagher, D. (1988). Relation of patient pretreatment characteristics to the therapeutic alliance in diverse psychotherapies. *Journal of Consulting and Clinical Psychology, 56,* 483–489.

Gaw, K. F., & Beutler, L. E. (1995). Integrating treatment recommendations. In L. E. Beutler & M. Berren (Eds.), *Integrative assessment of adult personality* (pp. 280–319). New York: Guilford Press.

Giles, T. R. (1993). *Managed mental health care: A guide to practitioners, employers, and hospital administrators.* Boston, MA: Allyn & Bacon.

Gotlib, I. H. (1993). Depressive disorders. In A. A. Bellack & M. Hersen (Eds.), *Psychopathology in adulthood.* (pp. 179–194). Boston: Allyn & Bacon.

Greenberg, L. S., & Korman, L. (1993). Assimilating emotion into psychotherapy integration. *Journal of Psychotherapy Integration, 3,* 249–265.

Greenberg, L. S., & Safran, J. (1987). *Emotion in psychotherapy*. New York: Guilford Press.

Groth-Marnat, G. (1997). *Handbook of psychological assessment* (3rd ed.). New York: John Wiley & Sons.

Gurman, A. S. (1977). Therapist and patient factors influencing the patient's perception of facilitative therapeutic conditions. *Psychiatry, 40,* 16–24.

Hamilton, M. (1967). Development of a rating scale for primary depressive illness. *British Journal of Social and Clinical Psychology, 6,* 278–296.

Henry, W. P., Schacht, T. E., Strupp, H. H., Butler, S. F., & Binder, J. L. (1993). Effects of training in time-limited dynamic psychotherapy: Mediators of therapists' responses to training. *Journal of Consulting and Clinical Psychology, 61,* 441–447.

Henry, W. P., Strupp, H. H., Butler, S. F., Schacht, T. E., & Binder, J. L. (1993). Effects of training in time-limited dynamic psychotherapy: Changes in therapist behavior. *Journal of Consulting and Clinical Psychology, 61,* 434–440.

Herink, R. (1980). *The psychotherapy handbook: The A to Z guide to more than 250 different therapies in use today*. New York: New American Library.

Higgins, S. T., Budney, A. J., & Bickel, W. K. (1994). Applying behavioral concepts and principles to the treatment of cocaine dependence. *Drug and Alcohol Dependence, 34,* 87–97.

Hoffman, G. W., DiRito, D. C., & McGill. (1993). Three-month follow-up of 28 dual diagnosis inpatients. *American Journal of Drug and Alcohol Abuse, 19,* 79–88.

Howard, K. I. (1989, May). *Patient and therapy interaction effects in drug abuse research*. Invited paper presented at NIDA, Washington, DC.

Howard, K. I., Krause, M. S., & Lyons, J. (1993). When clinical trials fail: A guide for disaggregation. In L. S. Onken & J. D. Blaine (Eds.), *Behavioral treatments for drug abuse and dependence* (NIDA Research Monograph No. 137) (pp. 291–302). Washington, DC: National Institute of Drug Abuse.

Imber, S. D., Pilkonis, P. A., Sotsky, S. M., Elkin, I., Watkins, J. T., Collins, J. F., Shea, M. T., Leber, W. R., & Glass, D. R. (1990). Mode-specific effects among three treatments for depression. *Journal of Consulting and Clinical Psychology, 58,* 352–359.

Jensen, J. P., Bergin, A. E., & Greaves, D. W. (1990). The meaning of eclecticism: New survey and analysis of components. *Professional Psychology: Research and Practice, 21,* 124–130.

Kang, S. Y., Kleinman, P. H., Woody, G. E., Millman, R. B., Todd, T. C., Kemp, J., & Lipton, D. S. (1991). Outcomes for cocaine abusers after once-a-week psychosocial therapy. *American Journal of Psychiatry, 148,* 630–635.

Kaplan, H. S. (1987). *The illustrated manual of sex therapy* (2nd ed.). New York: Brunner/Mazel.

Kiesler, C., & Sibulkin, A. (1987). *Mental hospitalization: Myths and facts about a national crisis*. Newbury Park, CA: Sage.

Lambert, M. J. (1989, May). *Contributors to treatment outcome*. Paper presented at the annual meeting of the Society for the Exploration of Psychotherapy Integration, Berkley, CA.

Lambert, M. J., & DeJulio, S. S. (1978, March). *The relative importance of client, therapist and technique variables as predictors of psychotherapy outcome: The place of "nonspecific" factors.* Paper presented at the midwinter meeting of the Division of Psychotherapy, American Psychological Association, Scottsdale, AZ.

Lazarus, A. A. (1981). *The practice of multi-modal therapy.* New York: McGraw-Hill.

Lefebrve, M. F. (1981). Cognitive distortion and cognitive errors in depressed psychiatric and low back pain patients. *Journal of Consulting and Clinical Psychology, 49,* 517–525.

Levy, S. J., & Rutter, E. (1992). *Children of drug abusers.* New York: Lexington Books.

Luborsky, L. (1984). *Principles of psychoanalytic psychotherapy: A manual for supportive-expressive treatment.* New York: Basic Books.

Luborsky, L., & DeRubeis, R. J. (1984). The use of psychotherapy treatment manuals: A small revolution in psychotherapy research style. *Clinical Psychology Review, 4,* 5–14.

Luborsky, L., Diguer, L., Schweizer, E., & Johnson, S. (1996, June). *The researcher's therapeutic allegiance as a "wildcard" in studies comparing the outcomes of treatments.* Paper presented at the annual meeting of the Society for Psychotherapy Research, Amelia Island, FL.

Luborsky, L., McLellan, A. T., Woody, G. E., O'Brien, C. P., & Auerbach, A. (1985). Therapist success and its determinants. *Archives of General Psychiatry, 42,* 602–611.

Luborsky, L., Singer, B., & Luborsky, L. (1975). Comparative studies of psychotherapies. *Archives of General Psychiatry, 32,* 995–1008.

Machado, P. P. P., Beutler, L. E., & Greenberg, L. S. (1999). Emotion recognition in psychotherapy: Impact of therapist level of experience and emotional awareness. *Journal of Clinical Psychology, 55,* 39–57.

Maki, R. H., & Syman, E. M. (1997). Teaching of controversial and empirically validated treatments in APA-accredited clinical and counseling psychology programs. *Psychotherapy, 34,* 44–57.

Marlatt, G. A., & Gordon, J. R. (1985). *Relapse prevention: Maintenance strategies in the treatment of addictive behaviors.* New York: Guilford Press.

McLellan, A. T., Luborsky, L., Woody, G. E., & O'Brien, C. P. (1980). An improved diagnostic instrument for substance abuse patients: The Addiction Severity Index. *Journal of Nervous and Mental Disease, 168,* 26–33.

McLellan, A. T., Luborsky, L., Woody, G. E., O'Brien, C. P., & Druley, K. A. (1983). Predicting response to alcohol and drug abuse treatments. *Archives of General Psychiatry, 40,* 620–625.

Meichenbaum, D. (1979). *Cognitive–behavior modification.* New York: Plenum.

Miller, W. R., & Rollnick, S. (1991). *Motivational interviewing: Preparing people to change addictive behavior.* New York: Guilford Press.

Millon, T., & Davis, R. (1995). Putting Humpty Dumpty together again: Using the MCMI in psychological assessment. In L. E. Beutler & M. Berren (Eds) *Integrative assessment of adult personality* (pp. 240–279). New York: Guilford Press.

Miranda, J., & Persons, J. B. (1988). Dysfunctional attitudes are mood-state dependent. *Journal of Abnormal Psychology, 97,* 76–79.

Mohr, D. C., Beutler, L. E., Engle, D. Shoham-Salomon, V., Bergan, J., Kaszniak, A. W., & Yost, E. (1990). Identification of patients at risk for nonresponse and negative outcome in psychotherapy. *Journal of Consulting and Clinical Psychology, 58,* 622–628.

Norcross, J. C., & Prochaska, J. O. (1988). A study of eclectic (and integrative) views revisited. *Professional Psychology: Research and Practice, 19,* 170–174.

Orlinsky, D. E., Grawe, K., & Parks, B. K. (1994). Process and outcome in psychotherapy—*Noch Einmal.* In A. E. Bergin & S. L. Garfield (Eds), *Handbook of psychotherapy and behavior change* (4th ed., pp. 270–376). New York: John Wiley & Sons.

Orlinsky, D. E., & Howard, K. I. (1986). Process and outcome in psychotherapy. In S. L. Garfield & A. E. Bergin (Eds.), *Handbook of psychotherapy and behavior change* (3rd ed., pp. 311–384). New York: John Wiley & Sons.

Orlinsky, D. E., & Howard, K. I. (1987). A generic model of psychotherapy. *Journal of Integrative and Eclectic Psychotherapy, 6,* 6–27.

Parelli, P. (1993). *Natural horse-man-ship.* Salt Lake City, UT: Publishers Press.

Peck, M. S. (1985). *The road less traveled.* New York: Simon & Schuster.

Perls, F. S. (1969). *Gestalt therapy verbatim.* Moab, Utah: Real People Press.

Regier, D. A., Boyd, J. H., Burke, J. D., Rae, D. S., Myers, J. K., Kramer, M., Robins, C. N., George, L. K., Karno, M., & Locke, B. Z. (1988). One month prevalence of mental disorders in the U.S. *Archives of General Psychiatry, 45,* 977–986.

Rogers, C. R. (1957). The necessary and sufficient conditions of therapeutic personality change. *Journal of Consulting Psychology, 21,* 95–103.

Rounsaville, B. J., Dolinsky, Z. S., Babor, T. F., & Meyer, R. E. (1987). Psychopathology as a predictor of treatment in alcoholics. *Archives of General Psychiatry, 44,* 505–513.

Rounsaville, B. J., Kosten, T. R., Weissman, M. M., Prusoff, B., Pauls, D., Anton, S. F., Merikangas, K. (1991). Psychiatric disorders in relatives of probands with opiate addiction. *Archives of General Psychiatry, 48,* 33–42.

Rounsaville, B. J., Weissman, M. M., Kleber, H. D., & Wilber, C. H. (1982). The heterogeneity of psychiatric diagnosis in treated opiate addicts. *Archives of General Psychiatry, 39,* 161–166.

Scogin, F., Hamblin, D., & Beutler, L. E. (1987). Bibliotherapy for depressed older adults: A self-help alternative. *The Gerontologist, 27,* 383–387.

Shoham-Salomon, V., & Hannah, M. T. (1991). Client–treatment interactions in the study of differential change processes. *Journal of Consulting and Clinical Psychology, 59,* 217–225.

Sloane, R. B., Staples, F. R., Cristol, A. H., Yorkston, N. J., & Whipple, K.

(1975). *Psychotherapy versus behavior therapy.* Cambridge MA: Harvard University Press.

Smith, M. L. Glass, G. V., & Miller, T. I. (1980). *The benefits of psychotherapy.* Baltimore: Johns Hopkins University Press.

Smith, P. H. (1992). The political economy of drugs: Conceptual issues and policy options. In P. H. Smith (Ed.), *Drug policy in the americas.* Boulder, CO: Westview Press.

Spielberger, C. D., Gorsuch, R. L., & Lushene, R. E. (1970). *The State-Trait Anxiety Inventory (STAI) test manual for form X.* Palo Alto, CA: Consulting Psychologists Press.

Spielberger, C. D., Gorsuch, R. L., Lushene, R., Vagg, P. R., & Jacobs, G. A. (1983). *State-Trait Anxiety Inventory.* Palo Alto, CA: Consulting Psychologists Press.

Spitzer, R. L., Williams, J. B. W., & Gibbon, M. (1986). *The Structured Clinical Interview for DSM III-R—Patient version.* New York: Biometrics Research Department, New York State Psychiatric Institute.

Strupp, H. H., & Binder, J. L. (1984). *Psychotherapy in a new key.* New York: Basic Books.

Strupp, H. H., & Binder, J. (in press). Therapist inner processes in the Vanderbilt project, and conclusions for future training. In F. Caspar (Ed.), *The inner processes of psychotherapists: Innovations in clinical training.* New York: Oxford University Press.

Wakefield, P. J., Williams, R. E., Yost, E. B., & Patterson, K. M. (1996). *Couple therapy for alcoholism: A cognitive-behavioral treatment manual.* New York: Guilford Press.

Weiss, R. D., Griffin, M. L., & Mirin, S. M. (1992). Drug abuse as self-medication for depression: An empirical study. *American Journal of Drug & Alcohol Abuse, 18,* 121–129.

Wright, F. D., Beck, A. T., Newman, C. F., & Liese, B. S. (1993). Cognitive therapy of substance abuse: Theoretical rationale. In L. S. Onken, J. D. Blaine, & J. J. Boren (Eds.), *Behavioral treatments for drug abuse and dependence.* (NIDA Monograph No. 137). Washington, DC: National Institute of Drug Abuse.

Yost, E. B., Beutler, L. E., Corbishley, M. A., & Allender, J. R. (1986). *Group Cognitive Therapy.* New York: Pergamon Press.

Young, J. (1995). *Early maladaptive schemas: EMS.* Unpublished manuscript, Cognitive Therapy Center of New York, New York, New York.

Index

avoidance (*continued*)
  of feelings, 85
  indirect interventions for, 111–113
  of knowledge, 85
  treatment strategy and, 84–86, 87
avoidant thoughts, 93
awareness, 85, 87
  interventions for, 105–106, 111–112, 123–124

Barrett-Lennard Relationship Inventory, 44
BDI-II. *See Beck Depression Inventory*
Beck Depression Inventory, 40, 152, 153
behavior
  consequential, 100, 121–122
  defensive. *See* defensive behavior
  destructive, 89, 90–93, 108–109
  disruptive, 77, 78, 81
  externalizing. *See* externalizing behavior
  homicidal, 89, 92
  internalizing. *See* internalizing behavior
  noncooperative, 66
  nonverbal. *See* nonverbal behavior
  obsessive-compulsive, 84
  passive, 94
  risk, 38–41
  ruminative, 48
  self-injurious, 89
  self-monitoring problematic, 89
  self-reflective, 48, 82, 86–87
  situational, 43, 45–46, 48–49
  state-like. *See* state-like behavior
  trait-like. *See* trait-like behavior
  unwanted, 77
  verbal. *See* verbal behavior
behavioral
  analysis, 86
  contracts, 86, 117
  skills, 74
  symptoms, 87
behavioral interventions
  for anxiety, 16–17
  for depression, 16–17
  for distressed patients, 142–144
  for drug abuse, 4–5
  for stress management, 136
  for substance abuse, 5
beliefs, 100, 102–103, 121–122, 143–144
bibliotherapy, 126
blame
  coping styles and, 76, 85
  externalizing, 47, 101
  resistance and, 118
BLRI. *See Barrett-Lennard Relationship Inventory*
body language. *See* nonverbal behavior
books, self-help, 125, 126
boundaries, 47
brainstorming, 92–93

California Psychotherapy Alliance Scales, 44, 45
CALPAS. *See California Psychotherapy Alliance Scales*

caring, 27, 55, 63, 64
catastrophic thoughts, 101, 102
cathartic methods, 142, 144–145
CEAS-R. *See Client Emotional Arousal Scale*
change
  distress level and, 49
  empathy and, 65
  indirect interventions for, 113–114
  knowledge and, 27–28
  principles of, 27–28, 34–35, 36
  process, 27
  resistance and, 49, 128
  situational, 45
  state-like, 28
  symptomatic, 88
  tears and, 57
  therapeutic, 17–18, 77, 116, 135–136, 149–150
  therapeutic relationships and, 56–57
  timing and, 28
chemical abuse. *See* substance abuse
choice, 60
chronic
  depression, 134
  emotions, 135
Client Emotional Arousal Scale, 138, 176–180
clinical
  experience, 28
  judgment, 51, 72
  setting, 38–40, 58–59
cocaine, 4, 5
cognitive
  dissonance, 76–77
  patterns, 40–41
  triad, 100–103
cognitive therapy
  for alcoholism, 5
  for anxiety, 16–17
  for depression, 16–17, 121
  for distressed patients, 142–144
  for drug abuse, 4–5, 121
  history of, 6
  recordkeeping for, 122
  for self-destructive behavior, 92
  for stress management, 136
  voice, 142
collaboration, 56, 58, 71–73
  in indirect interventions, 113
  language and, 61, 71, 73
  permission and, 62
common factors model, 27
comorbidity
  of depression, 4, 5, 9, 10
  psychosocial treatment and, 9–10
compliance, 5, 26, 115
computer software
  for patient assessment, 31–33
  for patient-treatment matching, 32–34
  STS, 22, 31–33
confrontations, 78, 115, 118, 125, 135–136, 146
consequential behavior, 100, 121–122

distress (*continued*)
 reactive, 136, 142
 state-like, 140–141
 subjective, 138, 141, 153
 trait-like, 140
 treatment strategy and, 16, 132–147
 verbal behavior and, 136–137, 138, 139
doctoral level training, 25
Dodo Bird Verdict, 8
dominance, 117, 118
downward-arrow techniques, 102
dropouts, 5
drug abuse, 4, 41, 89
 behavioral interventions for, 4–5
 case study, 150–152
 cognitive therapy for, 4–5, 121
 depression and, 4–5
 direct change interventions for, 92, 93–100
 indirect interventions for, 105–114, 109
 polydrug, 4
 relaxation training for, 95
 risk situations for, 95–98
 social support for, 95, 99, 100, 151
 stimulus control for, 96, 98
 treatment strategy for, 85, 90
 workplace, 4
drug addiction, 4, 41–42
drugs (therapeutic), 84
DSM-IV, 39, 78
DTR. *See Daily Thought Record*
dysfunctional thoughts, 90, 100–103
dysphoria, 4, 9, 40, 134

Early Maladaptive Schemas, 107
eclecticism, 6–7, 15
education. *See* training
ego defense, 75
emergency procedures, 91, 94
emotional
 arousal. *See* arousal
 confrontation, 15
 experience, 133–135
 intensity, 132–133, 134, 135–136, 138, 140
 pain, 134
 sensitivity, 111–112
 stress, 135–136
 threads, 124
 ventilating, 142
emotional states. *See also* state-like behavior
 assessing, 32, 45, 45–50
 reflection and, 66
 training and, 35–36
 treatment strategy and, 17, 20, 86, 87, 135–
  136
emotions
 absence of, 134
 avoided, 86, 112–113
 chronic vs. acute, 135
 complex, 133
 conflicting, 123, 124
 culture and, 133

diagnosis and, 133–134
 in drug abuse treatment, 96, 97
 motivation and, 132
 negative, 134
 primary, 66, 133, 134, 138
 problematic, 132–133
 reactive, 137–138, 140
 situational, 46
 state-like, 134–135, 136, 137–138, 140–
  141
 therapeutic use of, 132–133
 trait-like, 134, 135–136, 140
empathy, 63–64, 65, 66, 67
EMS. *See Early Maladaptive Schemas*
environmental
 response, 45–46
 support. *See* social support
epidemiology
 of drug abuse, 4
 of mental disorders, 3
escapism, 93, 143
evaluation, patient. *See* patient assessment
evidence analysis procedures, 102–103, 122
evocative work, 128–129
exercise, 104
expectations, 55, 58, 60
experiences, 75, 107
 emotional, 133–135
experiential treatment, 86, 123–124, 136, 145–
 146
exposure/extinction principle, 14, 34
 arousal and, 146
 change and, 14, 136
 coping styles and, 78, 84–85
 distress and, 140
 in indirect interventions, 112–113
external
 control, 13
 raters, 69
externalizing behavior, 15, 47–48, 77, 83, 140
 blame, 47, 101
 coping styles and, 42, 45, 47–48, 76–78, 80–
  83
 direct change interventions for, 88–105
 vs. internalizing behavior, 82
 treatment strategy and, 48, 84–87, 90, 149
extinction/exposure principle. *See* exposure/
  extinction principle
extroversion, 48, 81

facial expression, 138
facilities, 39–40, 58
family
 confrontation, 146
 functioning, 78–80
 support, 91, 95, 99
fantasy, directed, 111–112
FAST. *See Firestone Assessment of Self-Destructive*
 Thoughts
fear, 133, 153
 confronting, 78

indirect interventions for, 109, 112–113
internalizing behavior and, 86, 87
feelings
acceptance of, 58
acknowledgment of, 64
avoided, 85
coping styles and, 81
decisions and, 124
destructive potential and, 109
feared, 109
identifying, 66
interventions and, 113, 123–124
reflections of, 63, 66–68
thoughts and, 67, 103, 122
Firestone Assessment of Self-Destructive Thoughts,
40–41
for drug abuse, 93
for problem-provoking thoughts, 106–107
for suicide, 91–92
flexibility
creative, 155
cross-theoretical models for, 15
distress level and, 50
imagination and, 28–29
structure and, 23
treatment manuals and, 8
focus
symptomatic, 108
therapeutic, 106–108
freedom, 115, 120
Freud, Sigmund, 6
friendships
in drug abuse treatment, 95, 99, 151
impairment level and, 78–80
functional impairment, 15, 30, 151
assessing, 31, 37, 41–42
cues to, 78–80
treatment strategy and, 77, 149, 151

generalization, 101
Global Assessment of Functioning, 50, 78–80
GOF. *See Global Assessment of Functioning*
graded task assignment, 98
graduate level training, 29–30
group intervention, 146
groups, self-help, 126
guidance, 119, 120, 121
guided
discovery, 101
imagery, 93–94

Hamilton Rating Scale for Depression, 40
HAq-II. *See Helping Alliance Questionnaire*
health care costs, 3
Helping Alliance Questionnaire, 44–45
homework, 94, 99, 119, 152
resistance and, 117, 120–121
self-monitoring, 125–126, 152
homicidal
behavior, 89, 92
ideation, 90, 92

hope, 35
hopelessness, 91, 92
hospitalization, 91
hypnosis, 141

ideation, 90, 92
image refocusing/replacement, 94
imagery
distress and, 143
guided, 93–94
rehearsal, 98
imagination, 28–29, 35, 56, 155
imaging, mastery, 98
impairment, 19, 39, 79
coping styles and, 88–114
cues to, 78–80
functional. *See* functional impairment
social, 151
treatment strategy and, 46–47, 74–87, 132–
147
impulsivity, 15
assessing, 37, 42
controlling, 86
coping styles and, 81, 85
destructive, 90–93, 108
treatment and, 48, 84, 113
indirect interventions, 105–114
for anxiety, 112–113
for change, 113–114
for drug abuse, 105–114
inner voices, 124–125, 142, 144–145
insight
coping styles and, 82
interventions for, 74, 105–114
oriented treatment, 86, 87
themes and, 110–112
therapeutic change and, 77, 149
instruments, 40–42, 51. *See also* names of
specific instruments; psychological tests
administering, 50–51
for patient assessment, 38–45
integrity, 115
interaction. *See* social interaction
internal dialogue, 124–125, 142, 144–145
internalizing behavior, 48, 83, 101, 140
coping styles and, 76, 77–78, 80–83, 122
destructive behavior and, 108–109
direct change interventions for, 88–105
vs. externalizing behavior, 82
fear and, 86, 87
identification of, 47–48
indirect interventions for, 106–108
treatment strategy and, 48, 85–87, 90, 108,
149
interpersonal
interaction, 47–48, 89, 100, 136
styles, 20
therapy, 5, 6, 123
interpretation, 67, 86, 109, 119
interventions, 11, 36, 77. *See also* treatment
coping styles and, 16, 19, 74

interventions (*continued*)
    direct change. *See* direct change interventions
    directed, 115–116, 120, 121–124, 130
    downward-arrow, 102
    emotions and, 135–136
    group, 146
    impairment level and, 84
    indirect. *See* indirect interventions
    integrating, 7
    internally vs. externally focused, 77
    multicomponent, 13–14
    nondirective, 17, 116, 126–127, 130
    paradoxical, 17, 34, 127–128
    resistance and, 115, 121–123
    selection of, 25–26
    themes for, 110–112
    theory-driven, 23
    timing, 28
interviewing
    initial, 60
    motivational, 86, 144–146
intimate relationships, 80
introversion, 107
in vivo
    exposure, 136
    role playing, 112
isolation, social, 78–80, 91, 93

joy, 133
judgment, 51, 65, 72

kindness, 55
kinesic behavior, 50, 138, 139
knowledge
    avoided, 85
    therapeutic, 27–28, 35–36, 55

language, collaborative, 61, 71, 73
lifestyle, drug-related, 99
love, 133

manuals. *See* treatment manuals
mastery imagery, 98
meanings, 128
medical
    evaluation, 38–41
    history, 41
medication, 84
mental disorders, epidemiology of, 3
methamphetamines, 4
Minnesota Multiphasic Personality Inventory, 42
Minnesota Multiphasic Personality Inventory-2, 43, 48, 151
    for coping styles, 48, 80–81
    for defensiveness, 117
misattributions, 102
MMPI. *See Minnesota Multiphasic Personality Inventory*
MMPI-2. *See Minnesota Multiphasic Personality Inventory-2*
models. *See* theoretical models
monitoring, 122

moods, 46, 121
motivation
    distress level and, 49, 141
    emotions and, 132
    lack of, 144–146
    therapeutic relationships and, 63, 65–66
    treatment, 133, 146
motivational interviewing, 86, 144–146
movement, 50, 138, 139
multimodal therapy, 29–30
multitheorectical models, 8–9, 13

names, 59
narratives, 128–129
National Institute on Drug Abuse, 4, 9
negotiation, 72–73
NIDA. *See* National Institute on Drug Abuse
nondirective
    interventions, 17, 116, 126–127, 130
    therapists, 130
nonverbal behavior
    distress level and, 136–137, 138
    rating scale, 139
    resistance behavior and, 49, 118–119
    in therapeutic relationships, 56

observations, 51, 136
obsessive-compulsive behavior, 84
open-ended treatment, 136
outcomes
    evaluating, 44–45, 51
    patient characteristics and, 16
    treatment manuals and, 8
overgeneralization, 101
ownership, of problems, 61, 73

pain, emotional, 135
paradoxical interventions, 17, 34, 127–128
parents, 124
participation, patient, 60
passive
    behavior, 94
    resistance, 116
patient assessment, 37–51. *See also* instruments
    of anxiety, 43, 153
    clinical setting and, 38–39
    computer software for, 31–33
    of coping styles, 31, 37, 42, 45
    of depression, 40, 152
    of distress levels, 31, 37, 43–44, 45, 49–50, 136
    of emotional states, 32, 45, 45–50
    of functional impairment, 31, 37, 41–42
    of impulsivity, 37, 42
    measurement procedures, 38–45
    objectives of, 37–38
    psychological tests and, 31
    severity, 39, 43–44, 79
    standardized, 39
    training for, 25
patient(s)
    compliance, 5, 26, 115

therapists. *See also* psychotherapists
  anger at, 57–58
  directed activities, 115–116, 122–123, 130
  directive, 130
  evaluating, 14, 44–45, 114, 129–131, 147,
    153–155
  judgment of, 51, 65, 72
  nondirective, 130
  patient matching, 12–13
  patient-relationships. *See* therapeutic
    relationships
  qualities of, 63
  resistance and, 116–117
  training. *See* training
therapy. *See* treatment
thought(s)
  anxious, 92
  associated, 96
  automatic, 96, 97, 100–101, 121–122, 143,
    152
  avoidant, 93
  catastrophic, 101, 102
  as cues, 67
  depressive, 100–103
  disorders, 134
  distortion of, 152
  dysfunctional, 90, 100–103
  feelings and, 67, 103, 122
  indirect interventions and, 106–108
  insertion procedures, 98
  patterns, 94
  problem-provoking, 106–107
  replacement of, 96
  self-abusive, 91
  situation-specific, 100–101
  substitution, 95
threats, intentional, 76–77
timing, 28, 35–36, 56
tools, therapeutic, 28, 55–56
training, 22–36
  doctoral, 25
  graduate, 29–30
  manual-based, 8
  postgraduate, 30–34
  undergraduate, 25
trait-like behavior
  assessing, 40–41, 43, 45–50
  defensive, 117
  distress, 140
  resistant, 115, 118, 126
  vs. state-like behavior, 40, 51
  treatment decisions and, 48
trait-like emotions, 134, 135–136, 140
transference, 110
treatment. *See also* interventions
  compliance, 5, 26, 115
  context, 12
  contracts, 72–73
  coping styles and, 47–48, 74, 81–82, 84–87,
    88–114
  decisions, 36, 38–39, 45–51
  dropouts, 5

experiential, 86, 123–124, 136, 145–146
facilities, 39–40, 58
goals, 60, 72, 73
impairment level and, 46–47, 74–87, 88–114,
  132–147
initial, 89–90, 107, 108, 149
insight-oriented, 86, 87
intensity, 15, 77, 149
models. *See* theoretical models
motivation for, 133, 144–146
open-ended, 136
outcomes. *See* outcomes
patient matching. *See* patient-treatment
  matching
planning, 20, 72–73
preparation for, 58–61
prioritizing, 89–90
readiness for, 117
relevant characteristics, 24, 25–26, 75–76
systematic selection. *See* systematic treatment
  selection model
treatment manuals
  history of, 5–7
  patient variability and, 20
  problems with, 8–9
  single-theory, 13
Treatment of Depression Collaborative Research
  Project, 7
TRS. *See Therapeutic Reactance Scale*
trust, 35, 56
twelve step programs, 94, 109, 152
two-chair procedure, 145–146

undergraduate level training, 25
understanding, 64, 68, 121
unhappiness, 78, 136
unipolar depressive disorders, 4
unmotivated patients, 144–146
unwanted behaviors, 77
urges, 122

values, 13, 68
Vanderbilt projects, 65, 116
variability, patient. *See* patient variables
vegetative symptoms, 90, 103–105
ventilation, of emotions, 142
verbal behavior
  distress level and, 136–137, 138, 139
  resistance behavior and, 49, 50, 118–119
  in therapeutic relationships, 56, 66–69
victims, potential, 91
violence, 89, 91
voices, inner, 124–125, 142, 144–145
voice therapy, 124–125, 142, 144–145

waiting rooms, 59
withdrawal
  resistance and, 118–119
  social, 78–80, 86, 90, 95, 99–100
workbooks, self-help, 125
working relationship. *See* therapeutic relationship
workplace drug abuse, 4
worth, 68